The Bulb Book

The Bulb Book

a photographic guide
to over 800 hardy bulbs

by

Martyn Rix and
Roger Phillips

edited by Brian Mathew

Book Club Associates

London

Acknowledgements

It would not have been possible to complete this book without the help of many people. We are particularly grateful to Brian Mathew for checking the text and the identifications, and answering many questions; to the Royal Horticultural Society's garden at Wisley and especially to Chris Brickell and John Warwick, to Jack Elliott and to Harry Hay, all of whom put up with frequent visits throughout the season, and were always helpful and generous in lending their plants. We would like to thank Lord Skelmersdale of Broadleigh Gardens for giving us a large number of bulbs, Mrs J. Abel-Smith for the modern Daffodils, and Regents Park for the Tulip cultivars. We would also like to thank the following who have given us plants, lent transparencies or helped in other ways: Peter Barnes, Beverley Behrens, Igor Belolipov, Brinsley Burbidge, Tim Brotzman, Paul Christian, Jill Cowley, Jenny Deakin, Kath Dryden, Valerie Finnis, Nora Gabrielian, Alison Goatcher, Chris Grey-Wilson, Susannah Hamilton, Diana Hewett, John Holmes, Tinge Horsfall, Mary Knox-Finlay, Christopher Lloyd, Roger Macfarlane, Wessel Marais, John Marr, Leuren Moret, Kate Penoyre, Oleg Polunin, Charles Quest-Ritson, Ted Rix, Lyndsay Shearer, Ole Sonderhousen, Walter Stagg, Hugh Synge, John Templer, Romke van der Kaa, and Ursula Wide.

First published 1981 by Pan Books Ltd, Cavaye Place, London SW10 9PG

This edition published 1981 by Book Club Associates

© Martyn Rix and Roger Phillips 1981 CN 2127

Printed in Great Britain by Cripplegate Printing Company Ltd, Edenbridge, Kent

Four colour origination by Litra Machine Plates Ltd, Edenbridge, Kent

Contents

Introduction

Bulbs hold a particular fascination for me. It is always a thrill to go into the garden soon after Christmas, looking for the first signs of spring, and find a white Snowdrop, or a yellow Aconite or Celandine, pushing up out of the cold grass. Bulbs appear and flower in a few days at the first warm spell: the colder the winter, the faster the Crocuses or Snowdrops emerge, sometimes pushing up through the melting snow, or colouring the mountainsides white and mauve. In autumn Cyclamen and Colchicums come up leafless, giving the first hint of approaching winter. In fact there is a bulb in flower every day of the year.

In this book we hope to show something of the beauty and diversity of bulbous plants. No other group can provide such a display of colour with such ease and reliability. Few indoor plants are as welcome in mid-winter as the sweet-scented Hyacinths and graceful Paper Whites. Tulips make a spectacular show, in every colour except blue, within five months of planting with no intervening attention; while daffodils flower as quickly and go on improving year after year for twenty years or more, without any replanting or division. Few herbaceous plants are as stately as the 3-metre-high *Cardiocrinum* or formal bells of the Crown Imperial. Some bulbs are like small jewels; gentian-blue in *Tecophilaea*, ice-blue in *Puschkinia*, or golden in many Crocuses; while others, like many Fritillaries, are all sombre purples, greens and browns.

Over 800 different bulbs are shown here, all hardy enough to survive the cold of winter outdoors in North-west Europe. They have been chosen to include many familiar ones, and some unfamiliar, new or interesting to grow. The larger pictures, showing the whole plant, were taken in the studio; the field pictures (wherever possible) were photographed in the wild, though a few were taken in gardens. The plants are grouped in order of flowering, beginning with early spring; but within this framework, as many species as possible of one genus have been brought together. The dates on which the studio shots were taken are given, to aid identification and to help in planning a display.

The book is designed not only for gardeners, but also for those who like to find plants growing wild. In the text the distribution and habitat of each species is given, as a guide to where it might be found. These habitat notes also form a valuable adjunct to the notes on cultivation.

Most of the species shown can be bought from one of the specialist bulb nurseries listed on page 189. Any that cannot be bought can be found through one of the societies listed on that page and they will always welcome new members and help them obtain some rare plant. Most of these societies hold auctions among their members, and publish seed lists. The Royal Horticultural Society's journal, *The Garden*, even has a special column for members to advertise that they want to acquire a plant rare in cultivation.

The greatest number of bulbous plants are found in countries where the winter is rather cold and wet and the summers are hot and dry, with a short spring, and it is from this type of climate that nearly all the varieties of hardy bulbs have originated. The possession of a food reserve in the bulb enables a plant to grow up very quickly in spring, before annuals and slower growing herbs have had time to develop. In tropical climates, which have alternating dry and wet seasons, bulbs are also common, but very few of them can be grown outside in Northern Europe; those few that are hardy enough come from high altitudes.

The bulb itself can be formed in several different ways. Strictly speaking, a bulb, of which the onion is the best known example, consists of the swollen fleshy bases of leaves. Other storage organs may be formed by different parts of the plant: a corm is a swollen stem base, usually surrounded by the dry bases of old leaves as in a Crocus. There are also swollen underground stems, of which the potato is the best known, usually called stem tubers or rhizomes. A third common type is the fleshy root which may be single or branched. If very short it is known as a root-tuber. There is no definite line which can be drawn between a tuberous root and a non-tuberous root, or between a bulb and a plant with persistent leaf bases, and the decision as to which borderline plants to include in this book was necessarily a subjective one.

Hardiness is also very difficult to define with any precision, as it depends on the interaction of several different factors. Generally speaking, plants are included here which would grow outside in eastern England and North-west Europe and survive all but the very coldest winter. Those whose main enemy in Britain is winter damp were generally included in preference to those killed primarily by cold. It is easier to cover plants to keep them dry than to keep them warm; continental Europe does not have the same damp winters as are found in the British Isles, and a covering of snow will also help to protect them. Plants which generally require a greenhouse or need to be brought indoors in winter, such as Begonias, Dahlias and most cultivated Gladioli, have been omitted. They are a subject for a separate book.

Nearly all hardy bulbs come from areas with a Mediterranean-type climate; that is, a cool wet winter and a hot dry summer. Five areas of the world have this type of climate: the Mediterranean – extending eastwards into Central Asia; California; southern Chile; the south-western tip of South Africa; and western and southern Australia. In the southern hemisphere the Mediterranean climates are found at around 35°S, and in the northern hemisphere at around 40°N. Partly because of this difference in latitude, and partly because they have no continental land masses to their south, the southern hemisphere areas of Mediterranean climate have almost frost-free winters, so few of their bulbs are hardy here. In California the Mediterranean climate is confined by the N–S line of the Sierras and the Rockies, to a narrow strip along the coast. This is sometimes subject to a big freeze, such as occurred in 1972, when the Arctic air of Canada extended down the west coast; consequently many of the Californian plants are cold-tolerant. Others come from higher altitudes in the mountains and these, of course, also tolerate winter cold.

The majority of hardy bulbs come from the Mediterranean area in Europe, North Africa and Asia. The winter rainfall type of climate extends into Central Asia, almost to the Himalayas, because the mountain ranges, the Alps, the Caucasus, Tauros, Hindu Kush and Tien Shan, run roughly east-west and provide no barrier to the winter storms from the Mediterranean, Black Sea and Caspian Sea. At the same time the proximity of Siberia means that cold air can extend south-westwards, often as far as Turkey or northern Greece. Most plants from the Mediterranean mountains are also frost-tolerant. Small areas on the southern shores of the Black Sea and Caspian have some summer rainfall too – horticulturally significant as these plants will survive the intermittent summer rainfall of Northern Europe. North-west Spain and south-west France also have summer rainfall, and this transitional type of maritime-Mediterranean climate produces many of the bulbs, such as Narcissus, which will do well in the open garden in England. On their equatorial side, the Mediterranean climates merge into deserts: the Sahara, the Syrian desert, the Mojave in California, the Karoo in South Africa and the Atacama in Chile. These border zones, which are particularly rich in bulbs, provide plants which are most difficult to grow in England, as they are intolerant of excess damp in both winter and summer.

Fewer bulbs come from areas with summer rainfall. Most of the hardy summer-flowering South African bulbs come from high in the Drakensbergs in Natal. Other summer-flowering bulbs are mainly from the Himalayas, China and Japan, and to a lesser extent from the mountains of Europe. The Lilies (*Lilium* spp.) are the most important bulbs which come from summer rainfall areas. Most species with their loose-scaled bulbs are intolerant of summer drought.

Martyn Rix, July 1981

Conservation and collecting

Apart from surviving the rigours of the climate, bulbs in the wild have to survive two main threats: grazing by animals and collecting, by humans. Of these grazing is very ancient, collecting in evolutionary terms very recent.

In the short term grazing is less harmful because the bulb itself is not damaged, and many bulbs have evolved adaptations to protect themselves against it. In some, e.g. *Crocus* and

Collecting bulbs in Kurdistan in 1965

Colchicum, the seed head develops below ground, only emerging as the seeds ripen; in others, the plants produce bulbils which can propagate the plant when the seed pod is eaten. Others, e.g. *Eremurus*, are very slimy and avoided by grazing animals, while others, e.g. some Alliums, have a horrible smell and taste. In other cases the bulb can only survive when growing inside some spiny bush, or on an inaccessible rock ledge or in a narrow rock crevice. Fritillaries are common in this kind of habitat.

The threat from human collecting is twofold, for food and for horticulture. In the eastern Mediterranean, a popular gruel called Salep is made from orchid tubers: owing to the similarity of these tubers to testicles (Greek Ὀρχις = testicle) Salep is thought to have some aphrodisiac properties. Many species are used and this type of collecting probably keeps overall numbers down without threatening rare species in particular.

Horticultural collecting is the more dangerous because it is selective and threatens rare species more than common ones. While there are a few examples of bulbs known or believed to be extinct in the wild because of over-collecting – *Tecophilea cyanocrocus* is one – many are in potential danger of extinction by collectors. A topical example of the type of decimation which can occur is that of *Sternbergia candida*, recently discovered and described in 1978 as being rare and very restricted in distribution. Within two years hundreds of bulbs were offered in the trade, recently collected in the wild. If collecting on this scale is continued the plant could very soon become extinct in the wild. Cyclamen, especially the species of more limited distribution, e.g. *C. pseudibericum*, are also in great danger. The importation of collected corms of cyclamen into this country is supposed to be prohibited, but judging by the size and gnarled appearance of some of the corms seen for sale in shops the laws are being ignored.

Those hardy bulbs considered to be endangered are marked with an ⋆ in the index. These should on no account be collected if they are found. Most are in cultivation already, and obtainable through specialist societies or reputable nurseries who propagate their own stocks and do not import stocks directly from the wild.

All orchids have been excluded from this book. Some Pleione species are almost hardy, as is *Bletia striata*, and these are easily propagated, but the tuberous orchids from the Mediterranean and the rest of Europe have not been successfully grown from seed on a commercial scale, and propagation by division is very slow. Few species can be said to be established in cultivation, and gardeners should not collect them unless they are certain to be destroyed anyway, by road widening, ploughing, etc.

The pressures of urban development or agriculture do not threaten many species in the Mediterranean, but in California the possibility of extinction by this means is very real. *Fritillaria liliacea* is now restricted to about three sites on the outskirts of San Francisco because of the effects of housing developments and agriculture. Fortunately it is not difficult to cultivate and it should be carefully preserved and increased, by seed if possible, by anyone who grows it.

Seed is the best means of introduction of a new species and will result in the establishment of the plant sooner, but it is often not present at the time the plant is found. As a general rule bulbs of species which are obtainable in cultivation should not be collected, unless they are unusual individuals of common species. There is never any excuse for collecting more than three bulbs of a species from one area, especially if it does not occur in thousands. Three bulbs will be sufficient for a population to be established in cultivation, by hand pollination and seed sowing. One bulb, unless it is an individual or clone which increases very fast by bulbils or division, is a dead end and unlikely to result in the permanent establishment of the plant in cultivation. Twenty or more bulbs are no more likely to do well than three.

Iris cycloglossa (p.61)

Bulb bed showing railway sleepers and wire netting base, wth layers of gravel, peat and gritty planting compost; bricks indicate depth of layers.

Cultivation

Planting bulbs in the garden

Most bulbs should be planted when they are dormant in early autumn (August onwards) for spring-flowering bulbs, or in early spring for summer-flowering ones. Exceptions to this are snowdrops and snowflakes which are best moved while in flower. Snowdrops bought dry are often difficult to establish, but those transplanted while in flower will do well the following year.

It is important to plant bulbs at more or less the correct depth, and the right way up. As a general rule they should be planted at about their own depth in heavy soil, and in up to twice their own depth in light sandy soil or very dry places, but even the smallest bulbs should have about 5cm of soil above them.

Most bulbs require a well-drained rich soil with much sand and humus. A chalky one, or at least one which is not very acid is preferable. Many of the Dutch bulb fields consist of dune sand which has a large amount of shell in it providing lime, enriched with humus, so that it is both moisture-retentive and well drained, as well as alkaline and fertile.

If bulbs are used only for bedding, and are then discarded, the fertility of the soil is not important. If they are planted permanently, or meant to be used again, then it is essential that the soil in which they are grown is very fertile. The best fertilizers are low in nitrogen, high in potash and phosphate, e.g. bone meal, chrysanthemum or rose fertilizer. These should be applied either before planting or sprinkled on the surface immediately after planting, so that they are well incorporated into the soil before growth begins.

Bulbs in grass

Many bulbs will grow happily in grass, and look most natural in this setting. Snowdrops and Snowflakes are both happy, as are some Crocus species, especially *C. vernus*, *C. tommasinianus* and Dutch Yellow. These will grow happily in lawns even on heavy soil, but their leaves should not be mowed off until they have begun to go yellow, which is usually in May. Other later-flowering bulbs are less satisfactory in formal grass because their leaves last longer, but they will do well in rough grass which is not cut until July when the leaves of the latest flowers have died down. They associate well in a 'meadow garden' setting, which has been well described by Christopher Lloyd in *The Well-Tempered Garden* and can be seen at Great Dixter. The 'meadow garden' is rather similar in ecology to a subalpine hay meadow. The succession of flowers begins in early spring when the grass is short, with Snowdrops, Spring Snowflakes, Crocus and *Scilla bifolia*. As the grass becomes longer, larger bulbs flower, such as Daffodils, Summer Snowflakes and Fritillaries (*F. meleagris* and *pyrenaica*), *Tulipa sylvestris*, *Ornithogalum*, with Cowslips and Buttercups. Later come *Tulipa sprengeri* and other cultivated Tulips, and possibly *Lilium pyrenaicum*, *Lilium martagon* and *Iris latifolia*, which continue the succession until the end of June. By late July most of the bulbs will have disappeared, and the grass should be cut short and hay made before it is cleared away. One or two mowings, if the summer is wet, will suffice until September when the first of the Colchicums and autumn Crocus such as *C. speciosus* and *C. nudiflorus* appear, and a final mowing can be done in November after these have flowered, but before any of the bulbs' leaves have emerged.

If the soil is naturally acid and sandy a different range of bulbs can be grown. The Crocuses will do well and dwarf Narcissus can be grown, e.g. *N. bulbocodium* and *N. cyclamineus*, in the damper places, and *N. triandrus* in the drier areas. So-called 'alpine meadows' of this type can be seen at Wisley and at the Savill and Valley gardens, Windsor. In these cases the grass can be cut rather earlier, in early July or late June, and the wild flower range will resemble a heathy upland hay meadow.

Bulbs among shrubs and under trees

Many spring-flowering bulbs also grow well among deciduous shrubs and under deciduous trees. They make most of their growth before the tree leaves shade them too much. The roots of the trees and shrubs also help keep the soil on the dry side during the summer, which is beneficial to most bulbs. Snowdrops, Aconites (*Eranthis*), Cyclamen, Scillas, Bluebells (*Hyacinthoides*), *Trillium* and *Erythronium* grow well in these conditions, and the very tolerant *Lilium martagon* will also thrive in rather dry shade. The dryness and shade in summer also prevent the grass becoming too thick, and a thin ground cover of a small-leafed ivy can be encouraged. This provides a good foil for many bulbs, especially Snowdrops.

Other shade-tolerant bulbs prefer a moister soil such as is found among dwarf Rhododendrons, which have more restricted root systems and provide shade without drying out the surounding soil. This shade is particularly important in spring when the young shoots of lilies are often damaged by late frosts. If the bulbs are planted on the west side of an evergreen shrub or even partly under it, they are less likely to be damaged by the early morning sun. A peat bank is also a very good environment for plants of this type and many other bulbs will do very well in it.

The bulb frame

It will be seen in the text that the 'bulb frame' is often mentioned as a place to grow bulbs. Its purpose is primarily to keep the bulbs quite dry in summer and rather dry in winter. The protection the frame gives from cold is incidental. Aluminium frames are expensive to buy, but require no maintenance, and should last for many years. They are also much lighter than steel ones, should they need to be moved, and as they are bolted together, they can be dismantled easily. As much air as possible should circulate inside the frame, and the sides should be left open, except in very cold, frosty weather.

The bed in which to plant the bulbs should be raised above ground level to ensure good drainage. The sides may be made of brick, breeze blocks or old railway sleepers, which are the easiest. If there are moles in the garden it is advisable to cover the base of the frame with wire netting, and small-mesh netting will also keep out mice. The sides of the frame can vary in height from about 30cm upwards. Small bulbs can be seen better if the surface of the frame is about waist height.

The bottom 30cm or so should be made up of coarse stones, ash, clinker or gravel, to provide absolutely free drainage. Above this put a layer of peat, leaf-mould compost or old mushroom manure up to 10cm and above this the compost in which the roots will feed. It should consist of loam, peat or leaf mould, sand and grit in roughly equal proportions for bulbs which want a rich soil; and with more sand and grit for smaller bulbs and for those which

require exceptionally good drainage; the addition of crushed limestone, which is sold as poultry feed, is very beneficial to most bulbs. For a small frame, sterilized JIP3 may be used instead of the loam; otherwise a general fertilizer can be added to the soil as it is mixed: 15–20cm of this soil is ample for all bulbs. The bulbs themselves may be planted on top of this, and the delicate or difficult ones encased in coarse silver sand. This definitely seems beneficial for producing good root growth on Fritillaries,

Plastic lattice pots of different sizes, with aluminium labels attached

Crocuses and *Iris reticulata*. The soil around the bulbs can be similar to that for them to root in, or more sandy, and the frame can be topped with 3–5cm of gravel, so that drainage is especially good round the neck of the plant. The bulbs should be carefully labelled, and similar ones not put next to each other, so that they can be separated if they are moved while dormant. Similar species can also be separated by vertical tiles or pieces of slate, or planted in plastic lattice pots sold for planting aquatics. They hardly restrict the root system of the plant, but they prevent the bulbs going astray and make it very easy to move the bulbs while they are dormant. They also have the advantage that the labels can be attached firmly to them, and a Hartley aluminium label is especially suitable for this purpose.

Watering and feeding

Most hardy bulbs begin their season's growth in September when they make roots, and become dormant again in May. These are the ones that the bulb frame is designed to accommodate, and the watering regime should take this into account. A very thorough watering should be given in September, to soak the whole frame, and a second in October if the weather is hot and dry. No more watering is needed until spring when top growth begins to show and in March and April several waterings should be given, preferably on a sunny windy day, so that the leaves, if they have been wetted, and the surface can dry as quickly as possible. Liquid fertilizer can be incorporated into the spring waterings, using a low-nitrogen compound such as Tomorite. This will promote healthy growth and flowering, and not produce too much lush leafage, which can encourage botrytis in damp weather.

Bulbs in the alpine house

These will require the same regime as in the bulb frame, but watering will need to be more carefully done, so that there is no drying out while the bulbs are in growth. If they dry out, even for a short time, they become dormant, and nothing will induce them to start again before the following autumn. For this reason bulbs are safer if the pots are plunged in sand which can be kept well watered. The alpine house has the great advantage over the bulb frame that some frost protection can be arranged in exceptionally cold winters, and that winter-flowering bulbs can be admired in comfort. After bulb foliage has died down, the pots can be stored out of the way under the bench or in a warm shed until autumn.

9

Propagation

Most bulbs are easily propagated, by either division or seeds. Commercial stocks have usually been selected for their vegetative vigour and ease of propagation, so they usually cause little trouble, but the rarer bulbs are often slow to increase and may require more care.

Seed

Seed is the best method of increasing stock. Where several members of one genus are grown together, it is advisable to hand pollinate the flowers to make sure that the seed is true and, if necessary, cover the flower to prevent cross-pollination by insects. Most species of bulbs with showy flowers are normally self-sterile, so it will be necessary to use two flowers from different clones as parents. Seed of most genera germinates best when fresh, so if planted in September of the year in which it ripens, and kept outside, much of it will germinate the following spring. Some species require a cold period to stimulate germination, some, including many lilies, have more complex requirements, so that germination appears to be delayed for a year. The young bulbs will usually be found clustered around the sides at the base of the pot, so if germination has been good they should be repotted after the first year.

Division

Division of the bulb is necessary where especially good forms are to be increased or where seed is unobtainable. There are many different ways depending on the type of bulb.

A Daffodil, Hyacinth or *Allium* can be induced to form bulblets by making a cross cut in the base of the bulb through the basal plate, just into the scales and inserting a small stone to keep the sides apart. These bulblets should be treated as seedlings. The cutting is best done in summer while the bulbs are dormant.

Few-scaled bulbs such as Fritillaries can be easily increased by breaking the scales apart and planting each separately. The piece which contains next year's bud will probably flower as well as if nothing had happened, and the other half will make a flowering-size bulb in one year. For larger Fritillaries such as *F. imperialis* and *F. persica* the bulb may be cut into many pieces with a sharp knife and the resulting pieces treated like lily-scales. In many-scaled bulbs such as lilies, single scales can be broken off and planted in loose peaty soil with the tip of the scale just above the soil. A new bulb will soon form at the base, and this can be treated like a seedling.

Corms are more difficult. Crocuses can be induced to make more than one shoot by carefully cutting out the single main shoot, thus stimulating the producing of adventitious buds on the edge of the corm.

Tubers and rhizomes can sometimes be increased by cutting them into pieces, depending on whether they have one or several growing points. Tuberous roots will often make new plants if they are divided at their point of attachment, but will usually fail to grow if cut lower down. One method of vegetative propagation that may be used successfully with Trilliums is to remove the soil to expose the growing point of the rhizome, but without disturbing the roots. Then cut off the top at the ring showing the line of new growth; several small bulbs will then form which should be removed in the summer and planted in rich soil. If only a single bulb is available and it is required for flowering, a narrow wedge may be removed around the line of the new growth ring without damaging the growing crown and multiplication along this cut will occur.

Pests and diseases

When grown in small numbers by amateurs, bulbs are remarkably untroubled by pests or diseases, provided that the original bulbs were healthy. It is when a large number of bulbs are grown close together, especially if they are of one genus or family, that troubles are likely to become serious, or spread very quickly.

Pests

Many different animals often attack bulbs, but in my experience four or five are the most serious culprits. Sparrows can be very destructive, eating the flowers of Crocuses and other early bulbs. Mice sometimes eat a large number in a very short time once they have developed a taste for bulbs: at Wisley they have caused great damage, but in my own garden in Kent they do not seem to bother about bulbs. On rich or heavy soils slugs are the major

Various slugs, and a cutworm

problem, especially the very small black ones which live underground and eat the young roots and the softer parts of bulbs. Watering with liquid slug killer will kill some, but the best deterrent is to surround the bulbs with a good layer of coarse sand when planting. Lilies are particularly badly attacked, Daffodils and Snowdrops least affected. Surface-living slugs are less harmful and can be killed with blue slug pellets.

The larvae of vine weevils (*Otiorrhynchus sulcatus*) are very destructive, eating the roots of Cyclamen, Lilies and other plants grown in pots. At the first sign of attack, the plants should be carefully repotted and all the old soil burnt. The adults are about 1cm long, and emerge at night, feeding on leaves and flowers. They can be found with a torch. Other destructive night-feeders are 'cut-worms', the green or brown caterpillars of various noctuid moths, such as the Yellow Underwing (*Noctua pronuba*) and the Turnip moths (*Agrotis* spp.). They love the dry conditions and loose soil of a bulb frame and hide several inches down in the day. Again, they are best caught at night.

There are a few more specialized pests which are less common but can cause great damage. The Narcissus fly (about three species are involved) lays its eggs among the dying foliage and the larvae feed inside the bulb, finally killing it by eating out its heart. Any sick looking or soft Daffodil bulbs should be burnt. The Lily beetle is a beautiful bright red and eats the leaves and buds of Lilies; its larvae are horrible, covered in their own excrement, and can soon strip a Lily plant of leaves. They also attack Fritillaries. Greenfly or aphids can be very common in

Larva of large Narcissus fly

Larvae of the Vine Weevil

some seasons and, apart from causing distortion of the leaves and flowers, are the main carriers of virus diseases. Any colonies seen should be sprayed immediately, and a regular spraying programme with a persistent systemic insecticide such as Abol X will prevent the aphids getting a hold on the delicate young growths of Lilies, Irises, etc.

Diseases

Diseases caused by fungi, bacteria or viruses are less easy to identify, but are well described and illustrated in the Ministry of Agriculture bulletin, *Diseases of Bulbs*, ADAS HPDI (1979).

The worst diseases of hardy bulbs are the moulds of various species of *Botrytis*. They attack the leaves and stems, particularly in warm wet weather, starting with brown patches on the leaves or at soil level, and finally killing the whole plant. Removal of any infected plants and spraying the remainder with captan, benlate or some other fungicide will usually control an outbreak, but some plants, especially *Iris persica*, always seem to succumb in the end. Small black knob-like 'sclerotia' can often be found on infected bulbs in summer, and they should always be removed and burnt. Soaking the bulbs before planting in a systemic fungicide such as benlate is also helpful in controlling various rots.

Iris reticulata bulbs infected with Ink spot (*Mystrosporium adjustum*)

Iris pseudocaucasica and *Colchicum* infected with *Botrytis*

A common disease of *Iris reticulata* and related species is the so-called 'Ink Spot' disease, which forms black stains on the bulb tunic, before infecting the whole bulb and killing it. Infected bulbs are best burnt, and healthy ones nearby treated with a fungicide.

Virus diseases do not immediately kill the plants, but they weaken them and cause unsightly spotting and streaking on the leaves and flowers. Most cultivated clones are relatively resistant, and in the case of Tulips, the virus causes the beautiful 'broken' effects shown on p.131; these are sold as 'Rembrandt' Tulips and should not be planted near other healthy, more delicate bulbs. The same goes for bulbous Irises and many other bulbs where the virus shows up as pale yellowish patches on the leaves. Many Lilies are especially easily infected, while Fritillaries seem almost immune. Viruses can be controlled by ruthless burning of any infected plants, by control of aphids and by keeping newly acquired plants in quarantine, away from healthy ones until they have been 'passed'. There is now the possibility of producing virus-free stocks of infected cultivars by tissue culture, but it is still an expensive business. Viruses are generally not transmitted through seeds, so clean stocks can be raised from seed.

The photographs

When shooting wild flowers in the field it is essential to work from a tripod, so that you can take advantage of the opportunity to use a slow shutter speed and thus a smaller aperture, giving greater depth of field. In practice the best speed is normally 1/15 sec although if there is a strong wind you may have to go up to 1/30 or in extremes 1/60.

Glossary

annulate splitting into rings at the base (of a Crocus corm).
anther the part of the stamen (q.v.) that contains the pollen.
axil angle between a leaf stalk and the stem.
bract a modified leaf below a flower.
bulb an underground storage organ consisting of modified leaves.
bulbil a small bulb which can be detached from the larger bulb on which it grows and form an independent plant.
canaliculate u-shaped in section (of leaf).
chaparral a low, dense scrub, characteristic of California.
ciliate fringed or surrounded with hairs.
clone vegetatively produced progeny of a single plant.
corm bulb-like subterranean swollen stem of a plant, e.g. a crocus.
corona tubular structure on the inner side of the petals, e.g. the trumpet of a Daffodil.
cultivar a cultivated variety.
dehisce to burst open (of a stamen).
diploid containing twice the basic number of chromosomes (the usual complement).
emarginate with the apex indented.
fall the outer petals of an Iris.
filament that part of the stamen that supports the anther (q.v.).
garrigue scattered, low scrub common in limestone areas of the Mediterranean region.
glabrous smooth, i.e. hairless.
glaucous a greyish 'bloom' especially on leaves.
hybrid the offspring of two plants of different species or varieties.
inflorescence the part of the plant on which the flowers are borne.
loess a deposit of fine silt or dust (found in the arid interior of Asia, Eastern Europe and central USA).
maquis scrub consisting of small trees and shrubs and found in parts of the Mediterranean region.
nectary the part of the flower which secretes nectar, generally at the base of the petal.
ovary the lowest or innermost part of the flower, which ultimately becomes the seed vessel.
paniculate arranged in a panicle, i.e. a compound, pyramidal inflorescence.
papillose covered with small, fleshy projections.
pedicel the stalk of a flower.
perianth the outer ring of petals (q.v.).
petal generally the coloured part of the flower (often called tepals or perianth segments in the Lily family).
raceme a simple inflorescence (q.v.) in which the flowers are arranged on short nearly equal stalks on an elongated axis.
racemose arranged in racemes.
rhizome an underground modified stem, often swollen and fleshy.
scabrid rough, with small knobs.
scarious having a dry and papery appearance.
serpentine a dull green or dark reddish rock which, because of its mineral content, supports little but often interesting vegetation.
sessile without a stalk.
spadix form of inflorescence (q.v.) consisting of a thick, fleshy spike, closely set with minute flowers (in *Arum* family).
spathe large leafy bract wrapped round the inflorescence, particularly in the *Arum* family.
species group of individuals having common characteristics, distinct from other groups; the basic unit of botanical classification.
standard inner petals of an Iris flower, which are usually held erect.
stigma the part of the flower which receives the pollen, usually on the apex of the style which connects it to the ovary.
subspecies group within a species showing certain minor differences.
triploid with three times the basic number of chromosomes. (c.f. diploid q.v.). An unusual complement often producing a robust but sterile plant.
tuber swollen rhizome (see p.6).
tunic the outer skin of a bulb or corm, especially of Crocus.
umbel flat-topped inflorescence in which all the flower stalks arise from a single point.
whorl group of leaves or flowers arising at one level around the stem.

(a) **Galanthus plicatus** Bieb. (*Amaryllidaceae*).
Native of western Russia, eastern Romania and
the Crimea, growing in woods and scrub,
flowering in February and March. Height
12–25cm. Distinguished from other
spring-flowering snowdrops by having its
leaf-edges folded back in the leaf sheath: the
leaves are glaucous and there is a single green
spot on each inner petal (cf. *G. byzantinus* p.14).
There is also a double form, and an especially
fine clone c.v. 'Warham' collected during the
Crimean war. Easily grown in good moist soil, in
shade or half-shade.

(b) **Galanthus plicatus × nivalis**
(*Amaryllidaceae*). This is a robust garden
hybrid, the leaves are partly flat and partly
folded back, suggesting that the parentage is *G.
plicatus* (a) × *nivalis* (h) (cf. p.17). Baker named
plants of this parentage *G. × grandiflorus*, and
they are reported by E. A. Bowles to be
short-lived in cultivation.

(c), (e) **Galanthus elwesii** Hook. fil.
(*Amaryllidaceae*). Native of Yugoslavia,
Romania and the Ukraine south to Greece and
west Turkey, growing in woods, scrub and
among rocks, flowering from February to April.
Height 10–30cm. Distinguished from other
species by its glaucous leaves, one folded inside
the other, and inner petals with two spots which
sometimes join so that the whole inner petal is
green. Height and width of leaves are very
variable (see p.14). *Galanthus* 'Merlin', a
beautiful cultivar with a very dark green inner
segment, may be a hybrid between this and
another species. Easily grown, but better in
more well-drained soil than the other species.

(d) **Leucojum vernum** L. (*Amaryllidaceae*)
Spring Snowflake. Native of central Europe
from Romania and western Russia to the
Pyrenees and Belgium, and naturalised in south
England, Denmark and Holland. It grows in
woods and on steep shady hillsides often in great
quantity, flowering from March to May, as soon
as the snow melts. Height usually 15–20cm, but
up to 35cm. Plants from the western part of the
species range have a green spot on each petal,
whereas plants from the eastern part have a
yellowish spot, and are somewhat larger: they
have been called var. *carpathicum* Sweet (see
p.5). Var. *vagneri* Stapf from Hungary is also
robust usually with two flowers to a stem as
shown here. Easy to grow in any moist soil, in
shade or semi-shade.

(f) **Galanthus elwesii** subsp. **minor** D. A.
Webb, syn. *G. graecus* auct. (*Amaryllidaceae*).
Native of NE Greece, S Bulgaria and some of the
Aegean islands, growing in woods at
100–1300m, flowering in February and March.
Distinguished by its narrow twisted leaves and
pale yellowish-green ovary. The inner petals
have a large green basal spot. Stem 8–12cm.
Intermediates between this and subsp. *elwesii*
are common in Bulgaria. They have been called
G. maximus Velen. See also p.14 (e). Easily
grown, but better in a sunnier more open spot
than the other species, and in well-drained soil.

(g), (h) **Galanthus nivalis** L. (*Amaryllidaceae*).
Common Snowdrop. Native of almost the whole
of Europe except for the west, from Russia to
Spain and Sicily; naturalised but probably not
native in England, Scotland, Holland, Belgium
and Scandinavia. It grows in woods and scrub
and by streams, flowering from January to
March. Height usually 10–20cm. Leaves
glaucous, flat in the sheath; flower always with a
single green spot. Double forms are common in
gardens and some of the many named garden
forms and hybrids are shown on pp.14 and 17.

²/₃ life size Photographed 11 February

13

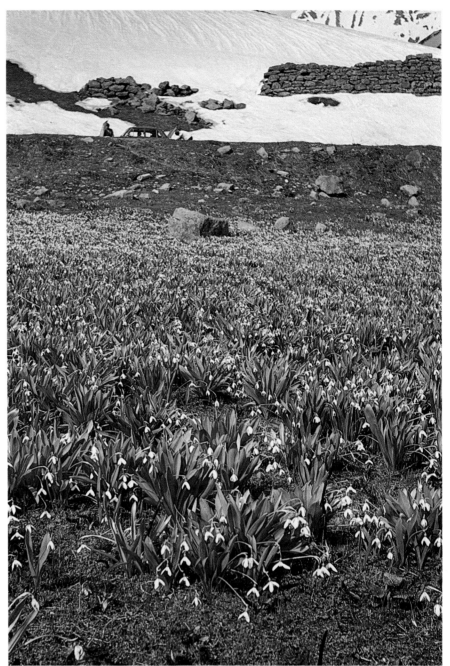

(a) Galanthus nivalis 'Scharlockii' (*Amaryllidaceae*). A late flowering clone of *G. nivalis*, characterised by its long bifid spathe and small flowers with a pale green mark on each outer petal. It was discovered by Julius Scharlock in the valley of the Nahe river, a tributary of the Rhine, in the mid nineteenth century.

(b), (c) Galanthus ikariae Baker (*Amaryllidaceae*). Native of the Aegean islands of Andros, Tinos and Ikaria, and of northern Turkey and the Caucasus, growing in woods and among shady rocks at low altitudes, flowering in February and March.
Two distinct forms are shown here: (b) with a tall stem and inner petals with a small green spot, was collected in northern Turkey. It is similar to a collection from Andros (see p.16); (c) is a cultivated form with shorter leaves at flowering, and larger flowers with the inner petal almost all green. It is illustrated in *Bot. Mag.* 9474, but its origin is not recorded. Both are distinct from other species in their broad shining green leaves, recurving at their ends, and lobed inner petals. Easy to grow in good soil, in shade or half-shade. Source (b) Turkey, Trabzon, Zigana pass, 1100m, Furse & Synge 178; (c) cultivated stock.

(d) Galanthus byzantinus Baker (*Amaryllidaceae*). Native of NW Turkey, growing at 100–500m, in fields and scrub, flowering from January to March. Very similar to *G. plicatus* (p.12), differing in its inner petals which have a green blotch at their base. Leaves folded back in the sheath, dark green, somewhat glaucous. Height 10–20cm. Easy to grow in good soil, in sun or shade. Source (d) cultivated stock.
Field shot photographed in NW Turkey, Abant, in March 1975 by B. Mathew 8511.

(e) Galanthus elwesii Hooker fil. (*Amaryllidaceae*). A small narrow-leaved form of this variable species (see pp.12 (c) and 2 (e)) collected in NW Turkey. The species is named after H. J. Elwes (1846–1922), an English sportsman and plant collector, author of 'A monograph of the genus *Lilium*' and with A. Henry *The Trees of Great Britain and Ireland* (see also p.94).
Source Turkey, Ankara, Elma Dağ, 1700m, Rix 1524.

Galanthus platyphyllus Traub & Moldenke, syn. *G. latifolius* Rupr. (*Amaryllidaceae*). Native of the central and western Caucasus where it grows in alpine and subalpine meadows, flowering in May and June. Very close to *G. ikariae* Baker, but plant usually larger, flowers on shorter pedicels and inner petals unlobed with a bold green spot.
Photographed in the central Caucasus, by the Georgian Military Highway on the south side of the Krestovje pass at 2500m, in May 1978.

Galanthus platyphyllus

Galanthus byzantinus

15

¾ life size Photographed 13 February

I. rosenbachiana ½ life size 2 February

Galanthus ikariae Photographed 21 March

½ life size Photographed 13 February

(a) Galanthus ikariae Baker (*Amaryllidaceae*) (see p.15 (b), (c).) The form shown here was collected on Andros, and is very similar to that from N Turkey shown on p.14(b); another form. Photographed in cultivation.

(b) Galanthus fosteri Baker (*Amaryllidaceae*). Native of Turkey and Lebanon where it grows among mountain rocks and in scrub, at around 1600m, flowering in February and March. It has rather broad dark green leaves like *G. ikariae* but there are two green spots on the inner petals. Reputed to be difficult in cultivation. It has survived well in a dry sunny bulb frame at Wisley. Source Turkey, Adana, above Haruniye, 1400m, P. Davis 26830.

(c) Galanthus rizehensis Stern (*Amaryllidaceae*). Native of north-eastern Turkey at c.150m in the foothills of the Pontus mountains above Rize and Trabzon, growing in woods, flowering in January. Very similar to *G. nivalis* in general appearance, but has bright shining green leaves. Easy to grow in the same conditions as suit most other snowdrops.

(d), (e) Galanthus caucasicus (Baker) Grossh.

(*Amaryllidaceae*). Native of the Caucasus and the Caspian coast where it grows in woods in the foothills, flowering from December to March. Very variable in leaf width, size and in flowering time in cultivation, but can be recognised by its glaucous leaves, one folded inside the other in the sheath. A robust and easy species in good soil in shade.

(f) Galanthus nivalis 'Magnet'. A large form of *G. nivalis* raised by J. Allen (see (i)) in the late nineteenth century. The flower hangs on a long graceful pedicel.

(g) Galanthus nivalis 'Atkinsii'. A large and robust form of *G. nivalis*, named by J. Allen (see (i)) after James Atkins of Painswick in Gloucestershire. The flower has an unusually short pedicel, almost hidden in the spathe.

(h) Galanthus nivalis 'Lutescens'. A pale delicate form of *G. nivalis*, requiring more care than the ordinary form. Originated in Northumberland in the nineteenth century.

(i) Galanthus allenii Baker (*Amaryllidaceae*). The origin of this species is something of a

mystery. It is intermediate between *G. caucasicus* and *G. ikariae* and was spotted by the great Snowdrop grower James Allen of Shepton Mallett, Somerset, in a consignment of bulbs from the Caucasus. Possibly a hybrid.

(j) Galanthus nivalis 'S. Arnott'. This fine form was named after Samuel Arnott, Provost of Dumfries (1800–1900) who introduced it into cultivation. The outer petals are very short and broad.

Iris. rosenbachiana Regel, syn. *I. nicolai* Vved. (*Iridaceae*, section *Juno*)). Native of Central Asia, especially the Pamir Alai, and NE Afghanistan, where it grows on stony hillsides and dry earthy slopes flowering from March to April. Plant about 10cm high at flowering, the leaves expanding later to about 15cm long. The form shown was that called *I. nicolai* Vved., and *I. rosenbachiana* was described as purple-flowered, but the two are now considered merely as colour forms of one species, cf. *I. persica* (p.58). Rare in cultivation and not easy, but should grow in a very well drained soil, kept rather dry and protected from rain in summer and in winter. Source Tashkent Botanic Garden.

(a) Crocus alatavicus Regel & Semenov (*Iridaceae*). Native of Central Asia, especially the Ala-Tau, the Tien Shan and the Pamir-Alai, growing in stony places and scrub in the mountains and flowering from February to May according to altitude. It often grows with the yellow *Colchicum luteum* (p.33), whereas the yellow *Crocus korolkowii* grows with the white *Colchicum kesselringii* (p.33). Easy in a bulb frame kept dry in summer. Source Central Asia, Chimgan valley, NE of Tashkent, 1700m, Rix 2765.

(b) Crocus korolkowii Regel & Maw (*Iridaceae*). Native of northern Afghanistan, Chitral and Central Asia, especially the Tien Shan and the Pamir Alai, growing in stony and grassy places in the mountains and foothills from 600 to 2600m, flowering from February to May. Easy in a bulb frame but possible in a place outside. Source Central Asia, foothills N of Dushanbe, 1200m, Rix 2728.

(c) Crocus graveolens Boiss. & Reut. (*Iridaceae*). Native of southern Turkey and Syria growing in stony fields, scrub and pine forest at c.1000m, flowering in February and March. Distinguished from other yellow-flowered species by its finely divided stigma (about twelve threads), and many narrow, grey-green leaves and parallel fibred corm tunic. The flowers smell of elder. The closely related *C. vitellinus* Wahl. has fewer deep green broader leaves. Cultivation as (a). Source S Turkey, Hatay, near Yayladağ, Rix 1365.

(d) Crocus nevadensis Amo (*Iridaceae*). Native of SE Spain and N Africa, growing in mountain meadows, scree, scrub and open pine forest from 1000 to 3000m, flowering from February to April. Petals sometimes, e.g. from the Sierra de Cazorla, unmarked. The whitish fimbriate stigmas are characteristic. Very susceptible to botrytis which infects the dead flowers and if not checked, can kill the leaves and bulb. Source S Spain, Sierra Nevada above Granada, Rix s.n.

(e) Crocus flavus Weston × **C. angustifolius** Weston. See pp.25 (f) and 29 (f). The slightly reticulate tunic shows this to be a hybrid. *C. flavus* is native of SE Europe and W Turkey and has a parallel fibred tunic.

(f) Crocus candidus Clarke (*Iridaceae*). Native of western Turkey growing in woods and scrub, flowering in February and March. It is especially common in scrub along the Dardanelles and in the pine woods above Troy. Leaves one or two, very wide (see p.25). Styles yellow-orange, much divided. Cultivation as (a). Source NW Turkey, NE of Çanakkale, 130m, N. M. G.Marr 198.

(g) Crocus sieberi Gay, syn. *C. atticus* Boiss. (*Iridaceae*). Native of Albania, S Yugoslavia, Greece and Crete, growing in stony places in mountains, woods and scrub usually above 1000m, flowering from March to June. Other colour forms are shown and described on p.24 (d), (e). Cultivation as (b). Source Greece, Elion Oros, S of Levadhia, 1100m, Rix 2176.

Crocus tommasinianus
Crocus tommasinianus Herbert (*Iridaceae*). Native of S Hungary, Yugoslavia and N Bulgaria, where it grows in woods and shady hillsides, especially on limestone, at around 1000m, flowering in January and February. The leaves are always well developed by flowering time. The combination of narrow leaves, purple flower and white tube distinguishes this species from *C. vernus* (p.26). Easily grown in well-drained soil or short grass.

Crocus tommasinianus

life size Photographed 11 February

(a) **Crocus melantherus** Boiss. & Orph., syn. *Crocus crewei* Hooker fil. (*Iridaceae*). Native of S Greece and western Turkey, growing in evergreen oak scrub and pine forests at 100–1000m, flowering from November till March. Grows outside in stony soil in full sun, but better in a bulb frame because it flowers so early. Source Turkey, Bergama, 260m, Marr 3282. See also p.175 (e).

(b) & (c) **Crocus chrysanthus** (Herbert) Herbert (*Iridaceae*). Native of Yugoslavia and Romania to Greece and southern Turkey, usually on bare stony or grassy slopes, at 1000–2000m, flowering from March to June, according to altitude. Cultivation as (a). Source Turkey, NW of Maraş, Berit Da., 2000m, Rix 700, and near Pazaçik, 1000m, Rix 1395.

(d) **Crocus biflorus** Miller (*Iridaceae*). This very variable species is native from Italy and Sicily eastwards to Georgia, Turkey, and N Iran, growing in damp woods, on dry open stony hillsides and alpine turf at up to 3000m, flowering from January to May. The lilac or blue flowers are characteristic of the species (see pp.23 and 25). Source SE Turkey, Bitlis, dry stony hillside, 2000m, Rix 707.

(e) **Crocus weldenii** Hoppe & Furnrohr, syn. *C. biflorus* var. *albus* Herbert (*Iridaceae*). Native of S Yugoslavia, growing in rocky woods especially on limestone at about 1000m. Cultivate as (a). Source Yugoslavia, Kičevo, Marr 45.

(f) **Crocus fleischeri** Gay (*Iridaceae*). Native of western and southern Turkey where it grows on dry rocky hillsides and in evergreen oak scrub at around 1000m, flowering from January till March. Source SW Turkey, Antalya, near Elmali, Rix 1315.

(g) **Crocus olivieri** Gay, syn. *C. suterianus* Herbert (*Iridaceae*). Native of Albania, Yugoslavia and Bulgaria to Greece and Turkey, growing on open hillsides in deciduous scrub, or in pine woods, from sea level to 1500m, flowering from January till March. Plants from Greece usually have broader leaves with some purple on the back of the flower. Subsp. *balansae* from W Turkey around Izmir has flowers usually purplish outside, and styles divided into twelve, not six branches. Source Turkey, between Istanbul and Ankara, Rix 651.

(h) **Crocus antalyensis** Mathew (*Iridaceae*). Native of south-west and west Turkey, near Antalya and near Bileçik, growing in evergreen oak scrub at c.1000m, flowering in early spring. Best kept in a bulb frame in full sun. Source S Turkey, mountains S of Antalya, 1000m, Rix 1318. (This is the type collection.)

(i) **Crocus minimus** DC. (*Iridaceae*). Native of south Corsica at low altitudes, and in Sardinia growing in scrub, flowering from January to April. Cultivation as (a).

(j) **Crocus cyprius** Boiss. & Kotschy (*Iridaceae*). Native of Cyprus, especially in the Troodos mountains, growing in stony places, flowering from January to April. Distinguished from *C. hartmannianus* (k) by its papery annulate corm tunic. Cultivation as (a).

(k) **C. hartmannianus** Holmboe (*Iridaceae*). Native of Cyprus, in the Troodos mountains where it is said to be rare, growing at about 880m, flowering in mid February. Very closely related to *C. cyprius* (j), but with a coarser tunic with parallel fibres. Cultivation as (a). Source Cyprus, coll. E. Hodgkin s.n.

life size Photographed 13 February

life size Photographed 13 February

Crocus gargaricus

Crocus scardicus Kosanin (*Iridaceae*). Native of south-western Yugoslavia, where it grows at altitudes of 1700–2500m, by late snow patches, flowering from May to July. Photographed in Yugoslavia, Sar Planina, by Oleg Polunin 7153B.

Crocus sieberi Gay (see p.19 (g)). Photographed in Greece, S Peloponnese, Taygetos mts, between Kalamata and Sparta, 1300m, 12 April 1972.

Crocus gargaricus Herbert (see p.25 (m)). Photographed in NW Turkey, Ulu Dağ above Bursa, 2000m, in March 1975 by Brian Mathew 8515.

Crocus biflorus
Crocus biflorus Miller (see p.21 (d)). A variable species native from Italy and Sicily eastwards to Georgia, Turkey, and N Iran, growing in damp woods, on dry open stony hillsides and alpine turf at up to 3000m, flowering from January to May. Photographed in central Turkey, Kuruca geçidi, E of Bingöl, 2000m, 10 May 1971.

Crocus chrysanthus cultivars
These were raised by crossing *C. chrysanthus* (p.21) with various forms of *C. biflorus* (pp.21, 25, 27, 31) and selecting far larger flowers and unusual markings and colour combinations. The breeding programme was initiated by John Hoog of the famous bulb firm of Van Tubergen at Zwanenburg Nurseries in Haarlem, and E. A. Bowles (1865–1954) author of *A Handbook of Crocus and Colchicum for Gardeners*, who exchanged bulbs and named their finest hybrids

Crocus sieberi

Crocus biflorus

in each other's honour. Other named cultivars are selected clones of either species. Bowles named many of his hybrids after birds, and some are still in commerce today. (**a**) **'Advance'** (hybrid), (**b**) **'Goldilocks'**, (**c**) **'Gypsy Girl'**, (**d**) **'Saturnus'** (hybrid), (**e**) **'Blue Bird'** (*C. biflorus*), (**f**) **'Blue Pearl'** (syn. 'Blue Giant'), (**g**) **'Snow Bunting'** (hybrid), (**h**) **'Zwanenburg Bronze'**, (**i**) **'Cream Beauty'** (hybrid), (**j**) **'Nanette'**.

Crocus scardicus

23

life size Photographed 18 February

(a) Crocus versicolor Ker-Gawler (*Iridaceae*). Native of the Alpes Maritimes, growing in scrubs and among rocks at up to 1200m, flowering from February to April. Grow in a bulb frame or sunny well-drained place outside. Source P. J. Christian 52.

(b) Crocus alexandri Ničić ex Velen. (*Iridaceae*). Native of Yugoslavia, especially around Skopje. This striking colour form of *C. biflorus* (p.21 (d)) has been in cultivation for many years. Cultivation as (a).

(c) Crocus etruscus Parl. (*Iridaceae*). Native of western Italy, growing in deciduous woods and stony fields, flowering from February to April. The form shown here is the cv. 'Zwanenburg'.

(d) Crocus sieberi Gay var. **sieberi**, syn. *C. sieberi* var. *heterochromus* Hal., *C. sieberi* var *versicolor* Boiss. & Held. (*Iridaceae*). Native of Crete, in the White Mountains, where it grows in the hills above the Omalos plain. Better grown in a bulb frame. 'Hubert Edelsten' is a hybrid between var. *sieberi* and var. *atticus* (p.19 (g)).

(e) Crocus sieberi Gay forma **tricolor** Burtt. This beautiful form originated in the northern Peloponnese on Mt Chelmos. The plant shown is abnormally small.

(f) Crocus angustifolius Weston, syn *C. susianus* Ker-Gawl. (*Iridaceae*). Native of the Crimea where it grows on hillsides, and in scrub and Juniper woods, flowering in February and March. Cultivation as (a).

(g) Crocus biliottii Maw (*Iridaceae*). Native of northern Turkey, especially the Pontus mountains, where it grows in grassy and stony places at c.2000m, flowering in May. The leaves are curved, rather stiff, and glaucous. Cultivation as (a). Source NE Turkey, pass from Bayburt to Of, Rix 1002.

(h) Crocus pestalozzae Boiss. (*Iridaceae*). Native of north-western Turkey on both the European and Asiatic side of the Bosphorus, near Istanbul, growing in fields and on low hills below 200m, flowering January to March. Has small black spots at the base of the filaments.

(i) Crocus candidus Clarke (*Iridaceae*) (see p.19 (f)). Source Turkey, near Çanakkale. H. & M. Crook 3026.

(j) Crocus ancyrensis (Herb.) Maw (*Iridaceae*). Native of western Turkey where it grows on dry hillsides at 1500–2000m, flowering in March and April. Source Turkey, near Ankara, Baytop.

(k) Crocus baytopiorum Mathew (*Iridaceae*). Native of western Turkey, especially Honaz Dağ, where it grows at about 1400m, flowering in February. The only member of the *C. vernus* group yet found in Turkey. For a bulb frame. Source Turkey, Honaz Dağ, A. & T. Baytop.

(l) Crocus reticulatus Steven ex Adam (*Iridaceae*). Native of SE Europe from NE Italy and Hungary to Bulgaria, S Turkey and the Caucasus, growing in woods and meadows up to 2000m, flowering from February to April. Source Caucasus, Ordzonikidze, M. Prasil 156–76.

(m) Crocus gargaricus Herbert (*Iridaceae*). Native of north-western Turkey, especially Ulu Dağ and Kaz Dağ, where it grows in great quantity on grassy slopes (see p.23). Easy to grow in a frame in peaty soil. Source Turkey, Ulu Dağ, above Bursa, 2100m, Rix 1209a.

life size Photographed 18 February

life size Photographed 18 February

(a) **Crocus vernus** (L.) Hill (*Iridaceae*). Native of the mountains of Europe from the Pyrenees eastwards to Poland and Russia, and south to Sicily and Yugoslavia, growing in grassland, scrub and open woods, flowering from February to June. Two subspecies are recognised: subsp. *vernus*, shown here, usually with purple flowers, occurs from Italy eastwards. Subsp. *albiflorus* (Kit.) Asch. & Graeb. is the common white crocus of alpine meadows, found from Czechoslovakia westwards. Subsp. *vernus* is easy in grass, and is the origin of the large Dutch purple crocus. Subsp. *albiflorus* has proved difficult. Source Italy, Naples, nr Giovanni, Mrs P. Saunders.

(b) **Crocus veluchensis** Herbert (*Iridaceae*). Native of Yugoslavia, Bulgaria, Albania and Greece, growing in rocky ground, on mountain grassland and by late snow patches at 2000m, flowering from April to July according to altitude. Easy to grow in well-drained soil in sun. Source NE Greece, Pindus Mts, Katara pass, coll. Mrs F. Baxter.

(c) **Crocus dalmaticus** Vis. (*Iridaceae*). Native of south-west Yugoslavia and north Albania, especially the area around Dubrovnik, growing in limestone hills among oak scrub and in rocky grassland, flowering from January to April. Colour varies from buff to dark violet. Grow in a bulb frame. Source Yugoslavia, above Kotor, B. Mathew 5174.

(d) **Crocus imperati** Ten. (*Iridaceae*). Native of western Italy from Rome southwards, growing in woods, scrub and rough grassy places, flowering from January to March. The form shown here is an albino. The flowers are usually purple to almost white, with the outer petals beautifully striped and feathered outside. Subsp. *imperati*, style deep orange; from Naples southwards. Subsp. *suaveolens* (Bertol.) Mathew, style yellow or orange; Naples northwards. Grow in a bulb frame.

(e) **Crocus malyi** Vis. (*Iridaceae*). Native of NW Yugoslavia, especially the Velebit mountains, growing in grassy places and at the edges of woods from 650 to 1000m, flowering in March and April. Source Yugoslavia, Karlobag to Gospič, P. A. Cox and J. Marr 6.

(f) **Crocus carpetanus** Boiss. & Reut. (*Iridaceae*). Native of central and north-west Spain and N Portugal, growing in stony places in the mountains from 1200 to 2000m, flowering in April and May. The leaves which are U-shaped in section are characteristic as is the very soft fibrous tunic and whitish style. Easy to grow in a bulb frame, but needs frequent replanting as the corms tend to get crowded and smothered by their thick tunic. Source C Spain, Sierra de Guaderrama, near Rascafria, Rix s.n.

(g) **Crocus danfordiae** Maw (*Iridaceae*). Native of central and southern Turkey, especially around Ankara and in the central Tauros mountains, where it grows in rocky places, usually on limestone, at 1200–2000m. Flowers may be yellow or bluish. Grow in a bulb frame. Source Turkey, between Kayseri and Malatya, Rix 1401.

(h) **Crocus biflorus** Miller (*Iridaceae*). This form of *C. biflorus* is found on the island of Rhodes, off the SW corner of Turkey. Source Mt Profitis Ilias, 600m, among limestone rocks under pines, Rix 1272.

(i) **Crocus vernus** var. **leucostigma**. This differs from normal *C. vernus* in its slender white stigma, rather than the usual orange one. It has been known in cultivation for many years, but its origin is unknown.

life size Photographed 13 February

¼ life size Photographed 25 February

Crocus corsicus ½ life size 13 March

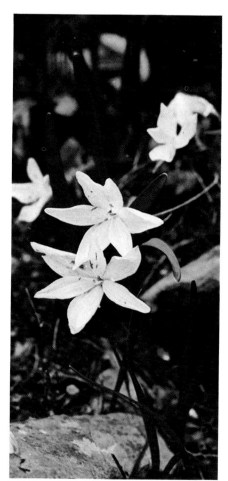

Sternbergia candida

(a) to (e) **Crocus vernus** cultivars (*Iridaceae*). These have been obtained by selection over several centuries from *C. vernus* subsp. *vernus*, p.27 (a). They survive well in grass, increasing by division to form solid patches. They should therefore be planted singly some distance apart, to produce a more natural effect. Shown here are:
(a) **'Pickwick'** (The flower is small because it has only just emerged and will expand).
(b) **'Remembrance'**.
(f) An old cultivated clone of *C. vernus*.
(g) **'King of the Whites'**.
(e) **'Little Dorritt'**.

(f) **Crocus 'Dutch Yellow'** or 'Large Yellow'. This old garden clone has been cultivated since the seventeenth century. It was formerly thought to be a form of *C. flavus*, but recent chromosome studies at Kew by C. Brighton and B. Mathew have shown it to be a triploid hybrid between *C. flavus* and *C. angustifolius* (p.25 (f)). Easily grown, but happier in better drained soil than the *C. vernus* cultivars.

(g) **Sternbergia fischerana** (Herb.) Roem. (*Amaryllidaceae*). Native of Iran and the Kopet Daǧ., to the Caucasus, Turkey and Syria, growing on stony slopes at 200–300m, flowering in February and March. A double-flowered form was recently collected in N Iran by Mrs A. Ala, and has been named 'Golestan'. Best grown in a pot or bulb frame where it can receive a good baking in summer to help initiate flowering.

(e) **Sternbergia colchiciflora** Waldst. & Kit. (*Amaryllidaceae*). Native of the Mediterranean region from Spain and France to Hungary, Turkey and Iran, where it grows on dry hillsides, flowering in autumn (see p.184). The leaves and seed pod shown here are highly characteristic. Easy to grow in a bulb frame, but

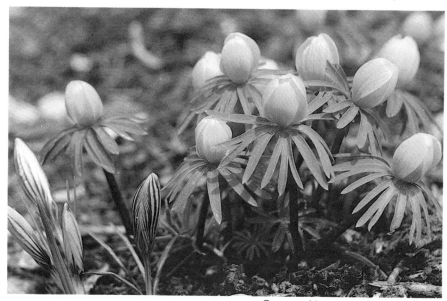

Crocus nubigenus and Eranthis cilicicus

rather too small and delicate to place outside. Source C Turkey, Kayseri to Gürün, 1500m, Rix 1599.

Crocus nubigenus Herbert (*Iridaceae*). This variant of the very variable *C. biflorus* (pp.20 (a), (d), (e) and 27 (h)) is found mainly in southern and western Turkey. It is very similar to *C. melantherus* but the ground colour is lilac rather than white. Growing with *Eranthis cilicicus* (see p.39). Photographed in S Turkey, Antalya, above Akseki, by O. Polunin.

Crocus corsicus Vanucci ex Maw (*Iridaceae*). Native of Corsica where it grows in stony and grassy places in the mountains, up to 2000m,

flowering from January till June according to altitude. Tunic fibrous and finely reticulate. Easy to grow in a bulb frame or in a dry sunny place outside in the south of England. Always one of the last crocuses to flower. Source Corsica, Monte D'Oro, c.1800m, Rix s.n.

Sternbergia candida Mathew & T. Baytop (*Amaryllidaceae*). Native of south-western Turkey, near Fethiye, where it was discovered as recently as 1976 by Oleg Polunin. It grows in scrub and among rocks at the edge of cedar forest, flowering in January and February. The only white *Sternbergia*. Petals 4.5–5cm; height 12–20cm. Photographed near Fethiye in February 1980 by O. Sønderhousen.

29

life size Photographed 25 February

(a) **Romulea columnae** Seb. & Mauri
(*Iridaceae*). Native of the Azores, western
England (Devon), and the Channel Is, S to Spain
and N Africa, Turkey and Israel, usually in
sandy places near the sea, flowering in February
and March. The flowers are always small, 1–2cm
long, and are usually pale lilac, with a yellow
throat. The inner bract is scarious. Easy to grow
in very sandy soil in a bulb frame or pot. Source
France, St Tropez, sandy cliff top, Rix s.n.

(b) **Romulea crocea** Boiss. & Held. (*Iridaceae*).
Native of southern Turkey, where it grows in
sandy places near the sea, flowering in March.
Easily recognised among Mediterranean species
by its yellow flowers, but otherwise very similar
to *R. bulbocodium*. Easy to grow in a very sandy
soil in a bulb frame. Source Turkey, Manavgat
to Alanya, fixed dunes by the sea, Rix 1334.

(c) **Crocus biflorus** Miller (*Iridaceae*). A
well-marked form of *C. biflorus* (see p.23 (c) etc.)
from Ulu Dag, north-west Turkey. Flowering
late, but easily grown and increasing well with
striking dark bluish flowers. In the wild it grows
with *C. gargaricus* (p.23). Source Turkey,
Bursa, Ulu Da, c.2000m, Rix 1209.

(d) (e) (h) **Romulea bulbocodium** (L.) Seb. &
Mauri (Iridaceae). Native of the Mediterranean
region from NW Spain and N Africa to
S France, Yugoslavia, Turkey and Israel,
growing in sandy and rocky places near the sea
and in scrub up to 1000m. Very variable in
flower size (20–35mm) and colour, varying from
white to pink and lilac. The flowers are often of
two sizes, the smaller flowers being
pollen-sterile, which makes the anthers appear
white – see (d) and (h): this phenomenon is
commoner in cultivation in some years than in
others. Easy to grow in a bulb frame, but not
long-lived in the open. Keep dry in summer and
replant regularly in good, very sandy soil.
Source (d) S Italy, above Matera, Rix 453; (e)
Greece, Corfu, 800m, Rix 459; (h) N Africa,
J. Archibald 839.

(f) **Romulea nivalis** (Boiss. & Kotschy) Klatt
(*Iridaceae*). Native of Syria (Anti-lebanon) and
the Lebanon, growing at 1400–2000m,
flowering in May and June near the melting
snow. Distinct in its rather stiff upright growth,
smallish flowers (20–25mm) with a very short
tube. Easy to grow in a bulb frame, but not
increasing as do many of the other species.
Source Mt Hermon.

(g) **Romulea tempskyana** Freyn (*Iridaceae*).
Native of SW Turkey from Izmir southwards,
Rhodes and Cyprus, growing on low hills and
sandy places up to 1000m, flowering in March.
Distinguished from other species by its dark
purple flowers 15–26mm long, with a long
slender tube, exserted from the bracts. Easy to
grow in a bulb frame and very striking when the
starry deep-purple flowers open wide in the sun.
Source Rhodes, dry sandy maquis, Rix 1243.

life size Photographed 11 February

life size Photographed 11 February

Iris pseudocaucasica

½ life size Photographed 25 February

Colchicum luteum

(a) Colchicum szovitsii Fischer & C. A. Meyer, syn. *C. nivale* Boiss. & Huet, *C. bifolium* Freyn & Sint. (*Liliaceae*). Native of Turkey, Iran, Soviet Armenia and the Kopet Dağ, growing in alpine meadows from 2000 to 3000m, and flowering from March to June. Flowers pink or white. Leaves usually two, glabrous. Easily grown in a bulb frame or raised bed, and probably better if not baked in summer. Source Turkey, Kayseri, Erciyes Dağ, alpine meadows, 2300m, Mathew & Tomlinson 4530.

(b) Colchicum fasciculare L., probably syn. *C. serpentinum* Woron. ex Miscz., *C. tauri* Siehe ex Stef. (*Liliaceae*). Native of the Caucasus and Turkey, growing on dry stony hills at c.1000m, flowering from February to April. Leaves sometimes hairy (*C. hirsutum* Stef.). Not difficult to grow in a dry bulb frame but slow to increase. Source Turkey, Malatya, limestone hills west of Darende, 1500m, Rix 1591.

(c) Colchicum kesselringii Regel (*Liliaceae*). Native of Central Asia, especially the Tien Shan and the Pamir Alai, and northern Afghanistan, from 1500 to 3000m, flowering from February to June depending on altitude, and growing on stony hillsides and alpine meadows. The flowers emerge as soon as the snow melts, and fade within a day or two to be followed by rather narrow leaves (up to 1cm wide). E. A. Bowles records that it grew well on a sunny bank until eaten by slugs. Cultivation as (a).

(d) Merendera hissarica Regel (*Liliaceae*). Native of Central Asia, especially in the Pamir Alai and the Tien Shan, N Afghanistan, growing in stony places at 2400–4000m, flowering in spring. Flowers rather similar to *Colchicum kesselringii*, but petals rounded and filamentous at the base. Anthers long compared with *M. trigyna* (g). Has survived and flowered in a bulb frame, but not increased. Source Afghanistan, SO623.

(e) Colchicum hungaricum Janka (*Liliaceae*). Native of south-eastern Europe, growing on stony hills, flowering from December to April. Leaves two or three, ciliate. Flowers purplish-pink to white. Leaves usually well developed at flowering. Cultivation as (a). Source Yugoslavia, Mathew & Tomlinson.

(f) Colchicum luteum Baker (*Liliaceae*). Native of Afghanistan, north-west India and Central Asia, especially the Tien Shan and the Pamir Alai, from 2000 to 3800m, growing on earthy slopes, flowering from March to July, at the edge of the melting snow. Not easy. The dead flowers are liable to botrytis which soon spreads to the developing leaves. Probably best planted in very gritty soil in a bulb frame and kept covered to protect from rain.

(g) Merendera trigyna (Adams) Woronow (*Liliaceae*). Native of the Caucasus, Turkey and N Iran, growing on dry slopes at about 1500–1800m, flowering from January to April. *Merendera* is close to *Colchicum*, but the petals are separate, so that the flower falls to pieces as it goes over. *M. kurdica* Bornm., from eastern Turkey and Iran, has broader petals and leaves. Easily grown in a bulb frame.

(h) Iris planifolia (Miller) Fiori & Paol., syn. *I. alata* Poiret (*Iridaceae*, section *Juno*). Native of the Mediterranean region from southern Spain and N Africa to Greece, Crete and Sicily, flowering from December to February. The plant shown here is unusually small. Not easy to grow, but will survive in a dry, sunny bulb frame. Source N Africa.

Iris pseudocaucasica Grossh. (*Iridaceae* section *Juno*). Native of N Iraq, north to Armenia, and N Iran, growing on stony hillsides from 600 to 3450m, flowering from April to June. Distinguished from *I. caucasica* (p.60) by the high wings on the erect part of the falls. The flowers vary from pale blue, through green to yellow. Photographed in Iran by B. Mathew, BSBE 744.

life size Photographed 18 February

(a), (c), (d), (e), (f) Cyclamen coum Miller, syn.
C. atkinsii T. Moore, *C. orbiculatum* Miller
(*Primulaceae*). Native of the Crimea, Bulgaria,
Turkey, NW Syria, the Caucasus and NW Iran,
growing in beech or pine woods and scrub from
sea level to 2000m, flowering from February to
May according to altitude. Very variable; pink
forms are commonest in S Turkey and N Syria,
dark pink or magenta forms from around
Istanbul and the Black Sea coast. From eastern
Turkey eastwards, the flowers become
progressively larger and the leaves more
heart-shaped. Plants from this area are called
var. *caucasicum* (C. Koch) Meikle (q.v.). The
easternmost forms from forest along the Caspian
coast of Iran have been called *C. elegans* Boiss. &
Buhse; its flowers are large and pale pink, the
leaves narrowly heart-shaped. Various
intermediate forms are found in the southern
Caucasus, and have been called *C. circassicum*
Pobed., *C. adzaricum* Pobed., and *C.
abchasicum* (Medw. ex Kusn.) Kulak.
Illustrated here are: (**a**) E Georgia, above Telavi,
1000m, Rix 2647; (**c**), (**e**) S Turkey, Hatay,
above Osmaniye, 1000m, Rix 1379; (**d**) cultivar
'Album'; (**f**) N Turkey, near Trabzon, 1800m,
Rix 1010. Easily grown in sun or light shade, in a
well-drained leafy soil. Will often produce
self-sown seedlings.

(b) Cyclamen trochopteranthum O. Schwarz,
syn. *C. alpinum* Saunders (*Primulaceae*). Native
of south-west Turkey around Muğla and
Denizli, growing in scrub and under pine trees
in stony ground from 350 to 1100m, and
flowering from February to April. Said to smell
of heather honey. Probably less hardy than
C. coum, and safer grown in a frame or a pot in
the alpine house.

(g) Cyclamen parviflorum Pobed., syn. *C. coum*
subsp. *alpinum* O. Schwarz (*Primulaceae*).
Native of northern Turkey, in the Pontus
mountains above Trabzon and Rize, where it
grows in pine forests, or under bushes of
Rhododendron from 1200 to 2300m, flowering
from April to June as soon as the snow melts.
The leaves appear in autumn and are uniformly
dark green with a slightly scalloped edge. Easy
to grow in rather dry peaty or leafy soil in semi-
shade, but easy to lose because it is so small. The
round tuber often has a long delicate shoot
on which grow the leaves and flowers. Should
not be dried out in summer. Source N Turkey,
above Of, under *R. caucasicum*, Rix 1003a.

(h) Cyclamen pseud-ibericum Hildebr.
(*Primulaceae*). Native of southern Turkey in the
Amanus mountains and in the Anti-Tauros, E
and NE of Adana, growing in pine forests and
beech and hornbeam woods, from 550 to 1500m.
Rather similar to *C. coum*, but with much larger,
always magenta, flowers. The flowers smell of vio-
lets. Should be grown in a pot, or in a rather dry
spot in sun or semi-shade. Good in a bulb frame,
where it can be kept rather dry in summer.

(i) Cyclamen libanoticum Hildebr.
(*Primulaceae*). Known only from the Lebanon
where it is very rare, growing in the mountains
E of Beirut from 750 to 1400m, among limestone
rocks and under trees. It was thought to be
extinct but was recently rediscovered in small
quantity. The young leaves appear in winter and
will survive slight frost but are safer if protected
in an alpine house or frame. The leaves are thick,
fleshy and heart-shaped, with well rounded
lobes; underneath they are deep shining red. Best
grown in a pot or pan in the alpine house, in leafy,
stony soil with limestone, and kept dry and
cool in summer. A careful watch should be kept
for vine-weevil larvae, which can do great damage
to the roots of all cyclamen, especially in pots.

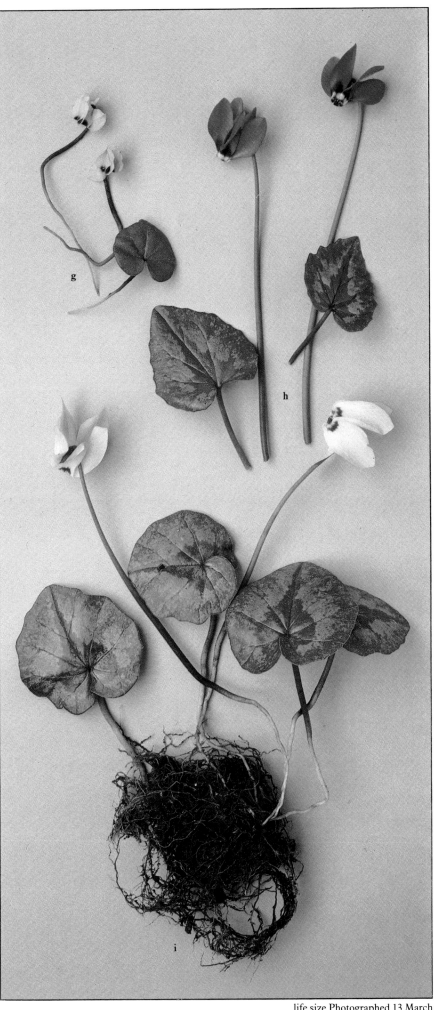

life size Photographed 13 March

a

b

c

d

e

½ life size Photographed 14 April

Leucojum trichophyllum

Cyclamen repandum (b)

Cyclamen repandum

Trillium nivale ½ life size 13 March

(a) Cyclamen persicum Miller (*Primulaceae*). Native of the eastern Mediterranean from Greece (where it is very rare) to Turkey, Cyprus and Lebanon, growing in woods, scrub and among limestone rocks, at altitudes of up to c.1000m, flowering from February to April. The tuber can be large, up to 15cm in diameter, rooting from the lower surface. The leaves appear in winter before the flowers, and are variously marbled with silver. The flowers vary from white to purple in the wild, and smell sweetly like lily-of-the-valley. The flower stalk does not coil and pull the seed head to the ground. Not reliably hardy. If grown in a pot, it should be kept dry in summer and very carefully watered while in growth. The cultivated florists' cyclamen have all been bred from *C. persicum* by selection.

(b)–(e) Cyclamen repandum Sibth. & Sm. (*Primulaceae*). Native of the north-east Mediterranean region from S France to Yugoslavia, Greece and Rhodes, growing among shady rocks and in walls, in woods or scrub, at altitudes up to 500m. The leaves appear in early

spring, the flowers from March to May. Very variable in leaf and flower colour. Var. *rhodense* Meikle from Rhodes has a greyish marbled leaf which appears in winter and white or pale pink flowers, usually with a darker eye. In Corsica and Italy, the leaves are dark green, marbled pale green and irregularly toothed, and the flowers are deep pink with no eye. In the central Peloponnese, the leaves are heavily marbled and spotted with white, and the flowers are pale pink with a deep pink eye. This form has received the cultivar name 'Pelops'. In the eastern Peloponnese, the flowers are crimson and the leaves are dark green, sometimes unmarked, sometimes faintly marbled. Other Mediterranean islands have closely related species; *C. balearicum* Willk. from the Balearic Islands and S France has marbled leaves emerging in spring, and whitish, small pink-veined flowers; *C. creticum* Hildebr. from Crete has pure white (or rarely pink) flowers and smaller leaves than *C. repandum*, which appear in autumn. All have a flattish corm, rooting from the middle. All forms of *C. repandum* are sensitive to hard frost and are better with

protection in cold areas. Source (b) Greece, SE Peloponnese, near Neapolis, Rix 2131; (c), (e) Greece, C Peloponnese, near Sparta, Rix 2107; (d) Corsica, near Ajaccio, Rix s.n.

Trillium nivale Riddell (*Liliaceae*) Native of eastern North America from Pennsylvania to Minnesota, south to Missouri and Kentucky, growing in woods, clearings and shady ledges, flowering from March to May. Grow in leafy soil in a cool, shady place, kept moist in summer. Good for a pot or pan in the alpine house.

Leucojum trichophyllum Schousboe (*Liliaceae*). Native of south-west Spain, S Portugal and Morocco where it grows in sandy places, often in dunes, flowering from January to April. Flowers usually white; petals 12–20mm long. The rather similar *L. longifolium* (Gay) Gren. & Godr. has smaller flowers about 10mm long and rounded petals. Best grown in a pan in the alpine house or in a bulb frame kept dry in summer. Photographed by Paul Furse.

37

½ life size Photographed 11 February

(a) Gymnospermium alberti (Regel) Takht., syn. *Leontice alberti* Regel (*Podophyllaceae*). Native of Central Asia, especially the Tien Shan and the Pamir Alai growing among shrubs and rocks at c.2000m, flowering in April and May, as soon as the snow melts. Height c.10cm at flowering, up to 20cm in fruit. Leaves digitate. Often considered to belong to the *Berberis* family. Should be kept rather dry at all times and completely dry in summer. Source C Asia, Tashkent, Chimgan valley, Rix 2768, and photographed in May, 1980.

(b) Hyacinthella lineata (*Liliaceae*). Native of Turkey, where it grows in rocky places in the mountains, flowering in spring. The specimen shown here is a very poor one. Leaves often with raised nerves, and ciliate, but glabrous in var. *glabrescens*. Easy to grow, but does not increase well, and is susceptible to botrytis. Source C Turkey, between Kayseri and Malatya, among limestone rocks, 2000m, Rix 1609.

(c) Scilla sibirica Haw. in Andrews (*Liliaceae*). Native of S Russia, the Caucasus and Turkey southwards to Syria, growing in woods, scrub

and among rocks, up to 2000m, flowering from March to May. Naturalised in E Europe. Very variable. The form shown here is a rather small pale one, from the south part of the species range. (See also pp.43 and 44). Easy to grow in a bulb frame or dry shady place outside. Source S Turkey, Gaziantep, Nurdağ pass, 1000m, Rix 1375. (Probably = *S. ingridae* Speta.)

(d) Eranthis hyemalis (L.) Salisb. (*Ranunculaceae*). Winter Aconite. Native of France, Italy, Yugoslavia and Bulgaria, but widely naturalised elsewhere in Europe. It grows in woods and rocky places, flowering from January to March. *E. cilicicus* (e) differs in its narrower leaves and larger flowers, and var. *bulgaricus* Stephanof from Bulgaria tends towards it. The garden form *E.* 'Guinea Gold' is also intermediate with extra large flowers. Easy to grow, and naturalises best in well-drained alkaline soil, under deciduous trees. Good under Horse Chestnuts (*Aesculus*).

(e) Ornithogalum fimbriatum Willd. (*Liliaceae*). Native of Romania and Bulgaria to Greece and Turkey, growing on dry hillsides,

flowering from February to May. Leaves hairy beneath and often ciliate at base. Easy to grow and increases well. Very early flowering in cultivation usually beginning in December. Source Greece, Euboea, Mt Dirphys, Rix s.n.

(f) Eranthis cilicicus Schott & Kotschy (*Ranunculaceae*). Native of Turkey, N Iraq and Afghanistan, growing on open hillsides and in pine and fir woods, flowering from February to May. Very similar to *E. hyemalis*, and now considered synonymous with it, but leaf segments usually narrower and flowers larger. See also p.29. Grows well in a bulb frame or pot and will tolerate drying in summer. Source Turkey, Mathew & Tomlinson 4138.

Leontice leontopetalum subsp. **eversmannii**
Leontice leontopetalum L. subsp. eversmannii (Bunge) Coode (*Podophyllaceae*). Native of E Turkey, N Iraq, Iran, Afghanistan and C Asia, growing in fields and on stony hillsides from 400 to 2200m, flowering from March to May. Subspecies *leontopetalum* has broader leaflets, which are usually orbicular, apiculate or emarginate. It grows further west than subsp. *eversmannii*, i.e. from Bulgaria, Greece and Turkey to Iran and Iraq, Israel and N Africa. Photographed in C Asia, Amankutan valley, S of Samarkand, April 1979, Rix 2378.

Eranthis longistiptitatus Regel (*Ranunculaceae*). Native of Central Asia, especially the Kopet Dağ, Pamir Alai and the Tien Shan, growing in woods and among scrub from 1000 to 2000m, flowering from February to May. A very small delicate plant with flowers about 15mm across. The seed pods are held on long slender stalks, not sessile as in *E. hyemalis*. Probably better in a bulb frame. The plants collected in 1979 have grown but not flowered yet. Photographed in C Asia, Tashkent, Chimgan valley, 1800m, in May 1980.

Leontice armenaica Boivin, syn. *L. minor* Boiss. (*Podophyllaceae*). Native of S Caucasus, Syria and Jordan to Iran, growing in stony places from 1500 to 2400m, flowering in spring. Differs from *L. leontopetalum* in its smaller size, up to 20cm, and unbranched inflorescence. Best grown in a bulb frame and kept on the dry side as it is susceptible to too much damp in winter. Keep dry in summer. Photographed in NE Iraq by Oleg Polunin.

Leontice armenaica

Gymnospermium alberti

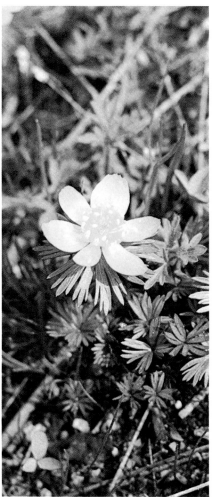

Eranthis longistiptitatus

Leontice leontopetalum subsp. **eversmannii**

39

¾ life size Photographed 13 March

(a), (b) × **Chionoscilla allenii** hort. (*Liliaceae*). This hybrid between *Chionodoxa luciliae* and *Scilla bifolia* is frequent in gardens where the two parents grow together and has also been found in the wild. Very variable, and many different forms have received cultivar names. The starry flowers are rather similar to *Scilla bifolia*, but the petals are joined at their base.

(c) **Scilla sibirica** Haw. in Andrews, c.v. **'Spring Beauty'** (*Liliaceae*). Native of S Russia southwards to Syria (see p.39 (c)). This robust cultivar has more purple in the flower than most wild forms. It is very similar to the original illustration of the species in Andrews' *Botanist's Repository*, a beautiful early nineteenth-century journal similar to the *Botanical Magazine*. Requires a rich sandy soil to grow well and tends to fade away if planted in thick grass (see p.43).

(d), (e) & (f) **Scilla bifolia** L. (*Liliaceae*). Native of central and southern Europe from Spain to Belgium and eastwards to the Ukraine, south to the Caucasus and Turkey, growing in woods, meadows and among rocks, flowering in spring. Very variable in size, chromosome number and flower colour, from pale violet to deep blue. The rather large starry flowers and two or three sheathing leaves are characteristic of the species. Easily grown in sunny places or half-shade in short grass or amongst shrubs, where it will naturalise itself if happy. Source (d) cultivated stock; (e) Greece, Euboea, Mt Dirphys, 1700m, Rix 626 (close to *S. nivalis* Boiss.); (f) forma *rosea*.

(g) **Chionodoxa luciliae** Boiss. (*Liliaceae*) Glory-of-the-Snow. Native of western Turkey, especially near Izmir, where it grows on stony hillsides, flowering in May and June by the melting snow at c.2000m (see also p.45 (c)). Leaves usually two. Flowers few, with a small white eye. The nomenclature of Turkish *Chionodoxa* is very confused, and most of the stocks in commerce are wrongly named. Easy to grow in well-drained soil in a sunny situation.

(h) **Scilla miczenkoana** Grossheim, syn. *S. tubergeniana* Hoog ex Stearn, (*Liliaceae*). Native of the southern Transcaucasia and NW Iran where it grows in mountain meadows and among rocks flowering from March to May. Like *S. sibirica* but flowers larger, palest blue or white, opening as soon as they emerge from the ground. Easily grown in a bulb frame, or a well-drained soil in the open where it will seed itself. The form sold as *S. tubergeniana* is slightly larger than the wild form shown here. Source NW Iran, pass from Ahar to Tabriz, 1800m, shady rocks, Rix 983.

(i) **Hyacinthella siirtensis** Mathew (*Liliaceae*). Native of south-east Turkey, growing on stony hillsides, flowering in early spring. The small pale sessile flowers are characteristic. The specimen here is rather smaller even than usual. Easy to grow in a bulb frame, flowering very early, often in December, and increasing well. Source Turkey, Siirt, pass between Eruh and Şirnak, Rix 417 (type collection).

(j) **Scilla messenaica** Boiss. (*Liliaceae*). Native of Greece, especially the Peloponnese, growing on rocky hillsides, at c.1000m, flowering in April. Like a robust small-flowered *S. bifolia* but has up to seven leaves per bulb and seven to fifteen pale blue flowers per stem. Easy to grow in well-drained soil in sun or half-shade. Source Greece, Peloponnese near Kalamata, H. & M. Crook 517.

¾ life size Photographed 18 February

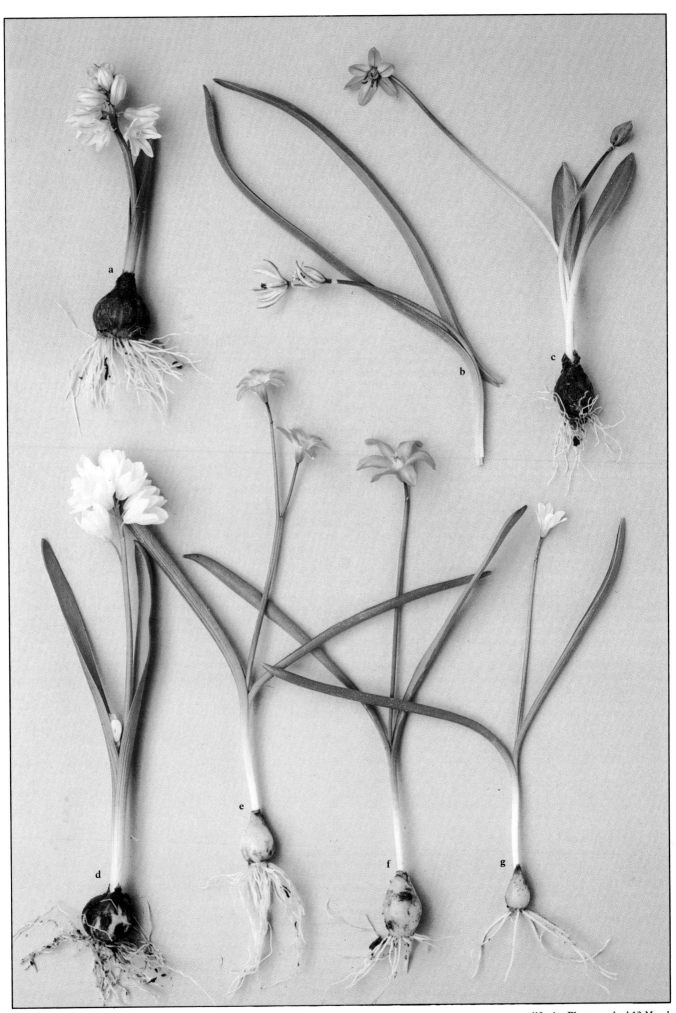

life size Photographed 13 March

Puschkinia Rix 1926   Scilla sibirica 'Spring Beauty'   Scilla puschkinioides

(a), (d) **Puschkinia scilloides** Adams, syn.
P. libanotica Boiss., *P. hyacinthoides* Baker
(*Liliaceae*). Native of the Caucasus, S Turkey,
N Iraq, Iran to Lebanon, growing in scrub, in
stony places and in meadows in the mountains,
at up to 3000m, flowering from April to July
according to altitude. Like *Chionodoxa* the
petals are united at their base, but the flower is
smaller and never opens flat. Easy to grow in
good, well-drained soil and very attractive if
planted in a large mass, as it often grows in
nature. The pure white form is common in
cultivation and very beautiful. Source Turkey,
Hakkari, near Yukşekova, 2000m, Rix 1943,
and photographed in May 1971.

(b) **Scilla puschkinioides** Regel (*Liliaceae*).
Native of Central Asia, especially the Pamir Alai
and the Tien Shan, growing above 1000m, in
scrub and stony places, flowering from March to
July, according to altitude. The stem may be up
to 20cm. Rather feeble, and has not done well in
cultivation, though often introduced. Source
C Asia, Tashkent, Chimgan valley, 1800m, Rix
2773, and photographed in April 1979.

(c) **Scilla armena** Grossh. (*Liliaceae*). Native of
the south Transcaucasus and NW Turkey,
where it grows on grassy places and stony slopes
from 1500 to 2400m, flowering in May and June,
usually by late snow patches. Close to *S. sibirica*
(p.41) but leaves short, lanceolate, and flowers
usually solitary with short, broad petals. Has
grown well in a shady bulb frame and would
probably be happy in a well-drained peaty soil
outside. Source NE Turkey, Tahir Dağ, 2500m,
Rix 1638.

(e) **Chionodoxa cretica** Boiss. (*Liliaceae*).
Native of Crete, especially the White
mountains, where it grows in *Berberis* scrub, at
c.2000m, flowering in April. The stem can have
several flowers, blue with a clear, white centre.
Rather small and delicate, and safer in a bulb
frame.

(f) **Chionodoxa lochiae** Meikle (*Liliaceae*).
Native of Cyprus, especially the Troodos
mountains, where it grows in stony soil under
pines. The flowers are usually one or two, but
may be up to six, blue without any white in their
centre, with a long tube at the base and usually
not opening fully. Easy to grow in a bulb frame

Puschkinia scilloides

or in a well-drained soil outside. Source Cyprus,
Troodos Mts, W. K. Aslet s.n.

(g) **Chionodoxa albescens** (Speta) Rix, comb.
nov., syn. *Scilla albescens* Speta in Naturk.
Jahrb. Stadt Linz 21: 19 (1976), *Chionodoxa
nana* auct. (*Liliaceae*). Native of Crete, growing
at 1200–1800m, in the White mountains, usually
among rocks. Flowers the smallest of the genus
and usually white, pinkish or pale blue. Small
and delicate and better in a bulb frame or alpine
house.

Puschkinia sp. (*Liliaceae*)
This green variant of *P. scilloides* is as yet

unnamed. It has been collected in Hakkari, and
Bitlis, south of Lake Van, and in Azerbaijan by
Brian Mathew. It grows in the same area as the
common form, but in separate populations and
usually at a rather lower altitude, flowering by
late snow patches. Photographed in Turkey,
Hakkari, near Yukşekova, May 1974, Rix 1926.
In cultivation the Turkish collections have
proved very sensitive to botrytis, but the
Azerbaijan collection has grown well in a bulb
frame.

Scilla sibirica 'Spring Beauty', syn.
'Atroviolacea'. Photographed in the RHS
Gardens, Wisley, April 1980, by Roger Phillips.

(a), (h) Gagea peduncularis (Presl) Pascher (*Liliaceae*). Native of Yugoslavia and Bulgaria to Crete, Greece and Turkey, growing in stony places and among rocks at up to 1000m, flowering in March and April. Distinguished from other species by its long and very slender basal leaves, which are solid, its long pedicels and its obtuse petals, up to 20mm long. Easy to grow in a bulb frame. Source (a) Cyprus, Halefka, H. & M. Crook 973; (h) Rhodes, Mt Profitis Ilias, 780m, Rix 1269.

(b) Scilla sibirica Haw. in Andrews (*Liliaceae*) (see also pp.41 (c), 39 (c)). This form is somewhat intermediate between *S. sibirica* and *S. cilicica* (p.71) having its leaves well developed before the flowers open, and a rather lax inflorescence. It seems close to *S. melaina* Speta. Easy to grow and striking in its relatively late flowering and beautiful pure blue colour. Source Turkey, limestone rocks west of Gaziantep, 600m, Rix 1380.

(c) Chionodoxa luciliae Boiss, syn. *C. gigantea* Whittall (*Liliaceae*). Native of western Turkey, especially the mountain of Boz Dağ, east of Izmir, where it flowers in May and June by melting snow at c.2000m, growing in very stony soil. The form shown here, usually called *C. gigantea*, is simply a larger form of *C. luciliae*. Flowers rather few per stem with a short tube, and outer petals much wider than inner. Easy to grow in well-drained rich soil in full sun.

(d) Chionodoxa siehei Stapf (*Liliaceae*). Native of southern Turkey, reputed to be from Ala Dağ above 2500m, flowering probably in May. The largest species in cultivation, and usually triploid, with a very large white centre to the flower, which is 12–19mm long. Rather smaller plants, diploid, are recorded from hills east of Izmir, from 900 to 1100m, flowering in March. They have shorter, broader petals. There is also a pink form in cultivation, called 'Pink Giant'. Easy to grow in well-drained soil in full sun, and good under deciduous shrubs.

(e) Chionodoxa sardensis Whittall ex Barr & Sugden (*Liliaceae*). Native of western Turkey, in the hills E of Izmir, in shady woods among mossy rocks, from 100 to 700m, flowering from February to April. This is one of the more distinct species, with rich blue flowers, 8–17mm long with only a small white eye, up to twelve on each inflorescence. Easy to grow in the same conditions as the other species.

(f) Ornithogalum balansae Boiss. (*Liliaceae*). Native of north-eastern Turkey at c.2500m. This is one of the more distinct and striking species with its short conical raceme of flowers, and rather broad leaves. Easy to grow in good soil in sun or semi-shade.

(g) Gagea pusilla (F. W. Schmidt) Schultes & Schultes fil. (*Liliaceae*). Native of central and southern Europe from Czechoslovakia and Hungary to Greece and Turkey, growing on stony hillsides, flowering from February to April. Characterised by its single narrow leaf, opposite stem leaves and glabrous flowers and stem. Easy to grow in well-drained stony soil in full sun. Source V. Horton 1795.

(i) Ranunculus kochii Ledeb., syn. *Ficaria fascicularis* C. Koch (*Ranunculaceae*). Native of S Transcaucasus, N Iran and the Kopet Dağ to S Turkey and N Iraq, growing in bare, stony places at up to 3000m, flowering from March to May. Cf. *R. ficaria*, Celandine (p.67). Easy to grow in a bulb frame, and better kept dry in summer. Source Turkey, Hakkari, Mor Da., 2800m, Rix 2440.

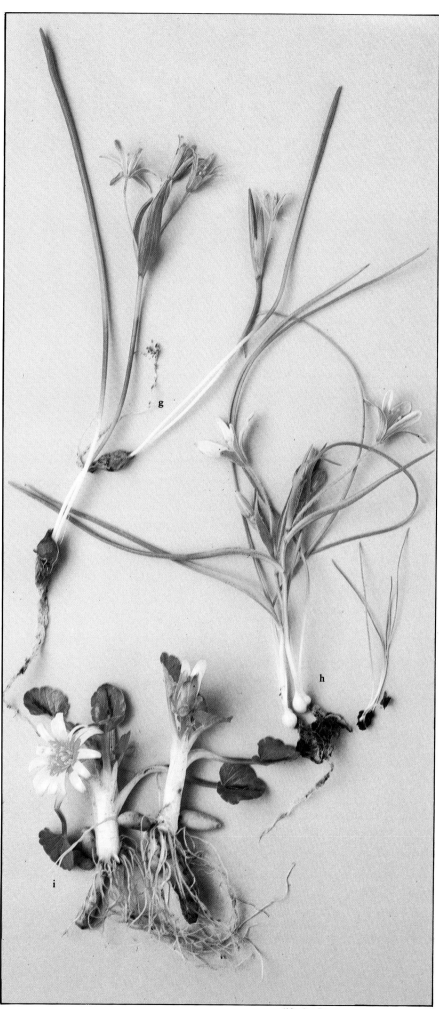

life size Photographed 25 February

½ life size Photographed 13 March

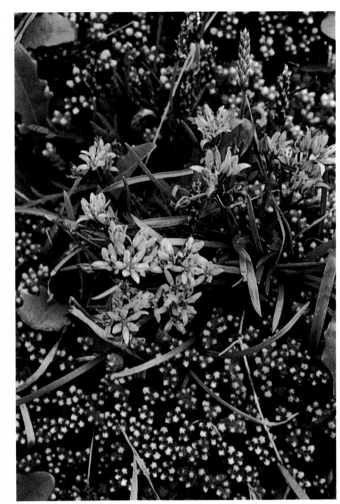

Tecophilaea cyanocrocus ½ life size Photographed 28 March

Scilla verna

(a) Muscari commutatum Guss. (*Liliaceae*). Native of Italy and Sicily and the east Mediterranean south to Israel, growing in scrub and rough grassland, flowering from February to June. Distinguished from other species by its very dark blackish flowers without white lobes. Easy to grow in well-drained soil in a sunny place. Source Greece, Argolis, near Didymi, 250m, Brickell & Mathew 8010.

(b) Hyacinthus orientalis L. (*Liliaceae*). Native of western Asia, in Turkey, Syria and Lebanon, growing among rocks, at up to 2000m, flowering from February to May. Close to the cultivated 'Roman Hyacinth' (p.185). Easy to grow in well-drained sandy soil in full sun. Source Turkey, Kayseri to Malatya, 1980m, among limestone rocks, Rix 1606.

(c) Muscari chalusicum Stuart (*Liliaceae*). Native of northern Iran, in the Chalus valley, where it grows on rock ledges from 300 to 1100m, flowering in March and April. The leaves lie flat on the ground. Grows easily in a bulb frame or sunny warm place outside. Source Iran, Chalus valley, P. Furse.

(d) Hyacinthus litwinovii E. Czem. (*Liliaceae*). Native of N Iran, and the Kopet Dağ in western Central Asia, growing at 1500–2000m, flowering in March and April. Distinguished from *H. orientalis* by its fewer broader leaves and narrow petals; in *H. transcaspicus* Litw. the tube is longer than the free part of the petals. Easy to grow in a bulb frame kept dry in summer. Source Iran, Kopet Dağ, stony slopes and rocks, P. Furse 7894.

(e) Hyacinthella leucophaea (C. Koch) Schur. (*Liliaceae*). Native of eastern Europe from

Poland southwards to Greece, Romania and S Russia, growing in dry grassland and on stony slopes, flowering in spring. Distinguished by its upright rather broad leaves, and flowers on spreading stalks (see p.39 (b)). Better grown in a bulb frame or pot in the alpine house where it can be kept rather dry in summer. Shown here is the variant which has been called *H. atchleyi* Feinbrun. Source Greece, Kozani to Grevena, Linzee Gordon, 0009.

Bellevalia atroviolacea Regel (*Liliaceae*). Native of Central Asia, especially the Pamir Alai, and NE Afghanistan, growing on bare dry hills and rocky places from 600 to 1500m (and rarely up to 2200m), flowering in April. Grow in a dry bulb frame, baked in summer. Photographed in C Asia, south of Samarkand, April 1979.

Tecophilaea cyanocrocus Leyb. (*Tecophileaceae*). Native of Chile in the Cordillera of Santiago at around 3000m, where it grows on stony slopes kept dry and protected by snow cover in winter, flowering in October and November. It is now possibly extinct in the wild through overcollecting. Shown here are the type form with flowers all blue, and var. *leichtlinii* in which the flowers are paler with a white centre. The closely related *I. violiflora* with purplish flowers grows on the coastal ranges north of Santiago, from Valparaiso to Coquimbo. Keep rather dry in winter, so that the leaves which are tender to hard frost do not develop in winter, or grow in a pot in the alpine house where it can be protected from frost. Requires a rich sandy soil. The best results have been obtained in mild gardens on the east coast of Ireland where it has grown well outside. Will set seed after careful hand pollination.

Bellevalia atroviolacea

Scilla verna L. (*Liliaceae*). Native of the Atlantic coast of Europe from Portugal to the Faroes, but absent from the south and west coasts of Ireland, growing on sea cliffs and grassy places, flowering from March to June. Distinguished by its short, 5–15cm stems and relatively large flowers, 10–16mm in diameter, usually purplish blue; bracts longer than the pedicels. Photographed in S Wales near St Davids by Roger Phillips.

47

Corydalis rutifolia

Corydalis glaucescens

Corydalis emanueli

Corydalis ledebouriana

(a) **Corydalis popovii** Nevski (*Papaveraceae*). Native of Central Asia, especially the Pamir Alai mountains, growing in scrub and rocky hillsides above 2000m, flowering from March to July according to altitude. Only recently introduced, but apparently not difficult to grow either in a pot in the alpine house, or in a bulb frame; will not require baking in summer. Source Central Asia, Ferghana district, Rix 2794.

(b) **Bongardia chrysogonum** (L.) Griseb. (*Podophyllaceae*). Native of western Asia from Turkey to the Pamir Alai and the Kara Kum desert, growing in cornfields and on stony hill-sides, flowering from March to May. *Bongardia* differs from *Leontice* (p.39) in having all the leaves arising from the tuber, not from the stem. Easy to grow in a bulb frame, but must be kept dry in summer, and not allowed to get too wet in winter. Source Turkey, near Gaziantep, Rix 1854.

(c) **Corydalis aitchisonii** M. Popov (*Papaveraceae*) Native of Soviet Central Asia in the Kopet Dağ and Badgis, and of NE Iran and Afghanistan, at 650–2300m, flowering from March to May. Tuber more or less spherical. Has grown well in a dry bulb frame at Wisley but

has not increased since 1964. Source Iran, near Meshed, 1800m, granite rocks, P. Furse 5280.

(d) **Corydalis solida** (L.) Swartz (*Papaveraceae*). Native of most of Europe, naturalised in England, Denmark, Norway and Turkey, growing on stony hillsides and woods, flowering from April to May. Very variable in flower size and in colour from white to pink and purple. The form shown here is a small one similar to var. *densiflora* (C. Presl) Boiss. The broad scale at the base of the stem is characteristic of *C. solida* and related species. Easy to grow in a bulb frame or well-drained soil in the open. Source Turkey, near Ankara, Rix 1532.

Corydalis rutifolia subsp. **erdelii** (Sibth. & Sm.) DC. Native of Crete and Turkey eastwards to Pakistan, growing in stony places from 1300 to 2800m, flowering from April to July. Distinguished from *C. bulbosa* (L.) DC. by its opposite, not alternate, stem leaves, and fewer-flowered raceme. Flower colour variable. Grow in a pot in the alpine house or a bulb frame, kept dry in summer. Photographed in central Turkey, near Malatya, 1900m, May

1970, Rix (1584).

Corydalis ledebouriana Kar. & Kir. (*Papaveraceae*). Native of Central Asia and NE Afghanistan, to Kashgar and Chitral, growing in rocky places and in scrub from 800 to 3700m, flowering from March to June. Characterised by strongly upward-curving spur and deflexed lower lip. Cultivation as (a). Photographed in Central Asia, S of Ferghana, c.2000m, in April 1979.

Corydalis glaucescens Regel. Native of Central Asia, especially the Tien Shan, the Pamir Alai and the Ala Tau, growing in woods and scrub at up to 1500m, flowering from March to June. Cultivation as for *C. popovii* (a). Photographed in Central Asia, in the mountains S of Frunze, c.2000m, May 1980.

Corydalis emanueli C. A. Meyer (*Papaveraceae*). Native of the Caucasus, from Taberda to Kasbek, growing among shady rocks at 2400–2500m, flowering in July and August. The thick, fleshy root has 2–5 lobes. Photographed in the Baksan valley, 2500m, in August 1975.

49

¾ life size Photographed 14 April

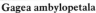
Gagea ambylopetala

Gagea fistulosa

Gagea bohemica

Lloydia serotina

Corydalis macrocentra

(a) **Corydalis caucasica** DC. (*Papaveraceae*). Native of the Caucasus where it is widespread, growing in forests and in scrub, flowering in April and May. Flowers usually pinkish-purple, but the white form shown here, var. *albiflora* DC., is common. Easily grown in shady places in peaty sandy soil.

(b) **Corydalis macrocentra** Regel. (*Papaveraceae*). Native of Central Asia, especially Tadjikistan and NE Afghanistan, growing on low sandy hills from 900 to 1300m, flowering in March and April. Source C Asia, Dushanbe, low bare sandy hills at mouth of Varsob gorge, 1200m, Rix 2723, and photographed in April 1980.

(c) **Gagea gageoides** (Zucc.) Vved. (*Liliaceae*). Native of eastern Turkey and Iran to Central Asia especially Tien Shan, Pamir Alai and Kopet Daǧ, growing on bare hills and rocks at up to 3000m, flowering in April and May. Easily distinguished by the numerous leafy bulbils in the leaf axils. Easy to grow in a bulb frame. Source Turkey, Hakkari, near Yukşekova, Rix 1954.

(d) **Gagea fibrosa** (Desf.) Schultes & Schultes fil., syn. *G. rigida* Boiss., *C. commutata* C. Koch (*Liliaceae*). Native of the S Caucasus, Turkey and Greece to Israel and N Africa, growing on dry hillsides, flowering in March and April. Distinguished by its very long tapering petals, flat spreading leaves, and stem which usually branches below ground. Cultivation as for (c). Source Greece, Parnon Oros, c.1000m, Rix 2143.

(e) **Gagea ambylopetala** Boiss. (*Liliaceae*). Native of Sicily and Crete to Yugoslavia and S Russia, and western Turkey growing in rocky places and in scrub, flowering in March and April. Distinguished by its two narrow basal leaves, small (less than 10mm) rounded petals, and glabrous stems with diffuse branching. Flowers often reddish outside. Source Greece, Elion Or. W of Thebes, c.1200m, Rix 2178, and photographed near Sparta by Roger Phillips.

Gagea fistulosa Ker Gawl., syn. *G. liotardii* (Stern.) Schultes & Schultes fil., (*Liliaceae*). Native of Europe from the Pyrenees to Russia, Greece, Turkey and the Caucasus, growing in damp grassy meadows in the mountains, flowering from May to July. Distinguished by its hollow fleshy leaves, opposite stem leaves and usually hairy pedicels. Sometimes produces bulbils instead of flowers. Photographed in the Serrat valley, Andorra, in June 1977 by Brinsley Burbidge 565.

Gagea bohemica (Zauschn.) Schultes & Schultes syn. *G. saxatilis* (Mert. & Koch) Schultes & Schultes fil. (*Liliaceae*). Native of Europe from Wales and France to Turkey and Syria and the Caucasus, at up to 1000m (in the south), growing in rocky places often in small pockets of soil, flowering from January to April. Distinguished by its narrow filiform basal leaves, rather large flowers with blunt petals, usually hairy pedicels and alternate stem leaves. Photographed in Wales on rock ledges in March.

Lloydia serotina (L.) Rchb. (*Liliaceae*). Native of the Arctic and mountains of Europe and the Caucasus, growing in tundra and on rock ledges up to 3000m, flowering from June to August. Very rare, and protected in Wales. Photographed in the Caucasus, Dongus Orun, in August 1976.

51

¾ life size Photographed 11 February

Iris × sindpers ⅓ life size 25 February

Iris wendelboi

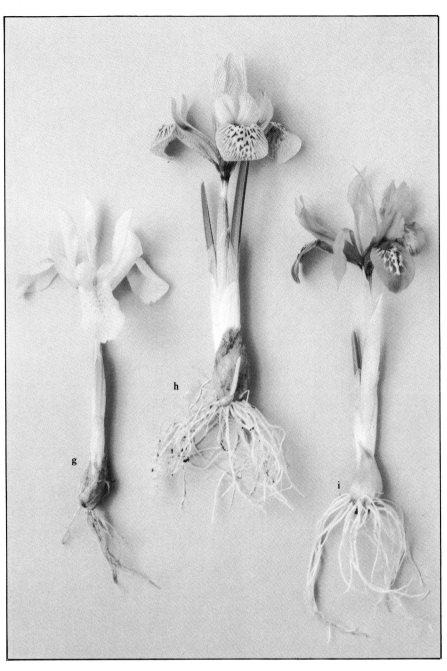

½ life size Photographed 25 February

(a) **Iris histrio** Rchb. fil. (*Iridaceae*, section *Reticulatae*). Native of S Turkey, Lebanon, Syria and Israel, growing on stony hillsides, and among rocks at up to 2000m, flowering in February and March. Flowers usually paler than shown here. Easy to grow in a bulb frame, kept rather dry and baked in summer. Benefits by frequent division. Source S Turkey, Nur Dağ pass above Osmaniye, 1000m, Rix 1557.

(b) **Iris histrio** var. **aintabensis** (*Iridaceae*, section *Reticulatae*). Native of S Turkey and Syria (?) growing in pockets on limestone rocks west of Gaziantep, at c.1000m. Like *I. histrio* but smaller with more delicate, paler flowers. Cultivation as (a).

(c), (i) **Iris histrioides** (G. F. Wilson) S. Arnott, c.v. 'Major' (*Iridaceae*, section *Reticulatae*). Native of central Turkey recorded from near Amasya and from Erzinçan district; very rarely collected probably because of its early flowering. Close to *I. histrio* but usually leafless at first flowering. Two or three very similar clones are in cultivation, one named 'Lady Beatrix Stanley' with more spotted falls. Cultivation as for (a).

(d), (e), (f) **Iris reticulata** M. Bieb (*Iridaceae*, section *Reticulatae*). Native of Turkey, Iran, S Transcaucasus and Iraq, growing on scree and bare stony places and among scrub from 600 to 2700m, flowering from March to May. Variable in colour, the pale blue forms from Talysh and N Iran (f) have been called *I hyrcana* Woron., but occur mixed with the normal purple form (d), (e). (See also pp.54 and 56.) Easy to grow in a bulb frame or in very sandy soil in the open, kept dry if possible in summer. Sources NW Iran, Tabriz district, Rix 875 and 973.

(g) **Iris winogradowii** Fomin (*Iridaceae*, section *Reticulatae*). Native of the southern Caucasus, in the west above Gagra, and in the south, inland from Batumi, growing in the subalpine zone, but very rare and poorly known. Very striking for its pale yellow colour, and the only species of the section better grown outside, in sandy peaty soil. New root growth begins in summer, so it should be replanted as soon as the leaves begin to fade, and never dried out completely.

(h) **Iris 'Katharine Hodgkin'**. This beautiful hybrid was raised in 1958 by E. B. Anderson and

named after the wife of Eliot Hodgkin (1900–1972), a great grower of rare bulbs. The parentage was said to have been *I. histrioides* 'Major' × *I. danfordiae*, but it looks as if *I. winogradowii* is a more likely parent because of its large standards compared with the minute ones of *I. danfordiae* (p.54). Easily grown and increases very quickly in a bulb frame, more slowly in the open.

Iris × sindpers (*Iridaceae*, section *Juno*). A hybrid between *Iris aucheri* (p.59) and *I. persica* (p.58) raised by the Dutch bulb firm of Van Tubergen, in an attempt to combine the robustness of *I. aucheri* with the dwarf habit and early flowering of *I. persica*. Probably better grown under cover in the British Isles.

Iris wendelboi Grey-Wilson & Mathew (*Iridaceae*, section *Juno*). Native of south-western Afghanistan, growing on dry sandy hills among *Pistachia* scrub, at c.1700m, flowering in March and April. Photographed in Afghanistan, ten miles NE of Gulestan, by C. Grey Wilson, G.-W./H. 575.

¾ life size Photographed 25 February

(a), (b), (d), (e) Iris reticulata M. Bieb.
(*Iridaceae*) (see pp.53 and 57). Four of the many
cultivars of *I. reticulata* are shown here. They
have been obtained by selection of collected
forms and by hybridisation. Some of them are
infected with virus, which shows itself by a dark
and light mottling of the young leaves, so they
should be kept separate from wild-collected
bulbs which may not be as resistant. They are
often also infected with 'Ink disease', a fungus
which forms dark stains on the tunic, before
infecting the whole bulb.
(a). Old commercial form, which is very sweetly
scented. It is very rare in the wild, being
recorded only once, in NE Iran by Paul Furse,
P. F. 5179
(b) 'Clairette'. Probably a hybrid with
I. reticulata var. *bakeriana.*
(c) 'Cantab'. Raised by E. A. Bowles.
(e) 'Joyce'. Raised by Van Tubergen. The large
blue flower and shorter stouter leaves suggest
that it may be a hybrid with *I. histrioides.*

(c) Iris danfordiae Boiss., syn. *I. bornmülleri*
Hausskn. (*Iridaceae*, section *Reticulatae*).
Native of central Turkey, where it has been
recorded from several widely separated areas, in
the Taurus, in west Malatya, in Amasya and in
Gümüsane, at 2000–3000m, on bare, earthy
hills, flowering probably in March and April.
Will flower well the first year after planting but
difficult to keep going in the open garden.

(f) Fritillaria stenanthera Regel (*Liliaceae*).
Native of Central Asia, especially the Pamir Alai
and the Tien Shan, where it grows in the
foothills up to 2000m on earthy slopes and
screes, flowering in March and April. Nectaries
all equal. Should not be difficult to cultivate in
good soil in a bulb frame kept dry in summer.
Source Central Asia, Tashkent, Chimgan valley,
c.2000m, Rix 2779.

(g) Fritillaria ariana (A. Los. & Vved.) Rix
(*Liliaceae*). Native of Central Asia, especially at
the southern edges of the Kara Kum desert, and
NE Iran and N Afghanistan, growing on sandy
steppes flowering in March. Not easy to grow
and probably best kept dry until late March,
when, if watered, it will grow and flower in a few
weeks.

(h) Crocus michelsoni B. Fedtsch. (*Iridaceae*).
Native of the Kopet Dağ in NE Iran, and
S Central Asia, where it grows on stony hills
from 1200 to 2300m, flowering in March and
April. The style is whitish; the flowers always
bluish or white inside, marked with blue purple
outside; corm tunic with reticulate fibres.
Best grown in a bulb frame, kept dry in
summer.

(i) Iris kolpakowskiana Regel, syn. *I. winkleri*
Regel (*Iridaceae*, section *Reticulatae*). Native of
Central Asia from the mountains near Tashkent
eastwards to Alma Ata from 1100 to 3000m,
flowering from April to June, growing on grassy
or stony slopes and in scrub. An atypical
member of the *Reticulatae* section in its flat
leaves and large standards, and found far to the
east of all other members of the section. Not easy
to grow, but the same treatment as given to other
delicate bulbous irises should suit it.

Fritillaria gibbosa Boiss. (*Liliaceae*). Native of
Iran and Afghanistan, south Caucasia and the
Kopet Da., growing on dry hills and steppes
from 1000 to 2000m, flowering from March to
May. Close to *F. ariana* (g) but has broader
leaves with less contrast between basal pair and
the rest, and papillose stems. Flowers usually
spotted. Cultivation as (g). Photographed in the
Elburz mountains by Paul Furse.

²/₃ life size Photographed 13 March

Fritillaria gibbosa

¾ life size Photographed 25 February

(a), (b), (c) **Iris reticulata** M. Bieb. (see p.53). These three forms are from further south than those shown on p.52, where there is a tendency for the flowers to be bi-coloured. Source (a) Turkey, Hakkari, gorge of Habur River, c.1200m, Rix 2437; (b) Iran, central Zagros Mts, Razan pass, E of Khorramabad, 1950m, P. Furse 1864; (c) Iran, Kuh-i-Sahand, P. Furse 2364.

(d) **I. reticulata** var. **bakeriana** (Foster) Mathew & Wendelbo (*Iridaceae*, section *Reticulatae*). This variety of *I. reticulata* is distinguished by its eight-ribbed leaves, not four-ribbed as in *I. reticulata* itself, but intermediates are found in the southern Zagros. Wild plants usually have pale blue flowers and dark falls without the yellow spot. Shown here is a commercial stock sold under the name *I. bakeriana*.

(e) **Iris pamphylica** Hedge (*Iridaceae*, section *Reticulatae*). Native of southern Turkey, confined to one small area NE of Antalya, where it grows in pine forest, among oak scrub and between limestone rocks at c.1250m, flowering in March. It has not proved easy to cultivate, but has survived and increased slowly in a sunny bulb frame in very sandy soil. Sensitive to botrytis, so it is wise to lift and treat with captan or benlate each summer. Source Turkey, Antalya, Rix 1340.

(f) **Hermodactylus tuberosus** (L.) Miller, syn. *Iris tuberosa* L. (*Iridaceae*). Snake's Head Iris, Widow Iris. Native of S France eastwards to Yugoslavia, Greece, Turkey and Israel, where it grows in scrub and on grassy banks and hillsides, flowering in March and April. It is naturalised in Devon and Cornwall. The long soft, *reticulata*-like leaves emerge in autumn. Easily grown in well-drained sunny places where it will sometimes increase greatly. Protect from slugs. Source Greece, Peloponnese near Githion, Rix 514, and photographed in March 1964.

Gynandriris sisyrinchium (L.) Parl., syn. *Iris sisyrinchium* L. (*Iridaceae*). Native of the Mediterranean region, from Portugal to Italy and Greece, Turkey and Israel and eastwards to Pakistan, growing at altitudes of up to 2000m, flowering from February to April. Very variable in size from 10 to 60cm. Flowers usually opening in the afternoon and faded by morning. *Gynandriris* is a mainly S African genus close to *Moraea* (p.152). The corm is rather similar to *I. reticulata*. Photographed in Greece, near Sparta, in April 1980 by Roger Phillips.

¹/₃ life size Photographed 28 March

Gynandriris sisyrinchium

Hermodactylus tuberosus

life size Photographed 13 February

Iris aucheri ⅓ life size Photographed 28 March

I. willmottiana ⅓ life size Photographed 28 March

Iris orchioides

(a), (d) **Iris persica** L. (*Iridaceae* section *Juno*). Native of southern Turkey, N Iraq, Syria and Lebanon, growing on bare eroded hills, on screes and among oak scrub at 600–2000m, flowering from February to April. Flowers usually solitary, greenish, brownish-yellow or greyish. The leaves should be kept as dry as possible at all times, dead flowers removed, and the centre of the leaves dusted with captan to prevent infection by botrytis. Source (a) Turkey, Adiyaman near Kahta, Linzee Gordon 5152; (d) Turkey, Silifke to Karaman, Linzee Gordon 5108.

(b) (c) **Iris stenophylla** Hausskn. & Siehe ex Baker, syn. *Iris tauri* Siehe ex Mallett (*Iridaceae*, section *Juno*). Native of central Turkey, where it grows on stony slopes and screes usually on limestone, at c.2000m, flowering in March and April. Very similar to *I. persica*, but is usually slightly smaller, and always a deep purple colour. Cultivation as for *I. persica*. Source Turkey, Eğredir to Beyşehir, Linzee Gordon 5065.

Iris aucheri (Baker) Sealy, syn. *I. sindjarensis* Boiss. & Hausskn. (*Iridaceae*, section *Juno*). Native of SE Turkey, W Iran, N Syria, and N Iraq, growing on rocky hills from 550 to 2600m, flowering in March and April. Height 15–40cm. Flowers pale blue crowded at the top of the stem above the lush leek-like leaves. Easy to grow in a bulb frame where it makes a dense clump. Keep dry in summer. Source SE Turkey, Bitlis, Pelli Da, 2600m, Rix 796.

I. willmottiana Foster (*Iridaceae*, section *Juno*). Native of Central Asia, especially low hills near Derbent where it flowers in May. This species is still in commerce, and is worth trying in good soil outside, preferably where it will become rather dry in summer.

Iris orchioides Carr. (*Iridaceae*, section *Juno*). Native of Central Asia, especially the Tien Shan, the Kara Tau and the Ala Tau, at up to 2000m on stony slopes, flowering from March to July. Grow in a sunny bulb frame in very gritty soil. Photographed in C Asia, Tashkent, Chimgan valley, c.1600m, in May 1980.

½ life size Photographed 14 April

(a) **Iris bucharica** Foster (*Iridaceae*, section *Juno*). Native of Central Asia, especially the Pamir Alai and Tadjikistan, and NE Afghanistan where it grows on stony and grassy hills from 800 to 2400m, flowering in March and April. Height 15–45cm. The form shown here is the usual commercial form. The wild form is shown on p.62. Easily grown in good well-drained soil in full sun.

(b) **Iris magnifica** Vved. (*Iridaceae*, section *Juno*). Native of Central Asia, especially the mountains south of Samarkand where it grows among limestone rocks at c.1600m, flowering in March and April. The largest species with stems up to 1m, and whitish or pale blue flowers. Easily grown in deep well-drained soil, in full sun. Photographed in Central Asia, Samarkand, Amankutan valley, April 1979.

(c) **Iris caucasica** Hoffm. (*Iridaceae*, section *Juno*). Native of S Caucasus, NW Iran, E Turkey and N Iraq, growing on screes and stony mountain steppe at 2400–3000m, flowering in May. The erect part of the fall is winged, but the wings are flat, not turned up as in *I. pseudocaucasica* (p.33). Has survived and flowered in a bulb frame but not increased. Possible outside in very well-drained soil. Sources Turkey, Agri, Tahir dağ, 2500m, Rix 1640, and photographed in NE Turkey, west foothills of Mt Ararat, 2000m, in May 1972.

Iris vicaria Vved. (*Iridaceae*, section *Juno*). Native of Central Asia, especially the Pamir Alai, growing on stony slopes and among rocks, at c.2000m, flowering in March and April. Height 20–40cm in the wild. Plants few flowered; flowers always pale bluish, the upright part of the falls without a wing. Probably not difficult in cultivation. Photographed in Central Asia, Dushanbe, 2000m, Rix 2701.

Iris cycloglossa Wendelbo (*Iridaceae*, section *Juno*) (see Introduction). Native of SW Afghanistan where it grows in low valleys flooded in winter, dry in summer, at 1450–1700m, flowering in April. Plant up to 40cm, with about six narrow leaves on the lowest part of the stem. Flowers scented and unusually shaped for a Juno Iris with wide flat falls, and horizontal standards. This seems likely to be one of the best Iris introductions of recent years, being easily grown in a bulb frame or outdoors. Source Afghanistan, near Farah, Wendelbo, Hedge & Ekberg 7727.

Iris magnifica

Iris caucasica

Iris vicaria

Iris drepanophylla

Iris microglossa

Iris bucharica

Iris warleyensis

(a) **Gagea glacialis** C. Koch (*Liliaceae*). Native of the Caucasus and northern Turkey, growing in wet places in alpine meadows, flowering in May and June. Like a small *G. fistulosa* (p.51). Source Caucasus, Georgian Military Highway, 2500m, Rix 2630.

(b) **Anemone caucasica** Willd. ex Rupr., syn. *A. blanda* var. *parvula* (DC.) Boiss. (*Ranunculaceae*). Native of the Caucasus, northern Iran and NE Turkey, where it grows in subalpine meadows from 500 to 2000m, flowering from April to June. Differs from *A. blanda* primarily in its small size. Suitable for a sink in a well-drained peaty soil. Source SW Caucasus above Sukhumi, c.2000m, Rix 2659, and photographed in April 1978.

(c) **Bellevalia hyacinthoides** (Bertol.) Persson & Wendelbo, syn. *Strangweja spicata* (Sibth. & Sm.) Boiss. (*Liliaceae*). Native of Greece, growing on rocky hillsides, olive groves and abandoned fields at up to 1000m, flowering in March and April. The flat leaves develop in autumn. Easy to grow in a bulb frame. Source Greece, Parnassus above Delphi, Rix 2130.

(d) **Anemone gortschakovii** Kar. & Kir. (*Ranunculaceae*). Native of Central Asia, especially the Tien Shan and the Ala Tau, growing on rocky slopes at up to 2000m, flowering in April and May. Distinguished from *A. petiolulosa* (p.65) by its very long flower stalk, and by the divisions of the basal leaves being sessile. Source C Asia, Ferghana, Chamsabad, 1800m, Rix 2784.

Iris bucharica Foster (*Iridaceae*, section *Juno*) (see p.61 (a)). Photographed in Central Asia, near Dushanbe, on dry grassy hills at c.1000m, in April 1979. Growing in great quantity; flowers all deep yellow with a variable amount of brown on the falls.

Iris warleyensis Foster (*Iridaceae*, section *Juno*). Native of the Pamir Alai mountains of Central Asia from Samarkand to Derbent, growing on sandy slopes at around 1300m, flowering in March and April. Height 20–40cm. Will grow outside in a well-drained sunny place. Photographed in C Asia, S of Samarkand, on steep, loose scree at 1500m, in April 1979.

Iris microglossa Wendelbo (*Iridaceae*, section *Juno*). Native of NE Afghanistan, where it grows on dry grassy hillsides often among Junipers from 1700–3000m, flowering from April to June. Height up to 60cm. Flowers pale blue to white. One of the easier of the Afghan species to cultivate, and some of the collections are reported to have grown well. Photographed on north side of Salang pass, 1900m, by C. Grey-Wilson, G.-W./H. 705.

Iris drepanophylla Aitch. & Baker (*Iridaceae*, section *Juno*). Native of NE Iran, NW Afghanistan and SW Central Asia, growing on dry slopes often of loess, from 600 to 1800m, flowering in April. The margin of the upright part of the falls is turned down, not turned up as in most species. Photographed in Afghanistan, Paropamissus, N of Herat, by C. Grey-Wilson, G.-W./H. 477.

Primula fedtschenkoi Regel (*Primulaceae*). Native of N Afghanistan and Central Asia, especially Uzbekistan, growing on dry grassy slopes from 700 to 1600m, flowering in March and April. Height 4–12cm. Has a tuft of tuberous roots, which become dormant in summer. Photographed in C Asia, S of Samarkand, Amankutan valley, at 1600m, in April 1979.

¾ life size Photographed 28 March

Anemone caucasica

Primula fedtschenkoi

a

b

c

d

life size Photographed 25 February

Anemone petiolulosa

Anemone petiolulosa × tschernjaewi

Geranium transversale

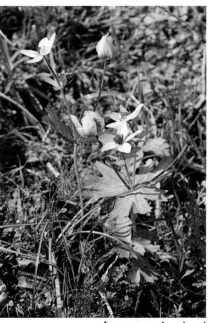

Anemone tschernjaewi

Anemone blanda Schott & Kotschy
(*Ranunculaceae*). Native of the eastern
Mediterranean region from Albania and Greece
to Lebanon, growing in rocky places and in
scrub at up to 2000m, flowering from March to
May. The flowers are usually white or dark blue
in Greece, and often a uniform pale blue in
Turkey. The leaves are hairless beneath.
A. appenina L., with a more elongated rhizome,
and leaves hairy beneath, is found from Corsica
to Yugoslavia and Greece. Several cultivars of
A. blanda have been selected and put into
commerce by Van Tubergen; shown here are:
p.64 (**a**) **'Radar'**, flowers rich pink with a white
centre; p.64 (**b**), (**c**), (**d**), wild forms from near
Delphi, Greece, Rix 563; p.66 (**h**) **'White
Splendour'**, large flowers up to 5cm across; p.66
(**i**) **'Atrocaerulea'**. All are easily grown in full
sun or light shade under deciduous trees. The
plants shown are at the beginning of their

flowering, and would become larger in a few
days.

Anemone petiolulosa Juz. (*Ranunculaceae*).
Native of Central Asia, especially the Tien Shan,
Pamir Alai and Kopet Dağ, where it grows on
stony steppes and mountainsides, flowering in
March and April. Close to *A. biflora* (p.67) but
flowers always yellow, smaller and less globular.
Divisions of the leaf more pointed. Not well
known in cultivation, but will probably require
bulb-frame treatment, kept dry in summer.
Photographed in C Asia, east of Dushanbe,
2000m, in April 1979.

Anemone tschernjaewi Regel.
(*Ranunculaceae*). Native of N Afghanistan and
Kashmir, and Central Asia, especially the Tien
Shan and the Pamir Alai, growing on rock ledges
and among scrub, from 900 to 2000m, flowering

from March to May. Flowers whitish to pale
violet, leaves three-lobed, the lobes almost entire.
Grow in a bulb frame or pot in the alpine house,
kept dry in summer. Photographed in Central
Asia, east of Dushanbe, 2000m, in April 1979.

Anemone petiolulosa × tschernjaewi. This
probable hybrid was a single plant growing with
the parents, and is close to the description of
A. eranthoides Regel, recorded from the same
area. Photographed in Central Asia, east of
Dushanbe, 2000m, in April 1979.

Geranium transversale (Kar. & Kir.) Vved.
(*Geraniaceae*). Native of W Siberia, Central Asia
and N China, growing on plains and low hills,
flowering in April and May. Leaves with 7–9
linear lobes. Photographed near Tashkent,
Chimgan valley, in May 1980.

½ life size Photographed 14 April

66

Anemone nemorosa L. (*Ranunculaceae*).
Native of northern Europe, eastwards to Turkey
and NW Asia, growing in woods and shady
hillsides, flowering from March to June.
Flowers usually white in the wild, often pinkish
outside, but in Ireland where some of the
cultivars originated, often bluish. Shown here
are: (**a**) '**Robinsoniana**', Named after William
Robinson, an influential Victorian gardener and
journalist, who found it in the Oxford botanic
garden to which it had come from Ireland.
Robinson himself came from Stradbally, Co.
Laois. Flowers pale blue, greyish outside; (**b**)
'**Vestal**', pure white button double. Origin not
recorded; (**c**) '**Bracteata**', a loose white double
in which some of the petals are green. Cultivated
since the sixteenth century; (**d**) '**Allenii**', named
after James Allen of Shepton Mallet, Somerset,
who raised it some time before 1890. Flowers
pale blue, pinkish outside; (**f**), a wild form from
Kent, S England; (**g**) '**Grandiflora**, a
large-flowered white form, possibly the same as
'Leeds' Variety' mentioned by Graham Thomas
in his account of the varieties. Other cultivated
varieties include 'Lismore Blue' (pale blue) and
'Lismore Pink' (a uniform pale pink), both
originating in Co. Waterford, Ireland. The
closely related *A. altaica* Fischer from Russia
and Siberia has flowers blue-veined inside. All
are easily grown in shade of deciduous trees in
moist leafy soil.

(**e**) **Anemone** × **lipsiensis** Beck, syn. *A.* ×
intermedia Winkler (*Ranunculaceae*). A variable
hybrid between *A. nemorosa* and *A. ranunculoides*
which is often found where the parents grow
together. Cultivation as for *A. nemorosa*.

(**h**), (**i**) **Anemone blanda** Schott & Kotschy (see
p.65); (**h**) c.v. '**White Splendour**'; (**i**) c.v.
'**Atrocaerulea**'.

(**j**), (**k**) **Anemone ranunculoides** L.
(*Ranunculaceae*). Native of northern Europe and
western Asia from Belgium and Spain eastwards
to the Caucasus and Siberia, growing in
deciduous woodland and heaths and flowering
from March to June. Two subspecies are
described: subsp. *ranunculoides*, a large plant,
up to 30cm tall, with a far-creeping rhizome, and
subsp. *wockeana* (Asch. & Graeb.) Hegi, a
smaller plant with a short rhizome, which makes
a dense clump. Cultivation as for *A. nemorosa*.

Anemone biflora DC. (*Ranunculaceae*). Native
of Iran, Afghanistan, Pakistan and Kashmir
growing on stony hillsides flowering from March
to May. Flowers either red or bronzy yellow,
larger than *A. petiolulosa* (p.65), up to 5cm
across. Leaves with obtuse segments. Grow in a
bulb frame, or pot in the alpine house, kept dry
in summer. Photographed in Iran, Zagros
mountains, Shuturunkuh, 2300m, BSBE 714,
by Brian Mathew.

Ranunculus ficaria L. (*Ranunculaceae*).
Celandine. Native of the whole of Europe except
the Atlantic islands, eastwards to Central Asia
(near Alma Ata), and Siberia, flowering from
January to May, growing usually on shady or
grassy banks or in woods. Very variable, each
form being able to spread widely by dispersal of
the tubers. Shown here are: (**l**), (**m**), two
semi-double forms; (**n**), a button-eye double
form; (**o**), a bronze-flowered form; (**p**) subsp.
ficariiformis Rouy & Fouc., a very large form,
native of S Europe, characterised by its
yellowish sepals and size; (**q**), a white form. All
are attractive plants for damp places in wild
garden, but are apt to become too invasive in
more cultivated parts of the garden.

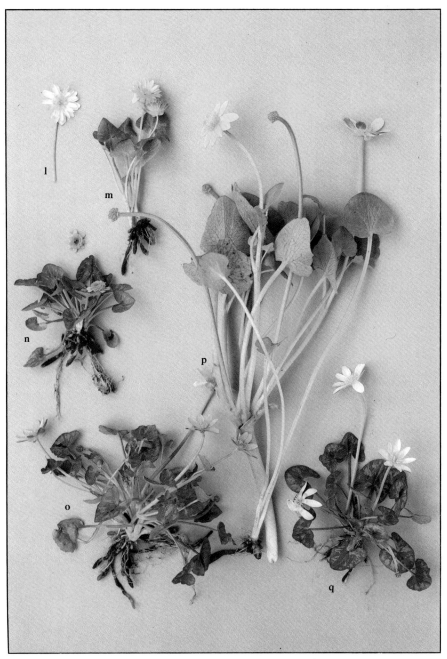

½ life size Photographed 17 April

Anemone biflora

67

½ life size Photographed 14 April

(a) Ornithogalum collinum Guss., syn.
O. tenuifolium Guss. (*Liliaceae*). Native of the
Mediterranean region, where it grows on
hillsides and in scrub flowering in April and
May. There are many very closely related dwarf
narrow-leaved species, differing in details of
bulb and leaf hairiness, in the presence or
absence of a white stripe, and in flowering time
(see pp.38 and 74). Most are easily grown in
sunny well-drained soil and among short grass.
Source Turkey, Hakkari, c.1200m, Rix 2443.

(b) Scilla lilio-hyacinthus L. (*Liliaceae*). Native
of central France and N Spain, growing in
woods and damp grassy places, flowering in
May. Easily recognised by its strange lily-like
bulb with several separate scales, and rather few
(up to fifteen) flowered inflorescence. The
specimen here is unusually short; stems
normally 15–40cm. Easily grown in moist rich
soil in shade, or half-shade.

(c) Anemone pavonina Lam. (*Ranunculaceae*).
Native of the Mediterranean region from France
eastwards to Turkey, flowering from February
to April, growing in fields and on hillsides, often
carpeting the ground under olive trees. Flowers
variable in colour, pink, purple or scarlet. Close
to *A. hortensis* (p.74) which has more (twelve to
nineteen) narrow petals, and *A. coronaria* (p.74)
which has more finely divided leaves. Easily
grown in full sun and well-drained soil. Source
Greece, SW Peloponnese, Rix 502a.
Photographed in Greece in April 1980 by Roger
Phillips.

(d) Muscari tubergenianum Hoog. ex Turrill
(*Liliaceae*). The native range of this plant is not
certain, but Brian Mathew says that it comes
from N Iran. It is very close to *M. aucheri*
(Boiss.) Baker from Turkey and may be a
selection of it. Flowers pure blue. Easy to grow
in any good soil in sun.

(e) Muscari armeniacum Leichtlin ex Baker
(*Liliaceae*). Native of Bulgaria and Yugoslavia,
Greece, Turkey and the Caucasus, growing on
grassy hillsides. Very variable. Leaves three to
five, up to 1cm wide. Flowers often have a
purplish tinge. Easily grown in well-drained
good soil in sun. There is a weird form c.v. 'Blue
Spike' in which each flower has become a
miniature inflorescence, giving a monstrous
effect. (See p.75.)

(f) Muscari botryoides (L.) Miller (*Liliaceae*).
Native of Europe from France, Germany and
Poland southwards, though rare in Greece.
Plants variable up to 30cm. Leaves shorter than
the stem, two or three. The form shown here is
an albino frequent in commerce. Easily grown in ·
any good soil.

Ornithogalum nutans L. (*Liliaceae*). Native of
Bulgaria and Greece to Turkey, growing in fields
and waste places, flowering in April and May.
Naturalised in many other parts of Europe. The
large (15–30mm long) nodding flowers are
characteristic, and appear long after the leaves.
Will survive in grass on well drained soil or
among shrubs, and naturalise itself if happy.

Anemone pavonina

Ornithogalum nutans

69

(a) **Muscari azureum** Fenzl (*Liliaceae*). Native of Caucasus and NW Turkey, growing in damp mountain meadows. Easily grown in good well-drained soil, in a sunny place or in a pot in the alpine house. Common in cultivation as is a very good white form.

(b) **Scilla furseorum** Meikle (*Liliaceae*). Native of NE Afghanistan, near Faisabad, growing on stony hillsides at c.1500m. The rather similar *S. griffithii* has a larger inflorescence and pendulous not erect flowers. Easily grown in a bulb frame or in a pot in the alpine house, kept dry in summer. Source Afghanistan, Faisabad, limestone slopes, 1600m, P. Furse 6254.

(c) **Bellevalia trifoliata** (Ten.) Kunth (*Liliaceae*). Native of S Italy to Greece, Turkey and Egypt (naturalised in S France), growing in fields and waste places, flowering in April and May. There are several very similar species in the Middle East. All are easy to grow in full sun. Source Adiyaman, near Kahta, Linzee Gordon 5150.

(d) **Scilla cilicica** Siehe (*Liliaceae*). Native of Cyprus and SE Turkey southwards to Israel, growing on limestone rocks at up to 1000m, flowering in spring. Distinguished by its long leaves which develop before the flowers appear, and purplish blue upright or horizontal flowers in a lax raceme. Easily grown in a bulb frame or semi-shaded place outside, kept dry in summer. Source Turkey, coll. P. H. Davis.

(e) **Allium paradoxum** (Bieb.) G. Don (*Liliaceae*). Native of the Caucasus, northern Iran and the Kopet Dağ, where it grows in forests from sea level to 2300m, flowering in April and May. Plant 15–30cm high with one flat leaf and one to four large white nodding flowers. Sometimes the flowers are replaced by bulbils. Differs from *A. triquetrum* (p.139) in its rounded petals and single leaf. Easily grown in shady places, and naturalised in NW Europe (esp. S Scotland) where it usually has many bulbils and only one flower. This form can become a weed, but some Iranian plants with no bulbils are very beautiful. Source N Iran above Chalus, coll. P. Furse.

(g) **Muscari neglectum** Guss. ex Ten., syn. *M. atlanticum*, Boiss. & Reut., *M. racemosum* (L.) Lam. & DC. (*Liliaceae*). Native of Europe, from north France southwards to N Africa, Lebanon and eastwards to the Caucasus, Iran and the Altai; naturalised in England. Distinguished by its blackish-blue flowers with white teeth. Very variable in size. Easy to grow in any well-drained soil, and increasing by numerous bulbils.

(f) **Muscari armenaicum** Leichtlin ex Baker (*Liliaceae*). Native of SE Europe, from Yugoslavia and Bulgaria southwards to Turkey and the Caucasus, growing in grassy or rocky places at up to 2000m, flowering in April and May. See also p.75 (a) and (b). Shown here is a commercial cultivated plant. Easily grown in well-drained soil in a sunny place.

(h) **Muscari commutatum** Guss. (*Liliaceae*). Native of N Africa and Italy, eastwards to Lebanon, Turkey and the southern Caucasus, growing in stony places and scrub, flowering from March to May. Distinguished from other species by its dark blackish flowers, with black teeth. Easily grown in any well-drained soil in a sunny place. Source Cyprus, coll. W. K. Aslet.

²/₃ life size Photographed 21 March

½ life size Photographed 2 May

(a) **Bellevalia pycnantha** (C. Koch) A. Los, syn.
Muscari pycnanthum C. Koch (*Liliaceae*). Native
of eastern Turkey, north-west Iran and Soviet
Armenia, growing in medows and marshy fields
in the mountains at 1000–2000m, flowering in
May and June. Easily grown in good soil in full
sun, wet in spring and will tolerate summer
drought, though it does not require it.

(b) **Bellevalia romana** (L.) Rchb. (*Liliaceae*).
Native of SW France and the Mediterranean
region from France to Greece and Turkey,
growing in meadows and waste ground,
flowering in spring. Easy to grow in well-drained
soil in a sunny position.

(c) **Muscari latifolium** Kirk (*Liliaceae*). Native
of NW Turkey, growing in open pine forests at
c.1000m, flowering in April. Very distinct with
its single broad leaf which encircles the stem at
the base. Cultivation as (b).

(d) **Iris × warlsind** hort. (*Iridaceae*, section
Juno). A hybrid between *I. warleyensis* (p.63)
and *I. aucheri* (syn. *I. sindjarensis*) (p.59), easily
grown in well-drained soil and full sun.

(e) **Ranunculus asiaticus** L. (*Ranunculaceae*).
Native of the eastern Mediterranean from Crete,
Rhodes and S Turkey to S Iran and Israel, and
N Africa, growing on stony hillsides and on
rocks, flowering in April and May. Usually red,
but also yellow, purple, pink or white. Easily
grown in a bulb frame or pot in the alpine house,
kept dry in summer, or in a dry place outside.
Source Rhodes, on limestone rocks, Rix 1240.

(f) **Muscari caucasicum** Griseb. ex Baker
(*Liliaceae*). Native of Turkey, south
Transcaucasus, N Iran and the Kopet Dağ, at up
to 3000m, growing in mountain meadows, on
stony slopes and in scrub, flowering from April
to July. Distinguished from *M. comosum* by its
shorter stemmed sterile flowers, which do not
elongate to form a tassel-like head. Cultivation
as (b). Source Iran, coll. P. Furse.

(g) **Fritillaria lusitanica** Wikstrom, syn.
F. hispanica Boiss. & Reut. (*Liliaceae*). Native
of E, C and S Spain, C and S Portugal, growing
in open pine forest at low altitudes, among rocks
and in alpine scree up to c.3000m in the Sierra
Nevada, flowering from March to July. Very
variable in leaf length and flower colour and
shape, but intermediates occur between all the
forms which have at some time been considered
distinct. Easy to grow in a bulb frame, or pot in
the alpine house, kept dry in summer. Source
Portugal, near Lisbon, open pine forest,
c.100m, R. Macfarlane.

(h) **Scilla ramburei** Boiss. (*Liliaceae*). Native of
Portugal, SW Spain and N Africa near Tangiers,
growing in sandy places at low altitudes
flowering from March to June. Sometimes
considered a subspecies of *S. verna* (p.47), but
taller with a looser inflorescence, and smaller
flowers on longer stalks. Easily grown in
well-drained sandy soil in a sunny place.

(i) **Scilla monophyllos** Link. (*Liliaceae*). Native
of Portugal, W Spain and N Africa around
Tangiers, growing on heaths, in pine woods and
sandy ground, flowering from February to June.
Easy to grow in sandy peaty soil in a sunny
position.

(j) **Scilla persica** Hausskn. (*Liliaceae*). Native of
SE Turkey, NE Iraq and W Iran, where it grows
in wet meadows at c.1700m, flowering in May.
Stem 15–20cm. Easy to grow in a bulb frame or
in a sunny place outside. Source Iran, Sanandaj,
P. Furse.

½ life size Photographed 17 April

(a) **Anemone coronaria** L. (*Ranunculaceae*).
Native of the Mediterranean region from Spain
and France to Greece, Turkey and Algeria;
found also in Central Asia, where it is often
called *A. bucharica* Regel. The flowers can be
bluish, pink, red or white. Cultivation as for (d).

(b) **Anemone hortensis** L., syn. *A. stellata*
Lam, *A. fulgens* Gay (*Ranunculaceae*). Native of
the central Mediterranean region from France to
Yugoslavia, growing in hedges, fields or in olive
groves, flowering from February to April.
Flowers usually purplish. The smallest
narrowest petalled form has been called
A. stellata. *A. fulgens* is larger, with broader
red petals, and possibly a hybrid between
A. hortensis and *A. pavonina*. 'St Bavo' is a strain
with pink or pale mauve petals (illustrated here).
Cultivation as (d).

(c) **Geranium tuberosum** L. (*Geraniaceae*).
Native of the Mediterranean region, eastwards
to the Caucasus and Central Asia, growing in
stony places, often as a weed in cornfields,
flowering from April to June. Shown here is
subsp. *tuberosum*. The N African *G. atlanticum* is
a better garden plant with larger flowers. Shown
here is *G. Macrostylum* Boiss.

(d), (e) **Muscari armeniacum** Leichtlin ex
Baker (*Liliaceae*). Native of SE Europe from
Yugoslavia and Bulgaria to Greece, Turkey and
the Caucasus, growing in grassy and rocky
places up to 2000m, flowering in April and May.
Easy to grow in a well-drained soil and sunny
position. Source (d) Turkey, Elma Da., above
Ankara (an albino), Rix s.n.; (e) between
Malatya and Kayseri, limestone plateau,
c.2000m, Rix s.n.

(f) **Gagea graeca** (L.) Terr., syn. *Lloydia graeca*
L. (*Liliaceae*). Native of Greece, Crete and
Turkey, growing in pockets of soil on rock,
flowering in March and April. Easily grown in a
sunny bulb frame or in a pot in the alpine house
in full sun, kept dry in summer. Source Turkey,
Izmir, Rix 1218.

(g) **Gagea confusa** Terr., syn. *G. minimoides*
Pascher (*Liliaceae*). Native of E Turkey,
N Iraq, W Iran, Kopet Dağ, and
S Transcaucasia, growing in grassy places,
usually by late snow patches from 1000 to
3000m, flowering from April to July. Easily
grown in a bulb frame, kept wet in spring, dry in
summer. Source Turkey, Van, near Hoşap.

(h) **Muscari macrocarpum** Sweet (*Liliaceae*).
Native of Greece, especially the Aegean islands
and Crete, and western Turkey, growing on
limestone cliffs flowering in April and May.
Distinguished from *M. moschatum* Willd. by its
yellow flowers, purplish in bud. Easy to grow in
a well-drained sunny place.

(i) **Bellevalia longipes** Post (*Liliaceae*). Native
of Turkey, Syria, Iraq and Iran, growing in
fields and on hillsides from 900 to 2000m,
flowering in March and April. One of a complex
group of species with pedicels which elongate in
fruit, close to *B. sarmatica* (Pallas ex Georgi)
Woron. from the steppes of S Russia and
Romania. Cultivation as for (h). Source Iran,
coll. by Paul Furse.

Muscari comosum (L.) Miller (*Liliaceae*).
Native of most of Europe, N America to
Lebanon, Turkey and Iraq, at up to 2200m,
flowering from March to July, growing
especially in dry meadows and as a weed of
cultivation. Photographed in Greece,
Peloponnese, near Sparta, in April 1980 by
Roger Phillips.

¹/₃ life size Photographed 22 April

Muscari comosum

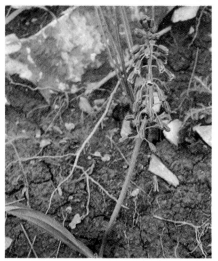

Bellevalia dubia

(j) **Ornithogalum fimbriatum** Willd. (p.38).

Bellevalia dubia (Guss.) Reichenb. (*Liliaceae*).
Native of Italy and Yugoslavia to Greece and

Turkey, growing on rocky hillsides on limestone
at up to 1000m, flowering in March and April.
Photographed in the S Peloponnese near
Githion, in April 1980 by Roger Phillips.

Bluebell wood in the Chilterns near Ibston, Buckinghamshire

¼ life size Photographed 2 May

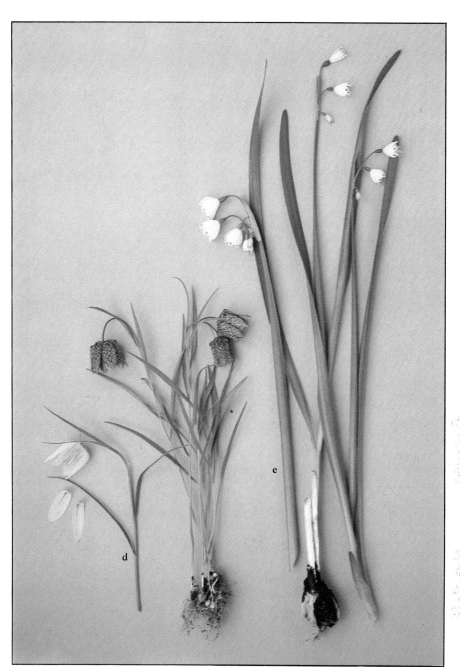

¼ life size Photographed 17 April

(b) **Hyacinthoides non-scripta** (L.) Chouard ex Rothm., syn. *Endymion non-scriptus* (L.) Garcke, *Scilla non-scripta* (L.) Hoffmans. & Link (*Liliaceae*). Bluebell. Native of W Europe from western France, Belgium and Portugal, growing in woods and meadows, flowering from April to June. Naturalised further east. Easily grown in leafy soil near the Atlantic coast of Europe, and requiring cool shady conditions further east. Photographed in S England, Chiltern Hills near Ibston, Buckinghamshire, by Roger Phillips.

(c), (a) **Hyacinthoides hispanica** (Miller) Rothm., syn. *Scilla hispanica* Miller (*Liliaceae*). Native of Spain, Portugal and N Africa, especially Morocco and Algeria, naturalised elsewhere, growing in woods and among shady rocks, flowering from March to May. Distinguished from *H. non-scripta* by its erect racemes, erect and more open flowers, as well as its broader leaves. Hybrids are common in cultivation and one is shown here (a) which has an infloresence intermediate between the parents. White (as shown) and pink forms are also common in cultivation.

(d) **Fritillaria meleagris** L. (*Liliaceae*). Snake's Head Fritillary. Native of most of Europe from N Yugoslavia and S Russia to Poland, central France and S England. Naturalised in Scandinavia. It grows in the flood plains of rivers usually in rather dry fen vegetation on alkaline soils, often in great numbers. The colour varies from dark purple to white. Easily grown in grass or in well-drained soil in sun or half-shade, not dried out in summer. Photographed in Gloucestershire in April 1964.

(e) **Leucojum aestivum** L. (*Amaryllidaceae*). Summer Snowflake. Native of Europe and SW Asia to north Iran, growing in wet fields, woods and swamps especially near rivers, flowering from March to May. Distinguished from *L. vernum* by the smaller flowers, and by having three to seven flowers in the umbel. The leaves emerge in winter. The seed pod is swollen and filled with air so that it will float and be dispersed by water. The larger flowered form, is c.v. 'Gravetye', named after the garden of William Robinson in Sussex. Easily grown in damp rich soil and happy in waterlogged conditions.

Fritillaria meleagris

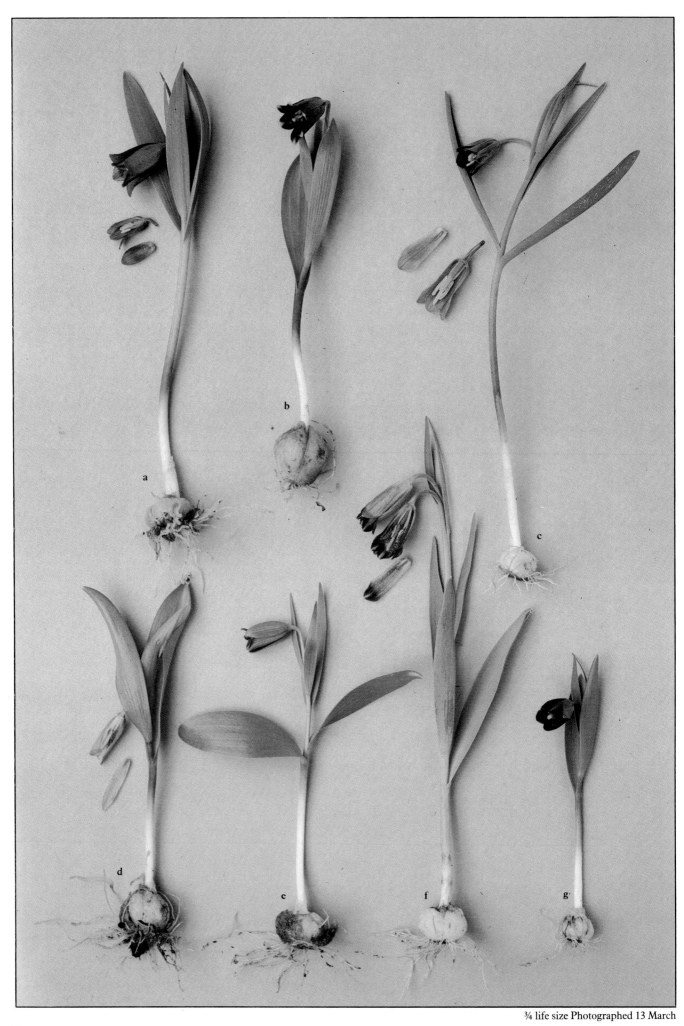

¾ life size Photographed 13 March

(a) **Fritillaria pinardii** Boiss., syn. *F. syriaca* Hayek & Siehe, *F. alpina* Freyn & Sint. (*Liliaceae*). Native of S Armenia, most of Turkey, Syria and Lebanon, growing on stony hillsides especially by late snow patches, at above 1800m, flowering in May and June (see also p.81 (d), (j)). Very variable, but characterised by its alternate rather broad leaves, purplish or reddish flowers, yellow or green inside, and papillose style. The short-stemmed form shown here was called *F. syriaca*. Easy to grow in a pot in the alpine house or in a bulb frame. Source Turkey, mountains south of Malatya, 2000m, Rix 1624.

(b) **Fritillaria zagrica** Stapf (*Liliaceae*). Native of Iran, especially the central Zagros mountains from 1800 to 3000m, growing in mountain steppe, often by late snow patches, flowering from March to May. Characterised by the small yellow tips to the otherwise dark purple petals, and rather slender, papillose style. Stem 4–12cm. Cultivation as (a).

(c) **Fritillaria assyriaca** Baker, syn. *F. canaliculata* Baker (*Liliaceae*). Native of E Turkey, W Iran, N Iraq and possibly S Armenia, growing in fields, on steppe and stony hillsides, from 100 to 2500m, flowering from March to May. Distinguished from *F. pinardii* by its narrower leaves, usually taller stem and very short stout style. (Height 10–35cm.) Cultivation as (a), but many forms have proved susceptible to botrytis. Keep rather dry. Source NE Turkey, Ağri, Tahir Dağ, 500m, Rix 1658.

(d), (e) **Fritillaria chlorantha** Hausskn. & Bornm. (*Liliaceae*). Native of Iran, especially the NW Zagros mountains, growing on steep and stony slopes from 1800 to 3000m, flowering in April and May. Characterised by its shining green, not glaucous leaves and green flower, sometimes marked with purple. Style short, stout, divided at the tip. Height 4–10cm. Cultivation as (a). Slow to increase. Source (d) Iran, Zagros, S of Thuin, 2310m, Archibald 1609; (e) Iran, SW of Arak, Shuturunkuh, 1800m, BSBE 695.

(f) **Fritillaria assyriaca × caucasica** (*Liliaceae*). Hybrids are rare in *Fritillaria*, but this form is frequent in NE Turkey around Erzurum and Kars. It has the tall stem of its parents, but broader leaves than *F. assyriaca*, and a stouter, more papillose style than *F. caucasica*. It is usually found near the parents, but often growing in separate colonies. Robust and easy to cultivate in a bulb frame, and might succeed outside. Source Turkey, Ağri, Tahir Dağ, stony slopes, 2400m, Rix 1641.

(g) **Fritillaria armena** Boiss. (*Liliaceae*). Native of north-eastern Turkey, especially around Erzurum, where it grows on stony hillsides in bare earth by late snow patches at 1800–2800m, flowering in May and June. Characterised by its small, deep purple flowers, dark inside, and stout papillose style. Cultivation as (a). Source Turkey, Erzurum, Çakmak Dağ, 2200m, Rix 855.

Fritillaria raddeana Regel, syn. *F. askabadensis* M. Micheli (*Liliaceae*). Native of NE Iran, and SW Central Asia, especially the Kopet Dağ, growing on rocks and among scrub, flowering from March to April. Like a small delicate Crown Imperial, with pale yellow flowers and a much smaller nectary. Easy to grow, but flowering so early that it is better in a bulb frame. Source cultivated stock, probably originating from a large seed collection by P. Furse in Golestan Forest, NE Iran.

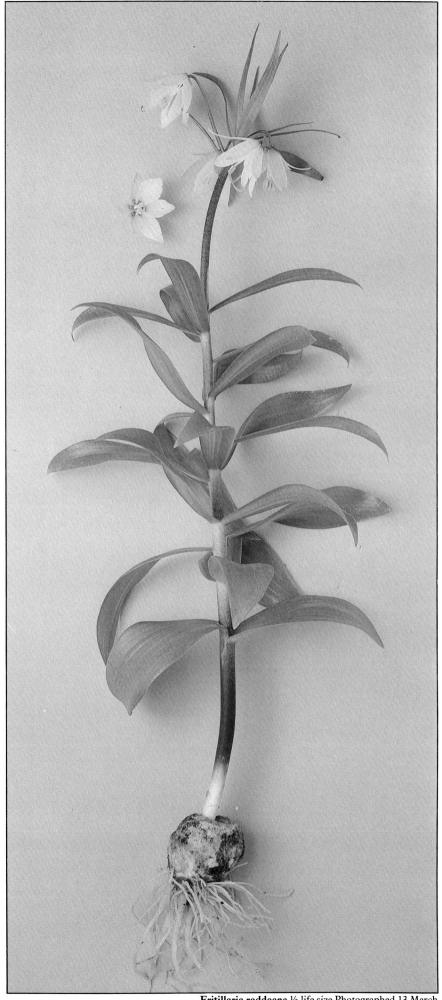

Fritillaria raddeana ½ life size Photographed 13 March

²/₃ life size Photographed 28 March

(a) Fritillaria conica Boiss. (*Liliaceae*). Native of S Greece, especially the Peloponnese, where it grows on limestone hills near the sea in low evergreen oak scrub, and at the edges of fields. Distinguished from other small yellow-flowered species by its tall stem, up to 25cm, and deeply divided style. Easy to grow in a bulb frame and in very well-drained, good soil outside, in full sun. Source Greece, near Pylos, Rix 485.

(b) Fritillaria uva-vulpis Rix, syn. *F. assyriaca* hort. non Baker (*Liliaceae*). Native of N Iraq, W Iran and SE Turkey, growing in cornfields and hay meadows from 1000 to 2500m, flowering in March and April. Distinguished from *F. assyriaca* Baker (p.79 (c)) by its few flat, shining green leaves; style very stout. This plant was misidentified as *F. assyriaca* and is widely cultivated under that name. Cultivation as (a). Source Iran, Rezaiyeh, SE of Mahabad, 1700m, Furse 2173.

(c) Fritillaria caucasica Adams, syn. *F. tulipifolia* M. Bieb. (*Liliaceae*). Native of NE Turkey, NW Iran and the Caucasus, growing in grassy subalpine meadows, and on shady rock ledges from 1700 to 3000m, flowering from April to June. Distinguished by its usually tall (up to 30cm) stem, few leaves and long, 9–17mm, slender usually smooth style and stamen filaments. Always grows in peaty soil in the wild, but difficult to cultivate satisfactorily. The specimen shown here is shorter than normal. Source USSR, Armenia, hills above Lake Sevan, Rix 2623.

(d) Fritillaria pinardii Boiss., syn. *F. alpina* Freyn & Sint. (*Liliaceae*) (see p.79 (a)). The form shown here is close to *F. alpina*, with its tall stem, and flowers yellow inside. It grows on stony hills in NW Turkey south to Ankara. Source Turkey, Elma Daǧ above Ankara, Rix 1526.

(e) Fritillaria forbesii Baker (*Liliaceae*). Native of the extreme south-western corner of Turkey around Marmaris, where it grows in scrub, usually on serpentine, flowering in February and March, from 50 to 350m. Requires careful treatment in a bulb frame or alpine house, as it tends to emerge very early and be damaged by frost. Collected plants grow poorly, and as the species is very restricted in the wild, it should not be dug up. The form shown here has been in cultivation for many years, and grows well, but increases slowly.

(f) Fritillaria carica Rix (*Liliaceae*). Native of south-western Turkey, Samos and Chios, where it grows on rocky hillsides, often among scrub, or in open pine woods from 200 to 1500m, flowering from March to May. Distinguished from *F. forbesii* by its broader leaves and shorter stem, and from *F. bithynica* which often grows nearby, by its fat, papillose style. Capsule not winged. Easily grown in a bulb frame or a pot in the alpine house. Source Turkey, Izmir, by the ruins of Ephesus, C.M.W. 2508.

(g) Fritillaria aurea Schott, syn. *F. cilicicotaurica* Hausskn., *F. bornmuelleri* Hausskn. (*Liliaceae*). Native of central Turkey, growing among limestone rocks and on cliffs, often by late snow patches from 1800 to 3000m, flowering from May to July. The large yellow flowers distinguish it from all other species except *F. collina* (p.85(e)), which has narrower leaves and petals greenish on the back, with finely ciliate margins, and the larger paler *F. tubiformis* subsp. *moggridgei* from the Alps. Cultivation as (f). One of the best small species, increasing well. Source Turkey, Sivas, Yildiz Daǧ, Rix 2030.

²/₃ life size Photographed 28 March

(h), (i) Fritillaria aurea × pinardii (*Liliaceae*). Two hybrid individuals and the likely parents are shown here. Hybrids are very rare, although two or more species often grow together. These two were growing with the parents in central Turkey. They have grown well in cultivation, increasing fast by bulbils, and hybrids have been made between (h) and *F. aurea*. Source (h) Rix 1602; (i) Rix 1601.

(j) Fritillaria pinardii Boiss. (*Liliaceae*) (see pp.79 (a) and 81 (d)). This form is found scattered across central Turkey, and is usually rather small and delicate with pronounced 'shoulders' to the narrow flower. It is called *F. fleischeri* by Boissier in *Flora Orientalis*. Source Turkey, between Malatya and Kayseri, 2000m, on rocky steppe, Rix 1600.

Fritillaria latifolia Willd., syn. *F. nobilis* Baker (*Liliaceae*). Native of the Caucasus and north-east Turkey, growing in alpine meadows and on stony hillsides by late snow patches from 1800 to 3000m, flowering from May to July. Similar to *F. tubiformis* from the Alps (p.87 (c)), but has shining green, not glaucous, leaves and the flowers are smaller, not greyish outside.

Fritillaria latifolia

Turkish collections have not grown well, but recent collections from the Caucasus, where it is more robust, may do better. Should do best in rich peaty soil outside. Photographed in NE Turkey between Yalnizçam and Ardanuç, in May 1970.

life size Photographed 21 March

a b c d

(a), (c) Fritillaria crassifolia Boiss. & Huet subsp. **kurdica** (Boiss. & Noë) Rix, syn. *F. karadaghensis* Turrill (*Liliaceae*). Native of SE Turkey, NW Iran and S Transcaucasia, growing on stony alpine steppes and on rocks from 1500 to 3500m, flowering from April to July. Nectary linear, 8–10mm long. One form shown here was named *F. grossheimiana* A. Los. Better grown in a bulb frame, in rich loose and very gritty soil. Source (a) NW Iran, Kuh-i-Sahand, Furse 2923; (c) SE Turkey, Hakkari, Yükşekova, 2150m, Rix 1936.

(b) Fritillaria straussii Bornm. Native of SE Turkey and NW Iran, growing among oak scrub and large herbs at 1500–2500m, flowering in May and June. Flowers dark purple, or green going purple with age; nectary linear. Cultivation as (a). Source Iran, Sanandaj to Marivan, P. Furse 3397.

(d) Fritillaria michailovskyi Fomine. Native of NE Turkey from Erzurum to Kars growing on screes and earthy slopes from 2000 to 3000m, flowering in May and June. The dead petals remain around the seed capsule. Cultivation as for (a). Source Kars, subalpine meadow in clearings among pine trees, 2100m, Albury, Cheese & Watson 1617.

(e) Fritillaria graeca Boiss. & Spruner. Native of S Greece, growing in rocky places among garrigue and *Abies* forest from 700 to 1800m, flowering from March to May. Shown here a rather stout, robust form which was called *F. guicciardii* Held & Sart. Cultivation as for (a). Source Greece, Athens, Mount Parnis, Rix 568.

(f) Fritillaria davisii Turrill. Native of the Peloponnese growing at low altitudes in scrub, olive groves and cornfields, flowering in March. Very close to *F. graeca*, differing mainly in habit, with the lowest leaves flat, at ground level, and in having a purple flower without a clear green central stripe. Cultivation as for (a). Source Greece, S Peloponnese, S of Githion, A. A. M. Batchelor.

(g) Fritillaria crassifolia subsp. **poluninii** Rix (*Liliaceae*). Native of NE Iraq, growing on limestone screes from 2200 to 2400m, flowering from April to June, often by late snow patches. Source NE Iraq near Suleimaniya, 2400m, Polunin 5063.

(h) Fritillaria crassifolia Boiss. & Huet, subsp. **crassifolia** syn. *F. ophioglossifolia* Freyn & Sint. Native of Turkey, scattered from the SW to the NE, usually growing on limestone screes, from 1500 to 2600m, flowering in May and June. Source Turkey, Erzurm, Kop Daǧ, 2600m, Rix 1710. See 93(c).

(i) Fritillaria crassifolia subsp. **hakkarensis** Rix. Native of SE Turkey and NE Iraq, growing by late snow patches from 1500 to 3500m, flowering from May to July. Close to subsp. *kurdica*, but has dark green shining leaves, and a smaller, more open flower. Source Turkey, Hakkari, Şemdinli, T. Baytop, ISTE 21620.

Fritillaria alburyana Rix, syn. *F. erzurumica* Kasapigil. Native of NE Turkey, growing in screes and in peaty soil among tussocks of grass, flowering in late May and June by late snow patches at 2000–3000m. Named after Sidney Albury, who died plant collecting in the Himalayas in 1970. This species has proved very difficult to flower well in cultivation, probably because it does not get a long enough cold period in lowland Europe. Photographed in Turkey, south of Erzurum, in May 1970.

life size Photographed 28 March

¼ life size Photographed 28 March

Fritillaria alburyana

83

½ life size Photographed 14 April

¹/₃ life size Photographed 28 March

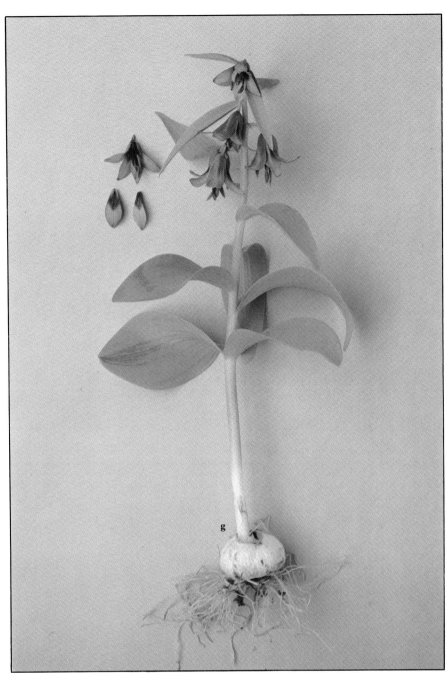

¹/₃ life size Photographed 2 April

(a) **Fritillaria sibthorpiana** (Sibth. & Sm.)
Baker (*Liliaceae*). Native of SW Turkey, near
Marmaris, where it grows in open pine forest on
limestone at c.400m, flowering in April.
Characterised by its small yellow flower, and two
large ovate-lanceolate stem leaves. Easy to grow
in a bulb frame or in a pot in the alpine house;
increase by seed. Source Turkey, near
Marmaris, Brickell & Mathew 8306.

(b) **Fritillaria alfredae** subsp. **glaucoviridis**
(Turrill) Rix, syn. *F. haradjianii* Briq.
(*Liliaceae*). Native of S Turkey, especially the
northern Amanus mountains, growing in oak
scrub and beech forest, at 500–1500m, flowering
in April and May. Stem 10–36cm; capsule
winged. Cultivation as for (a). Slow to increase,
but will set seed if pollinated. Source Turkey,
Amanus, Nurdağ pass, Rix 1357.

(c) **Fritillaria alfredae** subsp. **platyptera**
(Samuelsson) Rix (*Liliaceae*). Native of
S Turkey, and Syria in the southern Amanus
mountains, growing in oak scrub from 500 to
800m, flowering in April and May. Close to
subsp. *glaucoviridis*, but is more slender, with
longer upper leaves and narrower lower leaves.
Sub-species *alfredae*, a very rare plant from
Lebanon, is still slenderer and more delicate.
Source S Turkey, near Yayladağ, Rix 1360.

(d) **Fritillaria bithynica** Baker, syn. *F. citrina*
Baker, *F. schliemannii* Sint.,*F. pineticola*
Schwarz (*Liliaceae*). Native of western Turkey,
Samos and Chios, growing in open pine forest or
oak scrub from 100 to 1200m, flowering from
March to May. Characterised by its green
flowers, yellowish inside, occasionally with
purple markings, and slender, undivided style.
Cultivation as for (a). Source S Turkey, hills
south of Muğla, Rix 1298.

(e) **Fritillaria ehrhartii** Boiss. & Orph.
(*Liliaceae*). Native of the Aegean islands of
Euboea, Skiros, Andros and Siros, growing in
garrigue and among schistose rocks, from 180 to
800m, flowering from February to April. Differs
from *F. bithynica* in its purple flowers, with a
yellow point to each petal; cf. *F. zagrica* (p.79
(b)). Cultivation as for (a). Source Greece,
Euboea, near Karystos, Rix 2167.

(f) **Fritillaria minuta** Boiss. & Noë, syn.
F. carduchorum Rix (*Liliaceae*). Native of
eastern Turkey and NW Iran, growing on earthy
hillsides and among oak scrub from 1000 to
3500m, flowering from April to July, usually by
late snow patches. Distinguished by its small
narrow brick red flower, and deeply trifid
smooth style. Easy to grow in a bulb frame or pot
in the alpine house. Source Turkey, Bitlis,
towards Tatvan, 2300m, Rix 779.

(g) **Fritillaria severtzovii** Regel, syn. *Korolkovia
severtzovii* (Regel) Regel (*Liliaceae*). Native of
Central Asia, especially the Tien Shan and the
Pamir Alai, growing on cliff ledges, among
scrub and on steep earthy slopes from 1000 to
3000m, flowering from March to July. The bulb

is similar to many *Fritillaria*, and the branching
roots are similar to *F. imperialis*. The petal shape
and the nectary are closer to *Lilium*. Easy to grow
in a bulb frame or pot in the alpine house, kept
dry in summer. Source C Asia, mountains south
of Ferghana, Chamsabad, 2000m, Rix 2781.

(h) **Fritillaria collina** Adams, syn. *F. lutea* M.
Bieb. (*Liliaceae*). Native of the Caucasus, where
it grows in alpine meadows and birch scrub at
2000–4500m, flowering in May and June. Close
to *F. aurea* Schott, but flowers larger and paler,
and inner petals with finely toothed edges. Has
grown well in peaty soil in a bulb frame, but
should also grow happily in well drained soil
outside. Source USSR, N Caucasus, Dombai,
coll. D. Schlummel.

Fritillaria bucharica

Fritillaria walujewii

Fritillaria verticillata

(a) **Fritillaria minima** Rix (*Liliaceae*). Native of SE Turkey, where it grows on steep slopes among limestone rocks at 2900–3000m, flowering in June and July by melting snow patches. Has proved unsatisfactory in cultivation, as the flowers open before the stem has elongated. It has grown in a sunny bulb frame, in a peaty alkaline soil. Source Turkey, Van, above Gevaş, Rix 735a.

(b) **Fritillaria montana** Hoppe (*Liliaceae*). Native of SE France, Italy and the Balkans south to northern Greece, where it grows on limestone pavements, and on rocky slopes, at from 50 to 1600m, flowering from March to May. Easy to grow in a bulb frame or a raised bed outside, kept rather dry in summer. Source Yugoslavia, near Kičevo, 1250m, rocky limestone area in wood, J. R. Marr 3429.

(c) **Fritillaria tubiformis** Gren. & Godron, syn. *F. delphinensis* Gren. & Godron (*Liliaceae*). Native of SE France, and NW Italy, growing in alpine meadows from 1500 to 2000m, flowering in May and June. Subsp. *moggridgei* Boiss. & Reut. ex Rix has yellow flowers and longer nectaries. Easy to grow in peaty soil in a slightly shaded bulb frame or raised bed. Should not become absolutely dry in summer. Source France, near Gap, Col de Glaize, Rix s.n.

(d) **Fritillaria tuntasia** Heldr. ex Halacsy (*Liliaceae*). Native of Greece, especially the islands of Serifos and Kithnos, growing in rocky places and scrub, flowering in March and April. Cultivation as for (b).

(e) **Fritillaria reuteri** Boiss. (*Liliaceae*). Native of SW Iran, north and west of Esfahan, growing in wet rocky meadows at 2500–3000m, often in huge numbers, flowering in May and June. Flower colour and nectary rather similar to *F. michailovskyi* (p.83 (d)), but taller and more slender, and has two small bracts at the base of each pedicel. Not very robust in cultivation, but will grow in a pot in the alpine house, or in a sunny bulb frame. Source Iran, near Esfahan, F. Baxter.

(f) **Fritillaria bucharica** Regel (*Liliaceae*). Native of NE Afghanistan and Central Asia, especially the Pamir Alai, growing on cliffs and rocky slopes, at 1000–2400m, flowering from March to May. Easy to grow in a bulb frame or

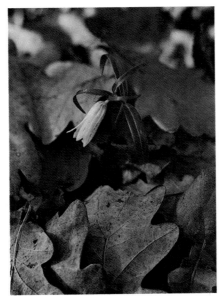

Fritillaria amabilis

pot in the alpine house, kept dry in summer. Source Afghanistan, Faizabad district, 1000m, P. Furse 6240. Photographed in Central Asia, Dushanbe, Varsob gorge, 1400m, 11 April 1979.

(g) **Fritillaria elwesii** Boiss. (*Liliaceae*). Native of southern Turkey, growing in fields, scrub and open pine woods along the coast at 500–1200m, flowering from March to May. Very close to *F. assyriaca* Baker (p.79 (c)), but usually taller, with a lobed style, and increasing well by numerous bulbils. Source Turkey, Içel above Mersin, 1200m, Davis 26500.

Fritillaria walujewii Regel, syn. *F. ferganensis* A. Los. (*Liliaceae*). Native of Central Asia, expecially the Dzungarian Ala Tau, the Tien Shan and the Pamir Alai, growing on cliffs and among Juniper scrub, at c.2000m, flowering in April and May. Nectary lanceolate. Only recently introduced into cultivation. In the wild growing in loose peaty soil, over limestone, often growing up through moss. Source Central Asia, mountains south of Ferghana, Chamsabad, 2000m, Rix 2780.

Fritillaria amabilis Koidzumi (*Liliaceae*). Native of S Japan, on the islands of Kyushu, Shikoku and SW Honshu, growing at

Fritillaria cirrhosa

600–800m, in woods in deep peaty soil, flowering at the end of March. Very difficult to grow, but has flowered grown in a pot in leafy soil, kept rather shaded and not allowed to dry out in summer.

Fritillaria cirrhosa D. Don. (*Liliaceae*). Native of the Himalayas from Nepal eastwards, growing in subalpine and alpine meadows and in scrub from 3000 to 4500m, flowering from May to July. Very variable. In the west this merges into *F. roylei* Hooker. Not easy to grow, but has thrived for many years outside in a sunny stony bed at Keillour Castle in Perthshire. Photographed in Nepal, trail to Annapurna, by Sir Colville Barclay.

Fritillaria verticillata Willd. (*Liliaceae*). Native of Central Asia and China, and naturalised in Japan where it is much used as a medicinal herb, and put in cough mixtures. The form shown here is *F. thunbergii* Miq., which is that usually cultivated; it probably originated in western China, and differs somewhat from the plants from eastern Central Asia. Grown best in a moist peaty soil in the open garden. Photographed in the Wild Garden at Wisley, Surrey, England.

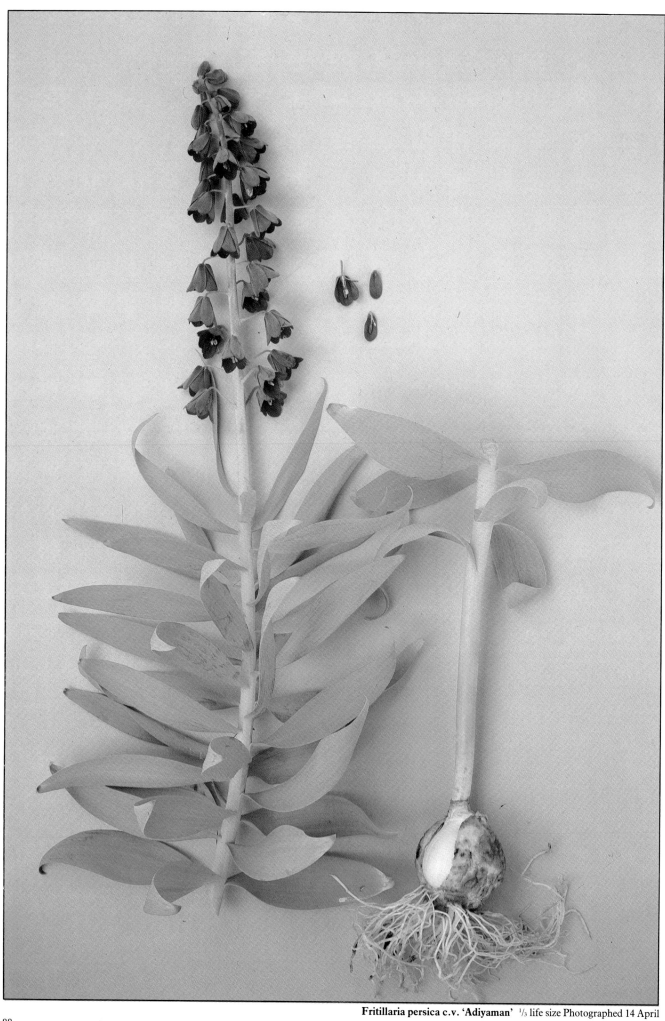

Fritillaria persica c.v. 'Adiyaman' ¹/₃ life size Photographed 14 April

Fritillaria persica L., syn. *F. libanotica* (Boiss.) Baker, *F. eggeri* Bornm. (*Liliaceae*). Native of S Turkey, Syria, Lebanon, Israel, Jordan, Iraq and W Iran, growing on rocky slopes, in scrub and at the edges of cornfields, from 700 to 2800m, flowering from April to May. Shown here is c.v. 'Adiyaman', which probably originated in S Turkey. The distinction between the Mediterranean *F. libanotica* and *F. persica* from the Zagros in W Iran is not clear. *F. arabica* Gandoger, from cliffs near Petra in E Jordan, is more striking in its very broad leaves and obovate petals. All require deep rich soil, either in a bulb frame, or in a very warm sunny place outside, such as a bed under a south wall.

Fritillaria imperialis L. (*Liliaceae*). Crown Imperial. Native of Turkey, especially the south-east, and W Iran, and found also in Afghanistan, Pakistan and Kashmir, growing on cliffs, rocky slopes and among scrub, from 1000 to 3000m, flowering in April and May. Easily grown in good well-drained soil in sun or in the shade of deciduous trees or shrubs. Cultivated in Europe since the sixteenth century, when it was brought from Constantinople to Vienna and thence to Holland and England. It is called in Persian 'Tears of Mary' because of the great drops of nectar at the base of each petal. Christian tradition tells that of all the flowers, only the proud Crown Imperial refused to bow its head at the Crucifixion; it has bowed and wept ever since.

Fritillaria eduardii Regel (*Liliaceae*). Native of Central Asia, especially Tadzikistan where it grows in scrub and rocky places in the mountains, at c.2000m, flowering in April. Intermediate between *F. raddeana* (p.79) and *F. imperialis*. Photographed in Central Asia, E of Dushanbe, 2500m, in April 1979.

Fritillaria eduardii

Fritillaria eduardii

Fritillaria imperialis ½ life size Photographed 14 April

89

a b c d e f g h

½ life size Photographed 14 April

(a) Fritillaria messanensis subsp. **gracilis** (Ebel) Rix, syn. *F. neglecta* Parl. (*Liliaceae*). Native of S Yugoslavia and N Albania, growing in rocky woods and on screes on limestone from 250 to 2000m, flowering from March to June. Distinguished from subsp. *messanensis* by having the flowers usually not tessellated, and the upper leaves not in a whorl of three. Easy to grow in a bulb frame, or in a rather dry place in half-shade under shrubs. Source S Yugoslavia, above Budva, c.900m, Marr 3130 and M.J.C./M. 33.

(b) Fritillaria messanensis var. **atlantica** Maire, syn. *F. oranensis* hort. (*Liliaceae*). Native of N Africa, growing in cedar forest and scrub from c.1200 to 3000m, flowering from March to June. The lowland fritillaries in N Africa seem inseparable from *F. messanensis*, but the subalpine and alpine forms have shorter broader leaves and a squat dark flower, and grow especially in the Middle Atlas, the Rif, and the High Atlas. Easy to grow in a dry bulb frame, or pot in the alpine house, but slow to increase. Source Morocco, High Atlas, A. Hamilton.

(c), (f)–(h) Fritillaria graeca Boiss. & Spurner, subsp. **thessala** (Boiss.) Rix, syn. *F. ionica* Halacsy (*Liliaceae*). Native of S Albania, S Yugoslavia and NW Greece as far south as Mt Parnassos, where it merges into subsp. *graeca* (see p.83 (e)). Leaves in a whorl of three at the top of the stem, flowers mostly green. Easy to grow in a bulb frame or a dry half-shady place outside. Source (c) Greece, near Meteora, W. K. Aslet; (f) Ziria, H. & M. Crook 3229; (g) origin not known, probably from Katara pass; (h) between Konitsa and Joannina, Marr 3213.

(d), (e) Fritillaria graeca Boiss. & Spruner subsp. **graeca** (*Liliaceae*). (See p.83 (e)). The forms shown here are from: (d) Peloponnese, Mt Chelmos, Polunin & Chater 13017; (e) Athens, Hymettos, 700m, Rix 572.

(i) Fritillaria verticillata Willd. (see p.87).

(j) Fritillaria messanensis Rafin, syn. *F. oranensis* Pomel (*Liliaceae*). Native of Sicily, Italy, Greece, Crete and N Africa, growing in scrub and in open pine and oak woods, flowering from January to May. The leaves are narrow with a whorl of three below the flower; the nectary is large 6–10cm long, and oval. *F. sphaciotica* Gandoger from Crete is similar, but slightly more delicate than the Greek form shown here. Easy to grow in a bulb frame, and would probably do outside in a dry sunny spot. Source Greece, lower slopes of Mt Olympus, c.800m, Rix 630.

(k) Fritillaria pyrenaica L. (*Liliaceae*). Native of the Pyrenees and NW Spain, growing in subalpine meadows, from 450 to 2000m, flowering from April to June. Distinguished by its short alternate leaves, and very dark flowers rather square at the base. There is also a beautiful pale yellow semi-albino form which grows among the normal form in some places (p.93 (i)). Easy to grow in well-drained soil and will do well in thin grass.

Fritillaria pallidiflora Schrenk (*Liliaceae*). Native of Central Asia, especially the mountains on the Sino-Soviet border, the Dzungarian Ala Tau, and the Tien Shan, flowering in May and June on subalpine slopes. The broad glaucous leaves and pale yellowish flowers are characteristic. Easy to grow in rich peaty soil in half-shade, and one of the best species for the open garden.

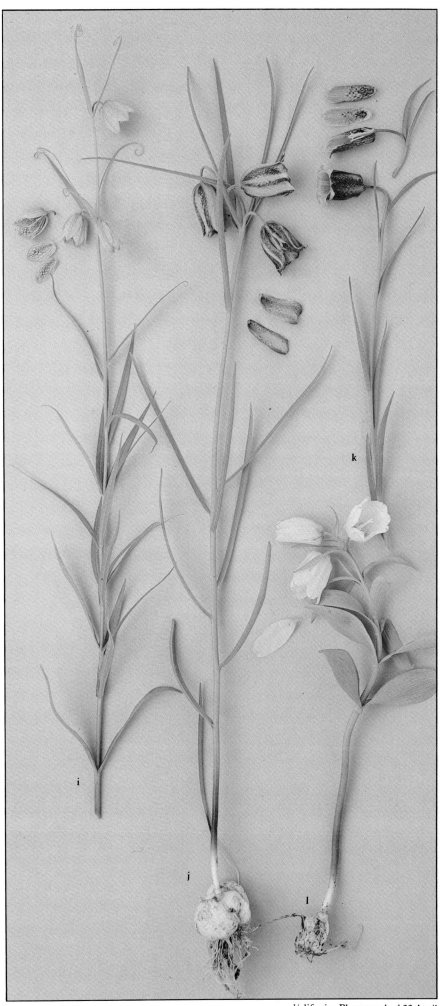

½ life size Photographed 22 April

91

⅓ life size Photographed 17 April

(a) Fritillaria latakiensis Rix (*Liliaceae*). Native of southern Turkey, Lebanon and Syria, growing in scrub and open pine forest at up to 1000m, flowering in April. Easy to grow in a bulb frame, and possibly also outside. Source S Turkey, V. Horton.

(b) Fritillaria drenovskii Degen & Stoyanoff. Native of S Bulgaria and NE Greece, growing in hazel scrub from 300 to 1000m, flowering in May and June. Similar to *F. armena* (p.79 (g)) in flower, but with narrower, glaucous leaves. Cultivation as for (a).

(c) Fritillaria crassifolia Boiss. & Huet subsp. **crassifolia** (see p.83 (h)). Source Turkey, Denizli, Honaz Dağ, limestone screes, 1750m, C.M.W. 2556 (the westernmost locality of the species).

(d) Fritillaria acmopetala Boiss., syn. *F. lycia* Boiss. Native of SW Turkey along the coast to Lebanon, and Cyprus, growing in open pine woods, scrub, and corn fields, at 20–2000m, flowering from March to May. Easy to grow in any good well-drained soil.

(e) Fritillaria pontica Wahl. Native of Bulgaria, Albania, S Yugoslavia, N Greece and NW Turkey, growing in woods and scrub, from 30 to 1000m, flowering in April and May. Capsule with narrow wings. Cultivation as for (d). Source Turkey, Bursa, Ulu Dağ, Rix 1207.

(f) Fritillaria gussichiae (Degen & Dörfler) Rix, syn. *F. graeca* var. *gussichiae* Degen & Dörfler. Native of S Bulgaria, S Yugoslavia and N Greece, growing in woods, on shady rocks and alpine pastures from 500 to 1500m, flowering from April to June. There may be up to six flowers in robust specimens; the capsules are narrowly winged. Cultivation as for (d).

(g) Fritillaria whittallii Baker. Native of SW Turkey, growing on limestone screes, or in cedar forest, from 1500 to 2000m, flowering from April to June. The leaves are usually narrower than in the specimen shown here. Cultivation as for (a). Source Turkey, Isparta, Dedegöl Da, 1600m, Sorger 66-46-42.

(h) Fritillaria involucrata Allioni. Native of S France and NW Italy, in the foothills of the Alpes Maritimes, growing in scrub and woods at c.1000m, flowering in April and May. Cultivation as for (d). Source S France, near Caussols, 1000m, Rix s.n.

(i) Fritillaria pyrenaica L. (see p.91 (k)). This pale yellow form of *F. pyrenaica* is easy to grow.

(j) Fritillaria olivieri Baker. Native of the northern Zagros mountains in Iran, where it grows in damp meadows by streams, from 1800 to 4000m, flowering in May and June. Up to 40cm in the wild, flowers usually not tessellated. Source Iran, Hamadan, Kuh-i-Alwand, BSBE 1666.

(k) Fritillaria grayana Rchb. fil. & Baker, syn. *F. roderickii* Knight, *F. biflora* var. *ineziana* Jepson. Native of California, especially Mendocino and San Mateo counties, growing in clay soil on open grassy slopes, usually near the coast. One of the easier American species in cultivation in Europe, growing well in good soil in a bulb frame. Source California, Mendocino Co., W. Roderick.

(l) Fritillaria pontica var. **substipelata** Candargy (see also (e)). This variety of *F. pontica* is from the island of Lesbos, off the west coast of Turkey. Coll. I. B. Barton.

½ life size Photographed 2 May

Fritillaria liliacea

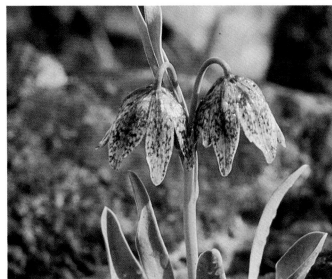

Fritillaria purdyi

¹/₃ life size Photographed 17 April

¹/₃ life size Photographed 21 March

(a) Fritillaria lanceolata Pursh (*Liliaceae*). Native of western N America from British Columbia south to central California and east to Idaho, growing in scrub and among oaks and pines, at up to 1000m, flowering from February to May. Grows best in a half-shaded bulb frame in stony, leafy soil, kept rather dry in summer. Source California, Sonamono Co., R. Macfarlane.

(b) Fritillaria gentneri Gilky. Native of Oregon where it grows in Jackson and Josephine counties, flowering in April and May. The style is divided in half, more deeply than *F. recurva*. Cultivation as for (a).

(c) Fritillaria biflora Lindl. subsp. **agrestis** (Greene) Macfarlane, syn. *F. agrestis* Greene. Native of California, especially the inner coast ranges, the Sacramento and San Joaquin valleys and the foothills of the Sierra Nevada, growing in grassland, flowering in February and March. The plant shown here is unusually small. Cultivation as for (a).

(d) Fritillaria liliacea Lindley. Native of central California, formerly common around San Francisco Bay but now almost extinct, growing in grassy places in heavy adobe soil on serpentine, on hills near the coast, flowering from February to April. The flowers are pale creamy white with green nectaries; the leaves shining green. Height 15–35cm. Grows best in rather heavy rich soil in a pot or bulb frame, not allowed to become very hot in summer. The leaves which emerge very early, are susceptible to damage by frost. Photographed in California by Roger Macfarlane.

Fritillaria pluriflora

Fritillaria recurva

Fritillaria atropurpurea

Fritillaria pluriflora

Fritillaria striata

(e) **Fritillaria pudica** (Pursh) Sprengel. Native of western N America, from British Columbia east to Wyoming and south to New Mexico, growing in sandy or gritty soil between 400 and 2000m, flowering by melting snow patches, from March to June. In flower and leaf remarkably similar to *F. minima* or some of the yellow west asiatic species, but very different in bulb, which is covered with bulbils. Not easy to grow, but has lasted for many years in a bulb frame, kept dry in summer.

Fritillaria purdyi Eastwood. Native of California, especially the inner coast ranges, from Humboldt Co. to Napa Co., growing in heavy stony soil on serpentine, from 600 to 2000m, flowering from February to June. Height 10–40cm. Distinguished by its primarily basal leaves, mottled flowers and divided style. Not easy to grow, but has been cultivated well in a pot in the alpine house, kept dry in summer. Photographed in California by Roger Macfarlane.

Fritillaria striata Eastwood. Native to

California, found only in the foothills of the Greenhorn Mts in Kern and Tulane counties, growing in heavy adobe clay at c.600m, flowering in March. Related to *F. pluriflora*, but nectary elliptical to ovate, not linear, and petals recurved at their tips. Height 20–40cm. Probably difficult to grow, requiring a hot dry summer, and not now cultivated in Europe. Photographed in California, 4 March 1967, by Roger Macfarlane.

Fritillaria pluriflora Torrey ex Benth. Native of northern California in the foothills bordering the upper Sacramento valley, growing in adobe clay in open fields, flowering in March. Stem up to 40cm high with one to four, rarely as many as twelve flowers. Nectary linear. Brian Mathew recommends a pot in the alpine house, but very difficult to cultivate successfully; the fields where it grows are very wet in winter and spring, baked hard in summer. Photographed in California, Colusa Co., Bear Valley, on 17 March 1979 by Roger Macfarlane.

Fritillaria recurva Benth. Native of S Oregon and N California, especially in the inner Coast

Ranges, and Sierra Nevada foothills, growing on dry hillsides, in scrub and open forest, from 700 to 2000m, flowering from April to July. Can be recognised at once by its whorled leaves and scarlet tubular flowers which are pollinated by humming birds. Not difficult to grow in a bulb frame or in a pot in the alpine house, kept dry in summer. Photographed in California, Mendocino pass, on 4 May 1966 by Roger Macfarlane.

Fritillaria atropurpurea Nuttall. Native of N America from Oregon and California east to the Dakotas and Nebraska, and south to New Mexico, growing in scrub and coniferous forest from 1500 to 3000m, flowering from May to July. Stem up to 50cm, with as many as fifteen flowers. Variable in habit, from the robust form named *F. adamantina* Peck to the delicate *F. gracillima* Smiley. Not easy to grow in spite of its wide distribution, requiring much moisture up to flowering and drought thereafter. Photographed in California by Roger Macfarlane.

½ life size Photographed 17 April

(a), (b) Erythronium revolutum Sm.
(*Liliaceae*). Native of western N America from
Vancouver Island south to N California, where it
grows near the coast in redwood forest and in
mixed evergreen forest, on the edges of bogs and
along wooded streams, up to 1000m, flowering
from March till June. Distinguished by its pink
flowers, swollen anther filaments and mottled
leaves. Two colour forms are shown here. The
darkest pink forms have been called var.
johnsonii. Grows best in sandy peaty soil, damp
in spring and in semi-shade. Naturalised in the
Wild Garden at Wisley.

(c) Erythronium 'Pagoda' (*Liliaceae*). A hybrid
between *E. tuolumnense* (p.101 (c)) and one of
the white flowered species. Very vigorous and
growing easily in rich leafy soil under the shade
of deciduous trees.

(d) Erythronium americanum Ker-Gawler
(*Liliaceae*). Native of eastern N America, from
New Brunswick to Ontario and Minnesota,
south to Long Island, Tennessee, Arkansas and
Oklahoma, growing in rich woods, valley
bottoms and meadows, flowering from late
March to June. Distinguished by its small size,
mottled leaves and yellow flowers which only
open in warm sun. The flowers are
brownish-orange in the form *castaneum*
L. B. Smith. Shy flowering in cultivation, but
growing well in moist sandy soil under
deciduous trees. Photographed in cultivation by
Brinsley Burbidge.

(e) Erythronium 'White Beauty' (*Liliaceae*).
This may be a hybrid between two of the
white-flowered species, or a very vigorous form
of *E. oregonum*. It is very strong growing and
easy, increasing fast in leafy soil under
deciduous trees or in half-shade.

Erythronium revolutum Sm. Photographed in
Oregon, on the Pioneer Mountain road, E of
Toledo, on 19 April 1980 by Roger Macfarlane.

Erythronium revolutum

Erythronium americanum

97

½ life size Photographed 22 April

Erythronium californicum

Erythronium oregonum

Erythronium montanum

Erythronium hendersonii

(a) **Erythronium californicum** Purdy (*Liliaceae*). Native of northern California, especially the coast ranges, growing in chaparral scrub, pine and evergreen woods, and mixed coniferous forest usually on north-facing slopes at up to 1000m, flowering in March and April. Very similar to *E. oregonum* (below), but has thin not swollen filaments, and usually white anthers. Easy to grow in shade, or semi-shade, in leafy well-drained soil. Photographed in California, between Boonville and Manchester, 14 April 1979 by Roger Macfarlane.

(b), (e), (f) **Erythronium oregonum** Appleg. (*Liliaceae*). Native of Vancouver Island southwards to Oregon and northwest California, growing in open fields, moist woods and in mixed evergreen forest at around 200m. Very similar to *E. californicum* Purdy (above), but has the filaments dilated at their base. Anthers usually yellow, but white in subsp. *leucandrum* Appleg., two forms of which are shown here. See also 'White Beauty' (p.97). Easy to grow in

half-shade in well-drained leafy soil. Photographed in Oregon, west of Philomath, on 19 April 1980 by Roger Macfarlane.

(c) **Erythronium helenae** Appleg. (*Liliaceae*). Native of NW California in the area of Mt St Helena, growing in woods and scrub from 500 to 600m, in moist volcanic soil, flowering from March to May. Close to *E. oregonum*, but has narrow or only slightly expanded anther filaments. Grows best in very well drained leafy soil on sand as it resents too much wet in winter.

(d) **Erythronium 'Jeanette Brickell'** (*Liliacea*). A very beautiful hybrid raised by E. B. Anderson at Porlock, and named after the wife of C. D. Brickell, Director of the RHS Gardens, Wisley, by Mrs K. Dryden. The crimson style and anthers suggest that *E. hendersonii* was one parent, possibly crossed with 'White Beauty' or some other white-flowered species, Hybrids between *hendersonii* and *oregonum* are reported to occur in the wild.

Erythronium hendersonii Watson (*Liliaceae*). Native of SW Oregon and N California, growing in glades in pine forest at 400–1500m, flowering from April to July. Distinct in its dark green leaves, pinkish lilac flowers with a purple centre, and purple anthers. Requires a rather well drained spot in partial shade. B. Mathew records that it grew well among the roots of a beech tree, wet in winter and spring, dry in summer. Photographed in California by Roger Macfarlane.

Erythronium montanum Watson (*Liliaceae*). Avalanche Lily. Native of western N America from Vancouver Island, south to the Olympic mountains and Cascades to N Oregon, growing in subalpine to alpine forest, and in alpine meadows, flowering from late June to September, according to altitude, near melting snow. Very difficult to grow successfully, like so many late-flowering snow patch plants. Photographed in Washington, on Mt Rainier, near Tipsoo Lake, by Roger Macfarlane.

a

b

c

d

²/₃ life size Photographed 2 April

Erythronium grandiflorum

Erythronium grandiflorum

Erythronium dens-canis

(a) **Erythronium albidum** Nutt. var.
mesochorium (Knerr) Rickett (*Liliaceae*).
Native of N America from Iowa and Nebraska to
Missouri, Oklahoma and Texas, growing in
woods, thickets and meadows, flowering from
March to May. In var. *mesochorium* the leaves are
narrow and folded, the flowers are pinkish to
bluish-white. In var. *albidum*, which grows
mostly to the north-east, the flowers are white,
the leaves mottled. Rather unsatisfactory in
cultivation because it emerges very early and the
flowers probably require more heat to open
properly.

(b) **Erythronium dens-canis** L. (*Liliaceae*).
Dog's-tooth Violet. Native of Europe from
Spain and Portugal to Austria, Romania,
Bulgaria and Turkey, growing in scrub, in
deciduous woods and rocky places and meadows
up to 1700m, on the south side of the Alps,

flowering from April to June. The amount of
spotting on the leaves is very variable, and some
forms from Italy have especially beautiful
leaves. Easy to grow in leafy soil or in thin grass
in half-shade. Photographed near Serrat,
Andorra, by Brinsley Burbidge.

(c) **Erythronium tuolumnense** Appleg.
(*Liliaceae*). Native of central California,
especially the foothills of the Sierra Nevada in
Tuolumne and Stanislaus counties, growing in
open pine and evergreen oak woods at
300–600m, flowering from March to May. The
plain green leaves and the small deep yellow
flowers are characteristic of this species. The
stigma is undivided. Grows best in a
well-drained peaty soil in partial shade, but does
not increase as quickly as some other species or
its hybrid 'Pagoda' (p.96 (c)), and can be
shy-flowering.

(d) **Erythronium japonicum** Dcne. (*Liliaceae*).
Native of Japan, on the islands of Hokkaido,
Honshu and Shikoku, growing in woods in the
lowlands and on low mountains, flowering in
April. Best grown in a shady spot in peaty or
leafy soil. Often damaged by slugs.

Erythronium grandiflorum Pursh (*Liliaceae*).
Native of western N America from S British
Columbia to N California, eastwards to Alberta,
Wyoming and Colorado, growing in sagebrush
and montane forest up to near the tree line
(c.2000m), flowering from March to August.
Leaves unmarked. Flowers cream to golden,
larger than *E. tuolumnense* (c); anthers white to
yellow, red or purple. Stigma lobed. Not easy to
grow, and probably best in well-drained soil,
wet in spring and rather dry in summer.
Photographed in Washington, July 1974, by
Brinsley Burbidge.

½ life size Photographed 22 April

(a) Trillium erectum L. (*Liliaceae*). Native of eastern N America, from Quebec to Ontario and Michigan, south to Pennsylvania, Georgia and Tennessee, growing in rich woods, often in large numbers, flowering from April to early June. Very variable, and subject to mutation; and green, white and yellow-flowered forms have been described (see (g) and p.105). Easily grown in loose leafy soil in the shade of deciduous trees. Source Ohio, near Madison, in woods, T. Brotzman.

(b) Trillium grandiflorum (Michx.) Salisb. (*Liliaceae*). Native of eastern N America, from Maine and S Quebec, east to Ontario and Minnesota, south to Georgia and Arkansas, growing in woods and thickets, often in huge numbers, usually on limestone, flowering from April to June. Very variable, and particularly subject to mutation. The double forms in cultivation are much sought after. Petals obovate to oblanceolate or suborbicular, rarely pinkish. Easily grown in leafy soil in shade or half-shade. Source Ohio, near Madison, in woods, T. Brotzman.

(c) Trillium ovatum Pursh (*Liliaceae*). Native of western N America from central California, north to British Columbia and Montana, growing in redwood forest and mixed evergreen forest, flowering from February to April. Close to *T. grandiflorum* from the eastern States, but the flowers are usually smaller, with petals 2.5–5.5cm long, ovate, tapering from a broad base. Grows best in well-drained leafy soil in the shade of deciduous trees.

(d) Trillium rivale Wats. (*Liliaceae*). Native of western N America from Del Norte and Siskiyou counties in N California to SW Oregon, growing in rocky places by streams, in the yellow pine forest from 400–1200m, flowering in March and April. Easily recognised by its long-stalked leaves and flowers, which become pendulous as they mature. Flowers white to pink. Grows best in well-drained leafy soil in half-shade or in a pot kept plunged in a shady frame.

(e) Trillium undulatum Willd. (*Liliaceae*). Painted Trillium. Native of eastern N America, from Nova Scotia and Quebec to Manitoba, south to the hills of Georgia and Tennessee, growing in acid woods and bogs, flowering from April to June, after *T. erectum*. Distinguished by the shortly stalked leaves and white petals marked with red. The specimen shown here is unusually small; stem usually c.30cm high. Grows best in a moist peaty soil in shade. Rarely seen in cultivation, so probably not easy.

(f) Trillium sessile L. (*Liliaceae*). Native of eastern N America from Virginia and New York to Ohio and Missouri and south to Georgia and Arkansas, growing in rich woods, flowering from April to early June. Easily grown in rich leafy soil in shade or half shade.

(g) Trillium erectum L. forma **albiflorum** R. Hoffm. A particularly beautiful form of *T. erectum*. The plant shown here is unusually small.

(h) Trillium luteum (Muhl.) Harbison. Very similar to *T. sessile*, but with yellowish or greenish flowers. The plant shown here is unusually small. Grows in woods from Kentucky and Missouri south to Alabama and Arkansas.

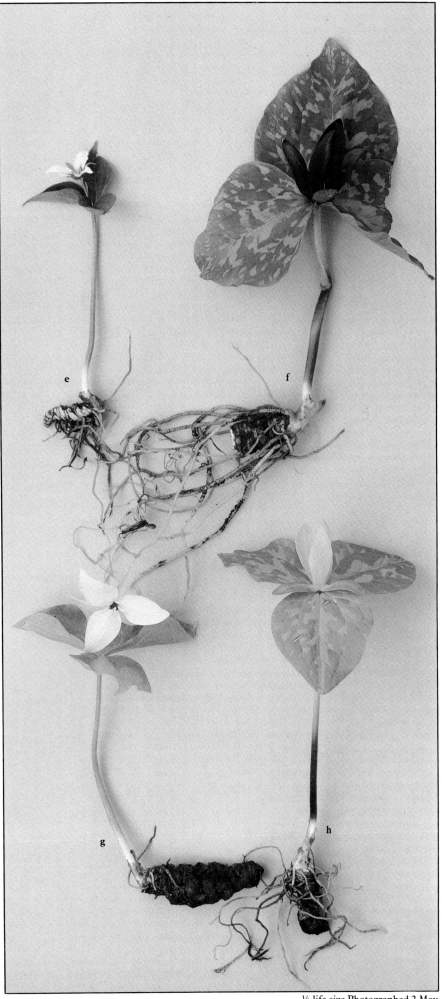

½ life size Photographed 2 May

½ life size Photographed 17 April

(a) **Narcissus pseudonarcissus 'Princeps'**, syn. *N. gayi* Jord. (*Amaryllidaceae*). An old garden variety.

(b) **Narcissus 'Carlton'** (2Y-Y). Raised by P. D. Williams at Lanarth, Cornwall, in 1927. Much grown for cutting and forcing.

(c) **Narcissus 'King Alfred'** (1Y-Y). Raised by J. Kendall from *N. pseudonarcissus* subsp. *major* (Curtis) Baker (syn. *N. hispanicus* Gouan), in about 1890.

(d) **Narcissus 'Telemoneus Plenus'**, syn. 'Van Sion', 'Vincent Sion'. A double *Narcissus pseudonarcissus*, introduced into England from Florence c.1620.

(e) **Narcissus 'Beersheba'**. Raised by the Rev. G. H. Engleheart of Andover and Salisbury, England, in 1923. One of the earliest Large White Trumpets, derived from selfing of pale forms of *N. pseudonarcissus*.

(f) **Narcissus 'Emperor'**. Raised by William Backhouse of Wolsingham, Co. Durham, c.1865. A hybrid of *N. pseudonarcissus* subsp. *pseudonarcissus* and *N. bicolor* L., a native of the Pyrenees in France and Spain.

(g) **Narcissus × medioluteus** Miller (*N. poeticus* × *N. tazetta*). The form shown here is close to 'Cragford', raised by P. D. Williams in 1930.

(h) **Narcissus poeticus 'Actaea'**. Raised by G. Lubbe & Son, Oegstgeest, Holland, in 1927.

(i) **Narcissus 'Butter and Eggs'**, syn. *N. × incomparabilis* var. *plenus*, 'Golden Phoenix', 'Yellow Phoenix', 'Incomparable' and '*aurantius var plenus*'. An old double form of *N. × incomparabilis*, grown in gardens since the seventeenth century.

(j) **Narcissus 'Sweetness'**. Raised by R. V. Favell in 1939. A hybrid of *N. jonquilla* L., other parent not known.

(k) **Narcissus tazetta** subsp. **italicus** (Ker-Gawler) Baker, syn. *N. canaliculatus* hort; *N. tazetta* subsp. *lacticolor* (Haw.) Baker. Native of the N and E Mediterranean.

(l) **Narcissus** cf. 'Dick Wellband' raised by Mrs Backhouse A.M. 1937

(m) **Narcissus × incomparabilis** Miller. A hybrid between *N. pseudonarcissus* and *N. poeticus*, and found wild where the parents grow together, especially in the Pyrenees. Also common in old gardens.

(n) **Narcissus 'Cheerfulness'**. A sport from *N. 'Elvira'* which appeared in 1923. The doubling is caused by the stamens becoming petaloid, the perianth and corona are unaffected.

(o) **Narcissus poeticus** L. Native of the mountains of central and southern Europe, growing in damp meadows, often in huge numbers, flowering from April to June. Easy to grow in moist soil, doing well in grass, but sometimes shy-flowering.

Trillium tschonoskii Maxim. (*Liliaceae*). Native of Japan especially Honshu and Shikoku, and Korea, growing in mountain woods, flowering from April to June. The petals are usually white, but may be purplish or pinkish in forma *violaceum* Makino. Photographed in Japan, Honshu, Oze-numa reserve, 1500m, in June 1978 by Peter Barnes.

Trillium sessile L. (*Liliaceae*) (see p.103 (f)). Photographed in the RHS Gardens, Wisley.

Paris polyphylla Smith (*Liliaceae*). Native of Afghanistan and the Himalayas, from Kashmir to central China and Formosa, and from Manipur to N Thailand, growing in forests from 1700 to 3500m, flowering from March to June. Very variable; leaves stalked, fruits splitting open to reveal a spectacular mass of fleshy red seeds. Easily grown in moist peaty soil in half-shade. Photographed in N India, Tunglu above Darjeeling, by Oleg Polunin.

Trillium sessile

Paris polyphylla

Trillium tschonoskii

(a) **Narcissus hedraeanthus** (Webb & Held.) Colmeiro (*Amaryllidaceae*). Native of south-east Spain, especially the Sierra de Cazorla, growing in stony places above 1500m, flowering in May as the snow melts. Distinguished by its very small size, long exserted stamens, and curving flower stalk. This is the most distinct of the 'hoop petticoat' daffodils. Easily grown in a bulb frame or pot in the alpine house, and would require a sunny place outside. Source Spain, Sierra de Cazorla, Tucker.

(b), (f) **Narcissus romieuxii** Br. Bl. & Maire (*Amaryllidaceae*). Native of Morocco, where it grows in cedar and oak forest, at 1700–2000m, usually on limestone or basalt, flowering in winter and early spring. Distinguished from *N. bulbocodium*, of which it is often considered to be only a subspecies, by its creamy sulphur-yellow flowers, and exserted stamens. The corona also appears to be wider at the mouth. Best cultivated in a bulb frame because it flowers so early, but will grow in a sunny well-drained place outside.

(c) **Narcissus asturiensis** (Jordan) Pugsley, syn. *N. minimus* hort. (*Amaryllidaceae*). Native of N Portugal, NW and NC Spain, growing at up to 2000m, in rocky meadows, flowering from March to May. Distinguished by its very small flowers 14–25mm long, and greenish spathe. Stem 7–10cm. Very early flowering in cultivation, often appearing in January, and should be protected from slugs. Grows best in sandy peaty soil, not drying out in summer.

(d) **Narcissus minor** L., syn. *N. pumilus* Pugsley (*Amaryllidaceae*). Native of the Pyrenees and N Spain, growing in mountain meadows and scrub, very close to *N. asturiensis*, but larger with stem 8–25cm, and flowers 25–40mm long. The form shown here flowers in midwinter, often starting in November and continuing until February. It has been named *N. minor* 'Cedric Morris', from whose garden it was distributed.

(e) **Narcissus cantabricus** DC. subsp. **monophyllus** (Dur.) A. Fernandes (*Amaryllidaceae*). Native of N Morocco and Algeria, growing in similar places to subsp. *cantabricus* (h). Distinguished by its white flowers with included stamens, and the single narrow leaf per bulb. Best grown in a pot or in a bulb frame, kept dry in summer.

(g) **Narcissus bulbocodium** L. (*Amaryllidaceae*). Native of Algeria, Morocco, Spain, Portugal and SW France, growing in scrub, rocky ground and peaty moorland, flowering from January to July. Very variable in size and in flower colour, from pale lemon yellow to golden; anthers not exserted. This species is particularly good for naturalising in grass on sandy soils; the lemon-yellow form is beautiful in Windsor Great Park, the darker yellow at Wisley. The early-flowering form shown here probably originated in Morocco.

(h) **Narcissus cantabricus** DC. (*Amaryllidaceae*). Native of S Spain, and Morocco, growing in oak and pine woods on limestone, flowering in early spring. Distinguished from *N. bulbocodium* by its white flowers. Stamens always included in the corona, not projecting. Grows best in a pot or bulb frame or in a very sunny place outside where it is dry in summer.

¾ life size Photographed 13 February

²/₃ life size Photographed 14 April

(a) **Narcissus rupicola** Dufour
(*Amaryllidaceae*). Native of central Spain and
N Portugal, growing in rocky places and in stony
mountain pastures at c.2000m, usually on acid
rock, flowering from March to May. Height here
10cm. Easy to grow in a bulb frame, a pot in the
alpine house, or a dry sunny place outside; does
not require acid soil. Source C Spain, Rascafria,
Sierra de Guaderrama, c.200m, Rix. s.n.

(b) **Narcissus cuatrecasasii** Casas, Lainz &
Ruiz Rejón, syn. *N. rupicola* subsp. *pedunculatus*
(Cuatrec.) Lainz ex Meikle (*Amaryllidaceae*).
Native of central Spain, growing in rocky and
stony places in the mountains, usually on
limestone. Like a slightly larger darker flowered
N. rupicola with a long (9–12mm) stalk to the
ovary. Cultivation as for (a). Source SC Spain,
Sierra de Cazorla, Rix. s.n.

(c) **Narcissus watieri** Maine (*Amaryllidaceae*).
Native of Morocco, growing in the Atlas
Mountains from 1800 to 2600m, in forest and
grassy places flowering in May and June. Not
difficult in a pot in the alpine house, but slow to
increase. The other North African species in this
group, *N. marvieri* Johand. & Maire, is closer to
N. rupicola with a paler yellow flower.

(d) **Narcissus requienii** M. J. Roemer, syn.
N. juncifolius auct. (*Amaryllidaceae*). Native of
S France, E and S Spain, growing on rocky
hillsides, often on limestone, flowering in April.
The plant shown here is rather larger than usual.
Flowers normally one or two per stem. Leaves
1–2mm wide. *N. jonquilla* L. is similar, but
larger in all its parts, with leaves 2–4mm wide.
Both are very sweet-smelling. Easily grown in a
dry sunny place. Source S Spain, Sierra Morena,
c.500m, C. Quest-Ritson, s.n.

(e) **Narcissus 'Hawera'** (*Amaryllidaceae*). This
beautiful plant is a hybrid between *N. triandrus*
(g) and *Narcissus jonquilla* L. Raised in New
Zealand by Dr W. M. Thompson in the 1930s.

(f), (g) **Narcissus triandrus** L. (*Amaryllidaceae*).
Native of Brittany, Spain and Portugal, growing
in scrub, woods and rocky hillsides, flowering
from February to April. (f) subsp. *pallidulus*
(Graells) D. A. Webb, syn. *N. concolor* (Haw.)
Link, has flowers yellow to cream, a shorter
corona and tube, with petals 10–18mm about
equalling the tube. Found in Portugal, central,
S and E Spain. (g) subsp. *triandrus*, syn.
N. cernuus Salisb., has flowers white to cream,
larger, with petals 15–30mm, and a longer
corona. Found in N Portugal and N Spain.
N. triandrus will grow well on a peat bank or in
thin grass on sandy soil in a sunny place. Good
drainage is important. Photographed in the
RHS Gardens, Wisley.

(h) **Narcissus gaditanus** Boiss. & Reut. Native
of S Spain and S Portugal, growing in rocky
places, flowering in March. *N. scaberulus*
Henriq. is very similar, but has leaves with two
keels and rough edges. Cultivation as (a). Source
S Spain, Granada near Almunecar, 1000m, C.
Quest-Ritson, s.n.

Narcissus cyclamineus DC. (*Amaryllidaceae*).
Native of NW Portugal and NW Spain, where it
grows on river banks and damp mountain
pastures, flowering in March. Grows best in
damp sandy peaty soil at the edge of water: some
very fine clumps grow in the roots of *Osmunda*
by the waterside at Wisley. Photographed in the
RHS Gardens, Wisley, by Roger Phillips.

Narcissus bulbocodium L. (*Amaryllidaceae*)
(see p.107 (g)). Photographed in C Spain, Sierra
de Urbion, c.2000m, 4 June 1967.

Narcissus cyclamineus

Narcissus triandrus

Narcissus bulbocodium

¾ life size Photographed 21 March

(a) Narcissus 'February Silver'
(*Amaryllidaceae*). A hybrid between
N. cyclamineus and probably a pale form of
N. pseudonarcissus raised by de Graaf in 1949 in
Holland. Outside it does not usually flower until
late March, even in S England.

(b) Narcissus pseudonarcissus L. Daffodil.
Native of Western Europe from England and
Holland to France, Switzerland, Spain and
Portugal, growing in woods, meadows and
rocky hillsides, flowering from March to May.
Very variable in flower colour, from white to
deep yellow, and in the shape and posture of the
flower, and in *Flora Europaea* divided into seven
subspecies. For cultivation see p.115. Shown
here is a pale form of subsp. *pseudonarcissus*.

(c) Narcissus 'Tosca'. Raised by Alec Gray and
introduced by Broadleigh Gardens in 1969.

(d) Narcissus cyclamineus DC. (see p.109).
N. cyclamineus crosses easily with forms of
pseudonarcissus, and various combinations are
common in gardens where the parents are
allowed to seed. They show the influence of
cyclamineus in their early flowering, narrow
trumpets and recurved petals.

(e) Narcissus 'March Sunshine'. A hybrid
between *N. cyclamineus* and *N. pseudonarcissus*
raised by de Graaf in Holland in 1923.

(f) Narcissus 'February Gold'. A hybrid
between *N. cyclamineus* and *N. pseudonarcissus*
raised by de Graaf in Holland in 1923. Good for
forcing, but usually March flowering outside in
England.

(g) Narcissus 'Tête à Tête'. Raised by Mr Alec
Gray of Camborne, Cornwall, in 1949. The
result of crossing *N. cyclamineus* with *N. tazetta*
'Soleil d'Or' was the doubtfully hardy
N. 'Cyclataz', and 'Tête à Tête' is an improved
and hardy form.

(h), (i), (j) Ipheion uniflorum (R. C. Graham)
Rafin., syn. *Triteleia uniflora* (*Liliaceae*). Native
of Argentina and Uruguay, where it is
widespread. Three colour forms are shown here:
(h) 'Froyle Mill' a dark-flowered form which
appeared in a garden of that name in Hampshire.
It is not as strong growing as the other forms; **(i)**
'Wisley Blue', named after the RHS Gardens at
Wisley, Surrey; **(j)**, a strong-growing pure white
form. The commonest form in cultivation is
smaller than 'Wisley Blue', and is a pale silvery
lilac colour. Easy to grow in a sunny place, kept
dry in summer. The crushed leaves smell faintly
of onion, the flowers of soap.

(k) Bulbocodium vernum L. (*Liliaceae*). Native
of the Pyrenees, the western and central Alps,
and one locality in Austria, growing in alpine
meadows, and flowering from April to June.
Bulbocodium is superficially similar to *Colchicum*
and *Merendera*, but the styles are trifid only at
the apex (in *Colchicum* and *Merendera* they are
divided to the base), and the petals fall apart as
the flower ages. *Bulbocodium versicolor*
(Ker-Gawler) Sprengel, from eastern Europe
and Western Asia, has smaller flowers and
narrower leaves, and is found in dry grassland.
Should be grown in good well-drained soil, and
replanted frequently, if it is to increase.

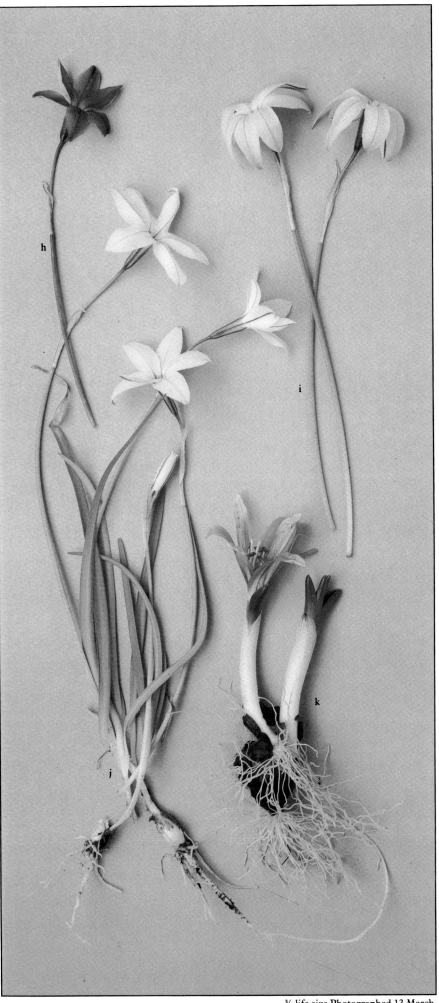

¾ life size Photographed 13 March

a

b

c

d

e

f

g

h

i

j

k

The text is on page 115 ²/₃ life size Photographed 22 April

The text is on page 115 ²/₃ life size Photographed 22 April

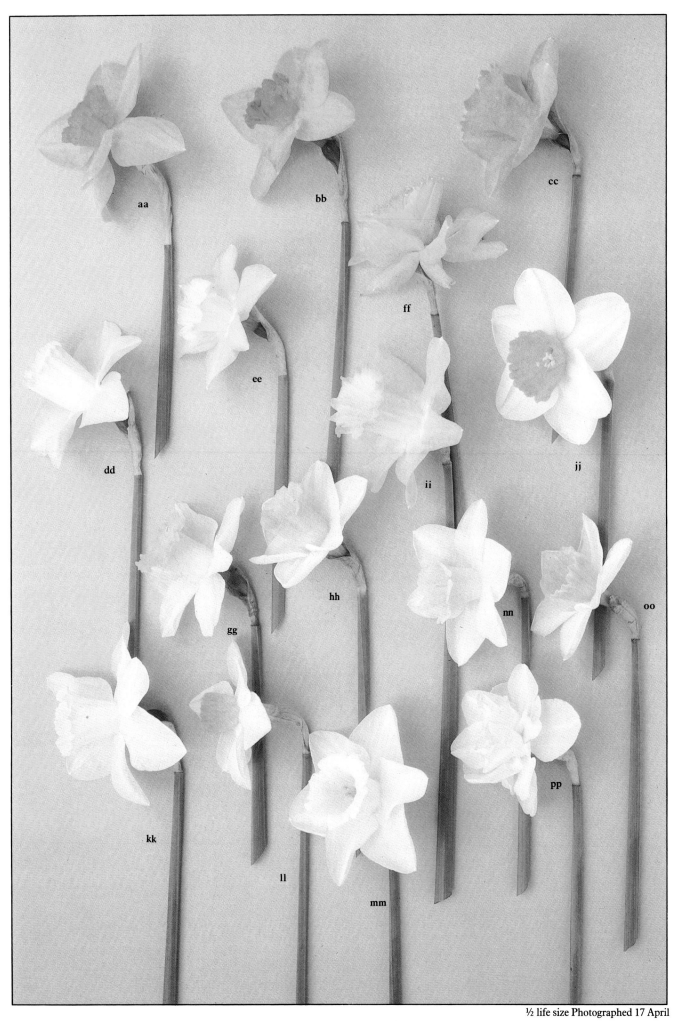

aa

bb

cc

dd

ee

ff

gg

hh

ii

jj

kk

ll

mm

nn

oo

pp

½ life size Photographed 17 April

Modern Daffodil Hybrids

The name is the name of the raiser; the date that of registration. All daffodils are easily grown in good soil in full sun or half-shade. It is important not to cut off the leaves until they begin to turn yellow (about six weeks after flowering), and better not to tie them in a bunch. On poor soil a tomato fertiliser applied in early spring will help growth and flowers for the following year.

Illustrated on the previous spread (pp. 112-113):
(a)	'Arctic Gold'	J. L. Richardson 1951
(b)	'Golden Aura'	J. L. Richardson 1964
(c)	'Ormeau'	W. J. Dunlop 1949
(d)	'Langwith'	Mrs J. Abel Smith 1969
(e)	'Dunmurry'	W. J. Dunlop 1958
(f)	'Grand Prospect'	Mrs J. Abel Smith 1974
(g)	'Irish Minstrel'	J. L. Richardson 1958
(h)	'Pipe Major'	F. E. Board, 1965
(i)	'Toreador'	J. L. Richardson 1961
(j)	'Rockall'	J. L. Richardson 1955
(k)	'Emily'	Mrs J. Abel Smith 1974
(l)	'Leonaine'	G. E. Mitsch 1959
(m)	'Knightwick'	J. L. Richardson 1963
(n)	'Farnsfield'	Mrs J. Abel Smith 1979
(o)	'Rufford'	Mrs J. Abel Smith 1975
(p)	'Langford Grove'	Mrs J. Abel Smith 1979
(q)	'Jewel Song'	Mrs Richardson 1967
(r)	'Aircastle'	G. E. Mitsch 1958
(s)	'Birchill'	Mrs J. Abel Smith 1974
(t)	'Suilven'	J. S. B. Lea 1956
(u)	'Tutankhamun'	Mrs J. Abel Smith 1972
(v)	'Vigil'	G. L. Williams 1947

Illustrated on this spread (pp. 114-115):
(aa)	'Devon Loch'	J. L. Richardson 1956
(bb)	'Patagonia'	J. L. Richardson 1956
(cc)	'Crocus'	P. D. Williams 1927
(dd)	'Chester'	Barr & Sons 1945
(ee)	'Binkie'	W. Wolfhagen 1938
(ff)	'Golden Ducat'	sport from 'King Alfred'
(gg)	'Polindra'	P. D. Williams 1927
(hh)	'Salome'	J. L. Richardson 1958
(ii)	'Spellbinder'	G. L. Wilson 1944
(jj)	'Brunswick'	P. D. Williams 1931
(kk)	'Dunlewey'	G. L. Wilson 1934
(ll)	'Blaris'	G. L. Wilson 1960
(mm)	'Knowehead'	G. L. Wilson 1954
(nn)	'Passionale'	G. L. Wilson 1956
(oo)	'Penvose'	P. D. Williams 1937
(pp)	'White Lion'	Le Graef-Gerharda 1949

(**qq**), (**rr**) **Narcissus minor** L. (see p. 107 (d)).

(**ss**) **Narcissus pseudonarcissus** subsp. **moschatus** (L.) Baker. Native of the Pyrenees and Cantabrian mountains of N Spain, in mountain meadows and open pine woods at c.1800m.

(**tt**) **Narcissus pseudonarcissus** subsp. **pallidiflorus** (Pugsley) A. Fernandes. Distribution as (ss).

$^2/_3$ life size Photographed 14 April

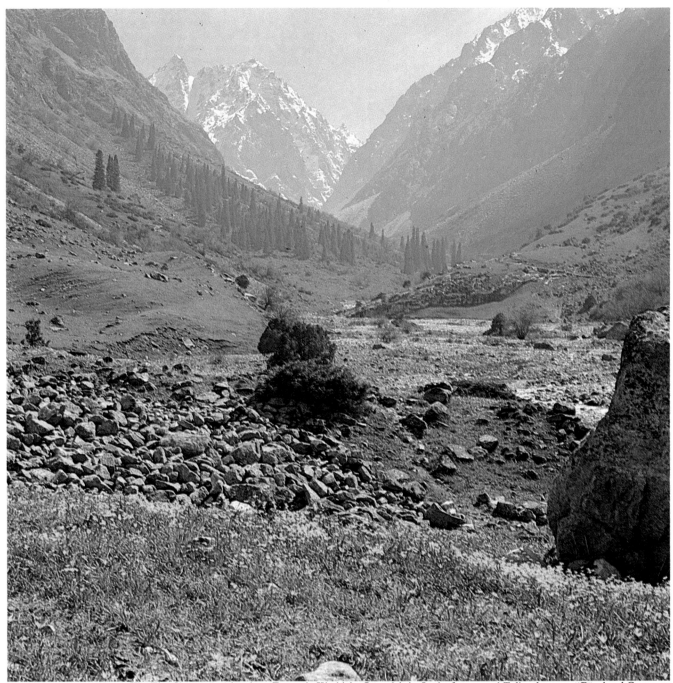

The Tien Shan mountains above Frunze in Kirghizia, Central Asia. In the foreground *Tulipa dasystemon* Regel and *Gagea* spp.

Tulipa dasystemon Regel (*Liliaceae*). Native of Central Asia, especially the Tien Shan and the Pamir Alai, growing in stony places and subalpine meadows at above 2000m, flowering in May and June. *T. dasystemonoides* is similar, but was described as having tunics with wool all over the inside, not only at the top of the bulb. *T. tarda* Stapf has a hairless tunic and three to seven leaves. Would probably grow best in a peaty sandy soil, kept dry but not baked in summer. Photographed in Central Asia, above Frunze, in May 1980.

Amana edulis (Miq.) Honda, syn. *Tulipa edulis* (Miq.) Baker (*Liliaceae*). Native of Japan and China, growing in meadows along rivers at low altitudes, flowering in March and April. *Amana* is close to *Tulipa*, but has an elongated style, and a pair of small leaves below the flower. Var. *latifolia* Makino, with broader and shorter leaves is found on wooded hills on Honshu. Easy to grow in a well-drained sunny position. Dormant in summer, but should not need protection from rain.

Tulipa heterophylla (Regel) Baker, syn. *Eduardoregelia heterophylla* (Rgl.) M. Popov (*Liliaceae*). Native of Central Asia, especially the Tien Shan, growing on stony slopes and in alpine meadows above 2500m, flowering in June and July. Between *Amana* and *Tulipa* with an elongated style, and two small leaves. The inner petals are much broader than the outer. Probably requires a light peaty soil, dry but not baked in summer. Photographed in C Asia, above Alma Ata, in June 1980.

Tulipa turkestanica Regel (*Liliaceae*). Native of Central Asia, especially the Tien Shan and the Pamir Alai, and NW China, growing in stony slopes, by streams and on rock ledges from 1800 to 2500m, flowering from March to May. *T. bifloriformis* Vved. is said to differ in its bulb tunics which are woolly all over the inside. *T. biflora* L. is smaller with glabrous stems. Easily grown in well-drained soil in full sun, kept dry in summer. Photographed in C Asia near Samarkand.

Tulipa turkestanica

Amana edulis ⅔ life size Photographed 23 February

Tulipa heterophylla

Tulipa dasystemon

117

½ life size Photographed 2 April

(a) Tulipa praestans Hoog (*Liliaceae*). Native of Central Asia, especially Tadzikistan in the southern Pamir Alai, growing on steep earthy slopes and in light woodland, flowering from April and May. Distinguished by its plain orange-red petals without a basal blotch and hairy stems which may have up to four flowers in cultivation. Shown here is 'Van Tubergen's Variety' with large orange-scarlet flowers (see also pp.123 and 125). Easily grown in well-drained good soil in a sunny place. A good species for the rock garden.

(b) Tulipa kolpakowskiana Regel (*Liliaceae*). Native of Central Asia, especially the northern Tien Shan and the southern Ala Tau, growing on rocky slopes and in scrub at up to 2000m, flowering in May. Flower stem curved, with orange-yellow petals shaded reddish and greyish-violet on the back. Easily grown in well-drained soil in a sunny position.

(c) Tulipa turkestanica Regel (*Liliaceae*) (see p.117). This plant, from commercial stock, shows the dark anthers supposed to be a character of *T. bifloriformis* Vved.

(d), (e) Tulipa humilis Herbert, syn. *T. pulchella* Fenzl, *T. violacea* Boiss. & Buhse (*Liliaceae*). Native of E Turkey, N Iraq and NW Iran, growing on stony hillsides, flowering from April to June. The flowers vary in colour from palest pink to crimson and almost purple, the central blotch may be yellow or black, as may the anthers (see pp.125 and 127). Easily grown in good well-drained soil. The flowers may abort if it is kept too dry in spring while the bud is developing. Source (d) commercial stock; (e) Iran, Mianeh, Tabriz–Tehran road, 1500m, BSBE 1310.

(f) Tulipa kurdica Wendelbo (*Liliaceae*). Native of NE Iraq, growing on stony slopes by melting snow from 2400 to 3000m, flowering in May and June. Very similar to *T. humilis*, but has bright brick-red to orange-red flowers, a colour not seen elsewhere in *T. humilis*. The small black basal blotch is also characteristic. The bulb here shows a 'dropper' forming, behaviour typical of Tulips if planted too shallow. A shoot descends several inches downwards and a new bulb is formed at its end. Cultivation as for *T. humilis*.

(g) Tulipa kaufmanniana Regel (*Liliaceae*). Native of Central Asia, especially the western Tien Shan, E of Tashkent, growing on stony slopes in the mountains, flowering in April and May (see p.121).

(h) Tulipa biflora Pallas, syn. *T. polychroma* Stapf (*Liliaceae*). Native of SE Russia, the Crimea, S Yugoslavia, the Caucasus, E Turkey and N Iran to Afghanistan and extending into Siberia, growing on steppes and stony and rocky hillsides, flowering in April and May. Very similar to *T. turkestanica* but usually smaller, and supposed to have a glabrous rather than pubescent stem; *T. biflora* is supposed to be diploid, *T. turkestanica* tetraploid. Easy to grow in well-drained stony soil, kept dry in summer.

½ life size Photographed 28 March

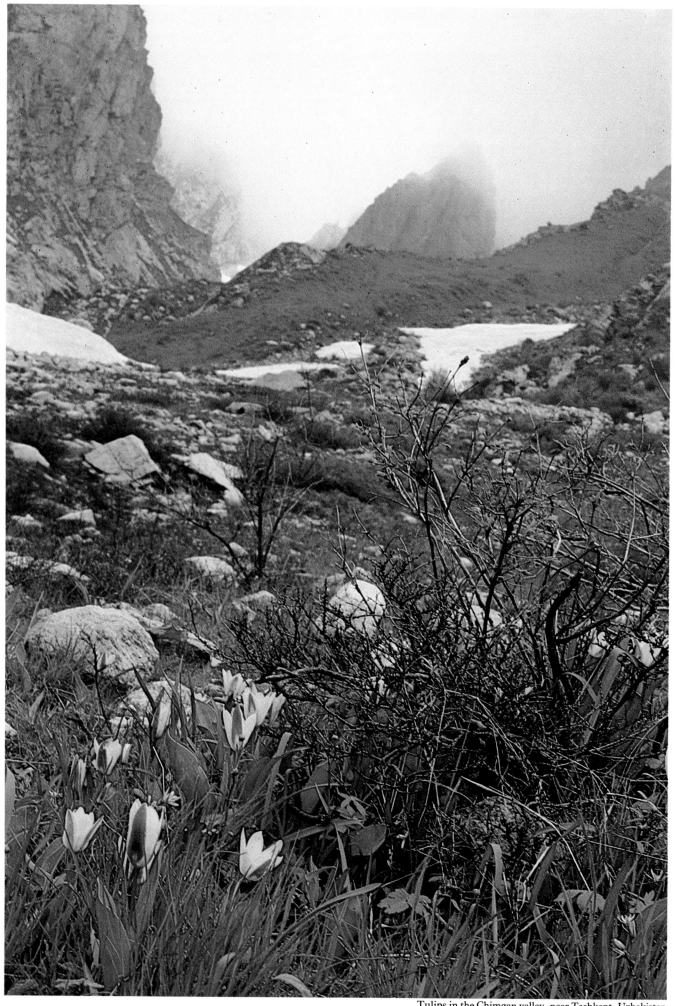

Tulips in the Chimgan valley, near Tashkent, Uzbekistan

Tulipa dubia

Tulipa kolpakowskiana

Tulipa ferganica

Tulipa kaufmanniana

Tulipa tschimganica

Tulipa tschimganica Z. Botsch. (*Liliaceae*).
Native of Central Asia, especially the Chimgan
valley NE of Tashkent, growing in rocky places
at c.2000m, flowering in May. Characterised by
its yellow flowers with a startling blotch of red
inside each petal. This is variable in size and can
be almost lacking or covering most of the petal.
T. dubia and *T. kaufmanniana* also grow here,
and *T. greigii* (p.125) is also recorded.
Intermediates are common, and *T. tschimganica*
has probably arisen by hybridisation.
Photographed in the Chimgan valley on 13 May
1980.

Tulipa dubia Vved. (*Liliaceae*). Native of
Central Asia, especially the western Tien Shan,
growing on earthy and stony slopes above

1800m, flowering in May and June. Leaves two
to four, spreading and with wavy edges; flower
yellow, tinged violet outside; bulb tunics
papery, hair all over inner surface.
Photographed in the Chimgan valley, NE of
Tashkent, in May 1980.

Tulipa kolpakowskiana Regel (*Liliaceae*). (See
p.119.) Reported in *Flora of the USSR* to
hybridise with the red-flowered *T. ostrovskiana*
Regel, but in this locality no red-flowered tulips
or possible hybrids were found. Photographed
in C Asia, above Alma Ata, near Medeo, at
c.1800m, in May 1980, growing exclusively on
rocky bluffs.

Tulipa kaufmanniana Regel (*Liliaceae*). (See

p.119.) Distinguished by its anthers which twist
as they dehisce from the top downwards.
Hybridising in the wild with *T. greigii*, *T. dubia*
and *T. tschimganica* (p.121). Many colour forms
have been produced in cultivation, in various
combinations of red, pink, yellow or white. Easy
to grow in well-drained sandy soil, kept dry in
summer. Photographed in Central Asia,
Chimgan valley, NE of Tashkent, in May 1980.

Tulipa ferganica Vved. (*Liliaceae*). Native of
Central Asia, especially the Alai, Fergana and
Chatkal ranges, growing on stony slopes at
c.1800m, flowering in April and May. Very close
to *T. dubia*, but differs in its dark leathery bulb
tunic, less hairy inside. Photographed in C Asia,
mountains S of Fergana, in April 1979.

121

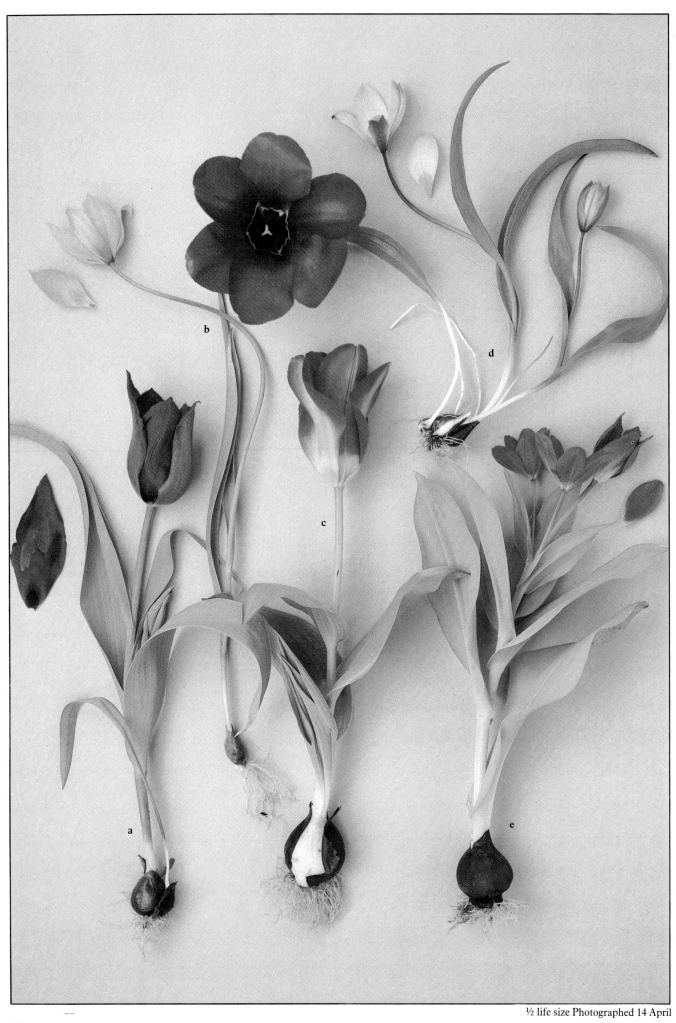

(a) **Tulipa sosnowskyi** Achverd. & Mirzoeva (*Liliaceae*). Native of Soviet Armenia, growing on open stony hillsides, flowering in May. Characterised by often having more than one flower, and by the narrowly pointed petals with a black basal blotch and a large greyish blotch in the centre of each petal. Height here 36cm. Easily grown in a sunny place in well-drained soil, kept dry or lifted in summer. Source Soviet Armenia, Meghri near Artzvaherd, E Gabrielian s.n.

(b) **Tulipa sylvestris** L. subsp. **sylvestris** (*Liliaceae*). Native of Italy, Sicily and Sardinia, and widely naturalised further north in Europe, including England and Holland, growing in meadows and open woods, flowering in April and May. Distinguished from subsp. *australis* (p.125) by the thicker stem, over 2.5mm in diameter, larger flowers with petals 36–63mm against 20–35mm long, greenish not reddish outside, and by the broader lowest leaf, over 1–2cm wide. Easily grown and will naturalise in grass on well-drained soil. Similar plants are found in N Iran, and are in commerce under the name 'Tabriz'. Subsp. *sylvestris* is variously reported as triploid or tetraploid, subsp. *australis* as diploid.

(c) **Tulipa fosterana** Irv. (*Liliaceae*). Native of Central Asia, especially the mountains S of Samarkand, growing in deep soil among limestone rocks at c.1700m, flowering in April. Distinguished by its usually shining green leaves and large red flowers which open out wide in the sun. Petals up to 12.5cm long, rounded. Many garden forms and hybrids are cultivated; shown here is c.v. 'Cantata' (see p.125 for wild form). Cultivation as for (a).

(d) **Tulipa cretica** Boiss & Held. (*Liliaceae*). Native of the mountains of Crete, especially in the 'hedgehog' scrub zone, flowering in April. Flowers pale pink or white, opening into stars; leaves usually two, shining green. Increasing greatly by stolons. Bulb tunic with few straight hairs inside, leathery. Grow in a bulb frame or very sunny place outside in stony soil, kept dry in summer.

(e) **Tulipa praestans** Hoog, c.v. **'Fusilier'**. A fine form with very glaucous hairy leaves and up to five rather small flowers. Cultivation as for (a). See pp.119(a), 125.

(f) **Tulipa batalinii** Regel (*Liliaceae*). This is a pale yellow colour form of *T. maximoviczii*. Intermediates between the two forms in various shades of bronze are found in cultivation. Height here 30cm.

(g) **Tulipa maximoviczii** Regel. (*Liliaceae*). Native of Central Asia, especially the Pamir Alai, growing on rocky hillsides, flowering from April to June. Very close to *T. linifolia* Regel which is said to have a large black blotch at the base of each petal. Cultivation as for (a).

(h), (i) **Tulipa julia** C. Koch (*Liliaceae*). Native of E Turkey, W Iran and the southern Transcaucasus, growing on stony hillsides, flowering from April to June. Bulb tunic very shaggy inside; leaves rather narrow. Outer petals longer than inner. Cultivation as for (a). Source (h) Turkey, near Agri, 2000m, Rix 869; (i) Turkey, Erzurum, Çakmak Da, 2250m, Rix 859.

½ life size Photographed 28 April

Tulipa humilis

Tulipa praestans Hoog

Tulipa fosterana

Tulipa hoogiana

Tulipa systola

(a) **Tulipa greigii** Regel (*Liliaceae*). Native of Central Asia, especially the Tien Shan, and the Syr Darya valley, growing on earthy slopes, flowering in April. Flowers usually orange-red, sometimes yellow; petals 3–10cm long. Leaves always marked with purple. The form shown here is c.v. 'Red Riding Hood', one of the many hybrids, raised in 1953. Easily grown in well-drained rich soil in full sun, either kept dry in summer or dug up and ripened under cover.

(b) **Tulipa vvedenskyi** Z. Botsch. Native of Central Asia, especially the western Tien Shan, SE of Tashkent, flowering in June. Characterised by its large orange-red flowers with a yellow basal blotch, and narrow glaucous leaves. Cultivate as for (a).

(c) **Tulipa primulina** Baker. Native of the Aures Mts in NW Algeria; close to *T. sylvestris* subsp. *australis* but flowers white. Cultivation as for (a).

(d) **Tulipa orphanidea** Boiss. ex Heldr., syn. *T. whittallii* A. D. Hall, *T. hageri* Heldr. Native of Greece, Crete, Bulgaria and W Turkey, growing in cornfields and stony places,

flowering in April. Flowers may be orange or red. Easy in good soil outside.

(e) **Tulipa urumiensis** Stapf. Probably native of W Iran, but not known in the wild. Common in cultivation, dwarf, many-flowered with green leaves.

(f) **Tulipa sylvestris** subsp. **australis** (Link) Pamp. Native of most of S Europe, N Africa, the Caucasus and N Iran, growing in scrub, stony hillsides, steppe and subalpine meadows, flowering in April and May (see p.23). Source Greece, Mt Hymettus, near Athens, Rix 574.

(g) **Tulipa armena** Boiss., var. **armena**. Native of NE Turkey and NW Iran, growing on stony hillsides, from 1300 to 2800m, flowering in May and June. The flowers are sometimes yellow. Bulb tunic with long silky hairs. Source Turkey, pass between Erzurum and Çat, Rix 1683.

(h) **Tulipa confusa** Gabrielian. Native of Soviet Armenia, in the Karabagh range, growing in steppe at c.1500m, flowering in May. Cultivate as for (a).

Tulipa systola Stapf. Native of N Iraq and W Iran, growing in fields and rocky places, from 200 to 3000m, flowering in March and April. Petals always acuminate, leaves wavy edged; bulb tunics very woolly. Photographed in NE Iraq, near Piramagrun, by Oleg Polunin.

Tulipa fosterana Irv. (see p.123). Photographed in Central Asia, S of Samarkand, Amankutan valley, on 13 April 1979.

Tulipa praestans Hoog (see pp.119, 123). Photographed in Central Asia, Tadjikistan, valley of Sorbo river, E of Dushanbe, 2000m, on 9 April 1979.

Tulipa humilis Herbert (see p.119). Photographed in SE Turkey, Hakkari, near Yukşekova, in May 1972.

Tulipa hoogiana B. Fedsch. Native of Central Asia, especially the Kopet Daǧ, growing on stony slopes, flowering in April and May. Leaves very glaucous; petals with a black, yellow edged blotch. Cultivate as for (a). Photographed in Tashkent Botanic Garden.

(a) **Tulipa tarda** Stapf (*Liliaceae*). Native of Central Asia, especially the Tien Shan, growing on stony and rocky slopes flowering in April and May. Flowers one to eight; bulb tunics glabrous. Easily grown in good well-drained soil, kept dry in summer, or lifted and ripened under cover.

(b) **Tulipa eichleri** Regel (*Liliaceae*). Native of south-east Transcaucasia and NW Iran, growing on dry slopes and in cornfields, flowering in April and May. Bulb tunic leathery, hairy inside. Petals with a small black blotch at the base, margined with yellow, up to 7cm long. Leaves glaucous, not striped. Easily grown in a sunny place outside, kept dry in summer.

(c) **Tulipa saxatilis** Sieber, syn. *T. bakeri* A. D. Hall (*Liliaceae*). Native of Crete, growing in fields and rocky places, flowering in April. Like a very large *T. cretica* (p.123). Increasing greatly by stolons, but often not flowering very freely. Requires a well-drained soil and a very warm sunny position. The shining green leaves appear in early winter. The plant known as *T. bakeri* has rather darker flowers.

(d) **Tulipa aucheriana** Baker (*Liliaceae*). Native of western Iran, but like *T. urumiensis* better known in cultivation than in the wild. Close to *T. humilis*, but with smaller more starry flowers, pink with a yellow centre. Easy to grow in well-drained soil in a sunny position, not requiring lifting in summer.

Tulip cultivars

(e) **'Pink Beauty'** (Single Early). Raised by Baars & Dibbits 1889.

(f) **'Big Chief'** (Darwin hybrid). Raised by A. Frijlink & Sons Ltd 1959.

(g) **'Gudoshnik'** (Darwin hybrid). Raised by D. W. Lefeber & Co. 1952.

(h) **'Apeldoorn'** (Darwin hybrid). Raised by Lefeber & Co. 1951.

(i) **'Diana'** (Single Early). Raised by A. van den Berg Gzn 1909.

(j) **Mr van der Hoef** (Early double). Sport of Murillo before 1911.

½ life size Photographed 17 April

a

b

c

d

e

f

g

h

i

½ life size Photographed 2 May

Tulip cultivars

(a) **'Maureen'** (Cottage). Raised by Segers Bros Ltd 1950.

(b) **'Big Chief'** (Darwin hybrid). Raised by A. Frijlink & Sons Ltd 1959.

(c) **'Purple Star'** (Triumph). Raised by S. J. Zandvoort 1952.

(d) **'Kansas'** (Triumph). Raised by Zocher & Co. before 1930.

(e) **'Lefeber's Favourite'** (Darwin hybrid). Raised by D. W. Lefeber & Co. 1942.

(f) **'Aristocrat'** (Darwin). Raised by Segers Bros Ltd 1935.

(g) **'Oranjezon'** (Darwin hybrid). Raised by C. V. Hybrida 1947.

(h) **'La Tulipe Noire'** (Darwin). Raised by E. H. Krelage & Son 1891.

(i) **'Copland's Magenta'** (Darwin). Sport of 'William Copland' raised by E. H. Krelage & Son 1891.

(j) **'White Triumphator'** (Lily-flowered). Raised by Van Tubergen Ltd 1942.

(k) **'West Point'** (Lily-flowered). Raised by de Mol-Nieuwenhuis 1943.

(l) **'Apeldoorn'** (Darwin hybrid). Raised by D. W. Lefeber & Co. 1951.

(m) **'Bellona'** (Single Early). Raised by H. de Graaff & Sons Ltd 1944.

(n) **'Vuurbaak'** (Double Early). Raised by C. Alkemade Azn 1980.

(o) **'Van der Neer'** (Single Early). Raised by G. Leembruggen 1860.

(p) **'Marechal Neil'** (Double Early). Sport of 'Murillo' 1930.

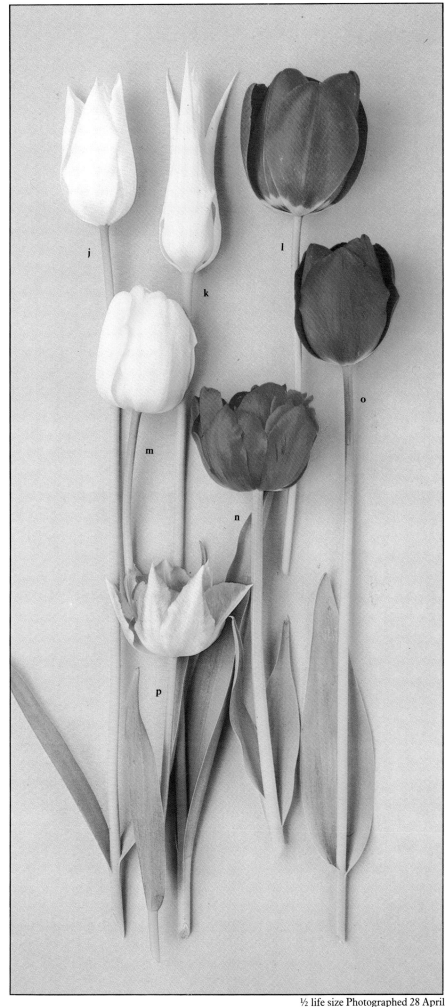

½ life size Photographed 28 April

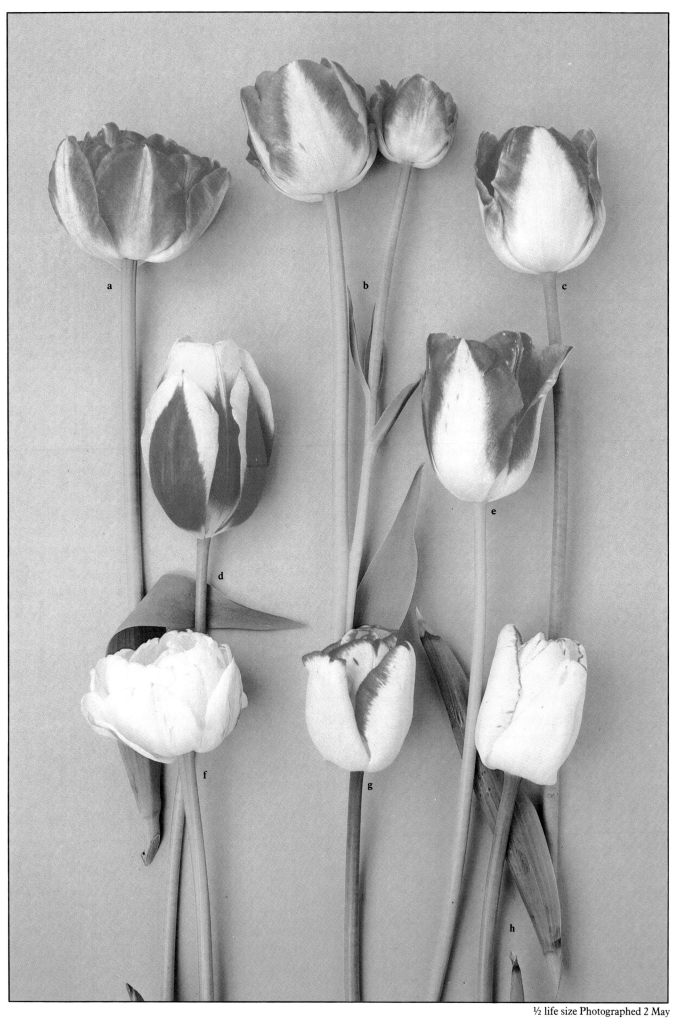

a

b

c

d

e

f

g

h

½ life size Photographed 2 May

Tulip cultivars

(a) **'May Wonder'** (Double Late). Raised by C. V. Hybrida 1951.

(b) **'Eros'** (Double Late). Raised by Zocher & Co. 1937.

(c) **'Ibis'** (Single Early). Sport of White Hawk 1910.

(d) **'Keizerskroon'** (Single Early). Raiser not recorded, 1750.

(e) **'Garden Party'** (Triumph). Raised by P. Hopman & Sons Ltd 1944.

(f) **'Mount Tacoma'** (Double Late). Raised by Polman Mooy before 1926.

(g) **'Rosy Dawn'** (Cottage). Raised by de Graaf Bros Ltd 1946.

(h) **'Ossi Oswalda'** (Darwin). Raised by J. J. Grullemans & Sons Ltd before 1939.

(i) **'K. & M.'s Triumph'**. Flamed flower from red original Triumph.

(j) **'Gudoshnik'** (Darwin hybrid). Raised by D. W. Lefeber & Co. 1952. The original is yellow, spotted and flamed red, but this flower shows more red flaming than normal (see p.87).

(k) **'Dreaming Maid'**. Flamed flower from violet-pink, white-edged original Triumph (see p.109).

(l) **'Artist'** (Green-flowered Cottage). Raised by Captain Bros 1947.

(m) **'Van der Neer'**. Flamed flower from purple original. Single Early (see p.106).

(n) **'Prins Carnaval'** 1930. Sport of Prince of Austria (see p.109).

(o) **'Garden Party'**. White sport of white, deep pink edged original Triumph (see p.110).

The 'breaking' of plain coloured tulip flowers into stripes and 'flames' of different colours is caused by infection with Tulip-breaking virus, which can be spread by aphids. For this reason the 'broken' varieties, often called 'Rembrandt Tulips', should be grown well away from other tulips. The appearance of different colours by 'sporting' is also a common phenomenon, and has been the source of many new varieties.

½ life size Photographed 2 May

a

b

c

d

e

f

g

h

i

½ life size Photographed 2 May

Tulip cultivars

(a) **'Dreaming Maid'** (Triumph). Raised by J. J. Kerbert 1934.

(b) **'Flying Dutchman'** (Darwin). Raised by Wamaar & Co. Ltd 1956.

(c) **'Orange Wonder'** (Triumph). Raised by A. Sabelis 1940.

(d) **'Clara Butt'** (Darwin). Raised by E. H. Krelage & Son 1889.

(e) **'Rosy Wings'** (Cottage). Raised by Van Tubergen Ltd 1944.

(f) **'Mrs John T. Scheepers'** (Cottage). Raised by Van Tubergen Ltd before 1930.

(g) **'Prince of Austria'** (Single Early). Raiser not recorded, 1860.

(h) **'Couleur Cardinal'** (Single Early). Raiser not recorded, 1845.

(i) **'China Pink'** (Lily-flowered). Raised by de Mol-Nieuwenhuis 1944.

(j) **'Blue Parrot'** (Parrot) Sport of 'Bleu Aimable' before 1935.

(k) **'Fantasy'** (Parrot) Sport of Clara Butt 1910.

(l) **'Firebird'** (Parrot) Sport of 'Fantasy' before 1939.

(m) **Narcissus poeticus** L. var. **recurvus** (Haw.) Fernandes (*Amaryllidaceae*). An old garden variety of *N. poeticus*, very late flowering, usually after all other Narcissus have finished. Easy to grow, but in some seasons flowers more freely than others. Very sweet-scented.

⅓ life size Photographed 6 May

½ life size Photographed 29 May

(a) Zigadenus micranthus Eastwood
(*Liliaceae*). Native of northern California and
Oregon, growing on dry slopes and valleys
below 1000m, flowering in May and June. Petals
4–5mm long, about equalling the stamens. Easy
to grow in a well-drained sunny position.

(b) Tulipa sprengeri Baker (*Liliaceae*). Native
of NW Turkey, near Amasya, but not seen
recently in the wild, though well known in
cultivation. Very late flowering, usually
35–45cm high. Brian Mathew records that it has
grown well in south-facing borders in full sun, at
the foot of north-facing peat banks, and in grass
under trees. Easy from seed.

(c) Pancratium illyricum L. (*Amaryllidaceae*).
Native of Corsica, Sardinia, Capri and
neighbouring islands, growing on rocks at low
altitudes, flowering in May. The bulb is large
with black tunics. Easily grown and flowering
freely at the foot of a south-facing wall, but slow
to increase. Source Corsica, near Porto Vecchio.

(d) Calochortus nuttallii Torr. (*Liliaceae*).
Native of eastern California, Oregon and
Montana to Colorado and New Mexico, growing
on dry slopes with grass and scrub at
1500–2800m, flowering from May to August.
The colour varies from white to deep yellow.
Grow in a bulb frame, kept dry in summer.

(e) Brimeura amethystina (L.) Chouard, syn.
Hyacinthus amethystinus L. (*Liliaceae*). Native of
the Pyrenees and mountains of north-east Spain,
and north-west Yugoslavia, in mountain
meadows up to the subalpine region, usually on
limestone, flowering in May and June. The
flowers vary in colour from white to deep blue or
violet. Cultivation as for (a).

(f) Calochortus pulchellus Dougl. ex Benth.
(*Liliaceae*). Native of central California where it
is frequent on wooded and bushy slopes in
chaparral and pine and oak forest above 200m,
flowering from April to June. One of the easier
species of the group. Grows well in good very
gritty soil in a bulb frame in sun or half-shade.

(g) Calochortus amoenus Greene (*Liliaceae*).
Native of central and S California, in the western
foothills of the Sierras to the Greenhorn Mts,
growing in leafy loam in partial shade, and on
grassy slopes from 500 to 1400m, flowering from
April to June. Cultivation as for (f).

(h) Calochortus albus Dougl. ex Benth.
(*Liliaceae*). Native of central California,
especially the coast ranges and the foothills of
the Sierras, growing in shaded and often rocky
places in evergreen oak and pine forest, and in
chaparral scrub, below 1500m. Cultivation as
for (f). Photographed in California, Butt Co., by
Roger Macfarlane.

(i) Calochortus caeruleus (Kell.) Watson, syn.
C. maweanus (*Liliaceae*). Native of northern
California in the western Sierra Nevada,
growing in open stony places in montane
coniferous forest from 1000 to 2200m, flowering
from May to July. Cultivation as for (f).

(j) Calochortus monophyllus (Lindl.) Lem.
(*Liliaceae*). Native of the foothills of the Sierras
in northern California on wooded slopes from
400 to 1100m, flowering in April and May.

Hyacinthella dalmatica
Hyacinthella dalmatica (Baker) Chouard
(*Liliaceae*). Native of western Yugoslavia,
growing in grassy places among limestone rocks.
Cultivation as for (a). Photographed in
Yugoslavia, near Dubrovnik, by Brian Mathew.

½ life size Photographed 28 April

Calochortus albus

Hyacinthella dalmatica

135

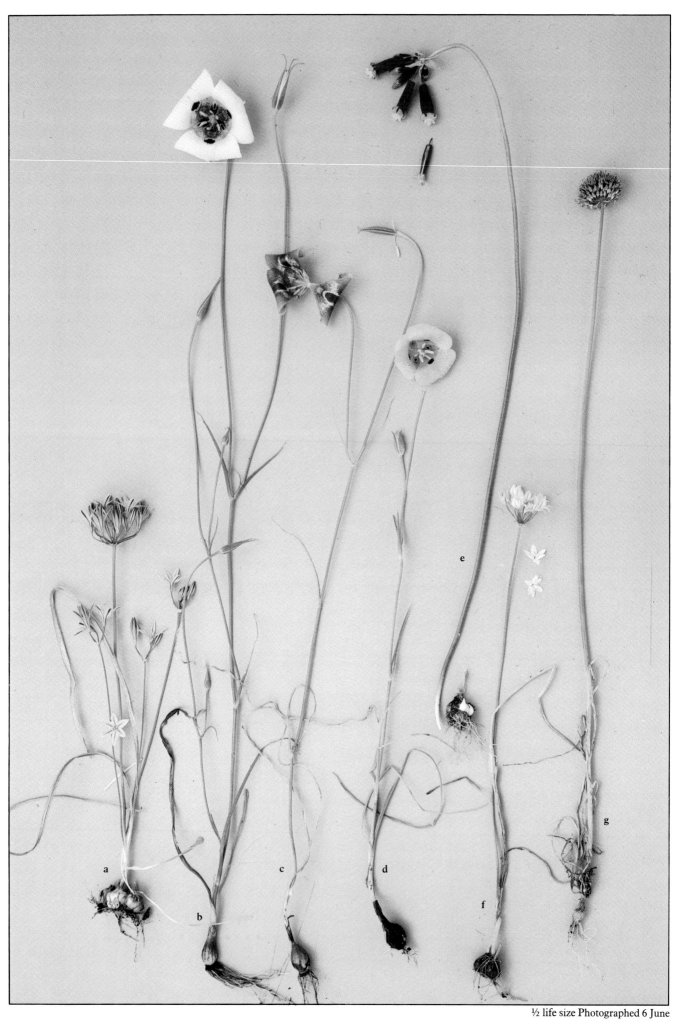

½ life size Photographed 6 June

Calochortus luteus

Calochortus venustus

Calochortus kennedyi

Calochortus amabilis

(a) **Triteleia ixioides** (Ait. fil.) Greene, syn. *Brodiaea lutea* (Lindl.) Mort. (*Liliaceae*). Native of central California, growing in sandy soil in pine and pine-oak forest up to 1500m, flowering from May to August. Easily grown in a bulb frame or warm sunny place outside. The stamens have a long tooth either side of the anther, which distinguishes it from *T. crocea* and *Bloomeria crocea* (Torr.) Cav.

(b), (c) **Calochortus venustus** Dougl. ex Benth. (*Liliaceae*). Native of central and S California, especially the Sierra Nevada and southern coast ranges, growing in grassland and in open evergreen oak and pine forest, in light sandy soil, usually decomposed granite, from 300 to 2600m, flowering from May to July. The flowers vary from white to yellow, pink, dark red or purple. Grows in well-drained sandy soil, kept rather dry in winter and watered until flowering, and so best in a pot in the alpine house, or in a bulb frame. Photographed in the Greenhorn Mts by Roger Macfarlane.

(d) **Calochortus luteus** Doug. ex Lindl. (*Liliaceae*). Native of central California in the Sierra Nevada and the coast ranges, growing in

heavy soils in open grassland, and in pine, evergreen oak and mixed coniferous woodland, below 650m, flowering from April till June. Close to *C. venustus* (p.136), but always clear yellow in colour. Nectary curved. Cultivation as for (b). Photographed in California, near Chico, by Roger Macfarlane.

(e) **Dichelostemma ida-maia** (Wood) Greene, syn. *Brodiaea ida-maia* (Wood) Greene (*Liliaceae*). Native of northern California and Oregon, growing in the redwood and mixed evergreen forest zone in open grassy places from 300 to 1200m, flowering from May to July. The leaves which are usually withered at flowering are normally three, 30–50cm by 4–8mm; flowering stem up to 90cm. Easily grown in a pot in the alpine house, a bulb frame or a very sheltered warm place outside.

(f) **Triteleia hyacinthina** (Lindl.) Greene (*Liliaceae*). Native of northern California north to Vancouver Is., and Idaho, growing in wet places, meadows and slopes up to 1800m, flowering from May to August, the large white-fld form from wet places, the smaller forms from drier slopes. Cultivation as (e).

(g) **Allium caeruleum** Pallas, syn. *A. azureum* Ledebour (*Liliaceae*). Native of the far east of Europe north of the Caspian, and Central Asia south to the Pamir and the Tien Shan, in steppes and salt marshes, flowering May to July. Leaves withered by flowering time, triangular in section. Easily cultivated in a dry place.

Calochortus amabilis Purdy (*Liliaceae*). Native of NW California, especially the coast ranges, where it grows in loamy or rocky soil on dry slopes in chaparral, scrub or evergreen mixed forest up to 1000m, flowering from April to June. Photographed in California, Lake Co., 23 April 1966, Roger Macfarlane.

Calochortus kennedyi Porter (*Liliaceae*). Native of S California, Nevada and Arizona, growing in heavy soil on open plains or on dry rocky or scrubby slopes, usually in desert conditions, at altitudes of 600–2000m, flowering from April till June. Variable in colour, being usually scarlet, but orange in the E Mojave desert and yellow at high altitudes. Has not proved amenable in cultivation in England. Photographed in California, near China Lake, M. Williams.

½ life size Photographed 2 May

(a) **Allium circinatum** Sieber (*Liliaceae*). Found only on Crete, on dry rocky hillsides, where it flowers in March and April. Unusual in its coiled leaves covered with long silky hairs, and hairy stem. Best cultivated in a bulb frame or pot, kept dry in summer.

(b) **Allium neapolitanum** Cyr. Native of the Mediterranean region from Spain to Turkey and Egypt, growing in grassy places and fields, flowering from March to May. Anthers dark, filaments flattened. Easily grown in sunny places, but said to be rather frost-tender. Source Spain, J. Pym s.n.

(c) **Allium ursinum** L., Ramsons. Native of most of Europe from Scotland and Finland to Spain and Greece, and east to the Caucasus. Found in damp woods, often in great quantity, flowering from April to June.

(d) **Allium trifoliatum** Cyr. Native of the Mediterranean region from France to Sicily, Crete and Israel, growing on stony hillsides, flowering in April and May. Like *A. subhirsutum*, but has flowers tinged with pink, yellow not brown anthers, pedicels 15–20mm as opposed to 25–40mm. Forms a dense clump.

(e) **Allium roseum** L. Native of the Mediterranean region from Spain and Portugal to Turkey and N Africa, growing in rocky places, dry open woods, and cultivated ground, flowering from April to June. The bulb tunic is hard and brittle; the leaves 1–14mm wide. Some forms have bulbils in the inflorescence. Cultivation as (b). Source Spain, coll. Linzee Gordon.

(f) **Allium zebdanense** Boiss. & Noë. Native of the eastern Mediterranean region from Syria to Israel, growing in rocky places in the mountains, flowering in May and June. Umbel short-stalked; stamens with wide-based filaments. Leaves glabrous. Cultivation as (b).

(g) **Allium triquetrum** L. Native of the western Mediterranean region from Italy to France and N Africa, where it grows in damp shady places, often by streams. Naturalised in Britain. Stem triangular. Easily grown in cool leafy soil.

(h) **Leucojum nicaeense** Ardoino (*Amaryllidaceae*). Native of SE France east of Nice, and possibly Italy, growing on rocky hills, flowering in spring. Dislikes disturbance, so best sown thinly and carefully potted on.

(i) **Notholirion thomsonianum** (Royle) Stapf (*Liliaceae*). Native of the western Himalayas from Afghanistan to Kumaon, growing in scrub and rocky places at 1600–2300m, flowering in March and April. Grow in well-drained rich soil, kept dry in summer to ripen the bulbs and encourage flowering.

(j) **Tulipa clusiana** DC. (*Liliaceae*). Native of Iran, near Shiraz eastwards to the Himalayas and Tibet, and naturalised in S Europe. It grows on stony mountain sides, flowering from April to June. The ground colour is usually white, with pink on the outer petals. Shown here is c.v. 'Cynthia' raised by Van Tubergen in 1959.

(k) **Ixiolirion tartaricum** (Pall.) Herbert, syn. *I. montanum* (La Bill.) Herb., *I. pallasii* Fisch. & Meyer (*Amaryllidaceae*). Native of western Asia from Turkey and Egypt eastwards to western Siberia and Songaria, growing in fields and on hillsides from 200 to 2700m, flowering from April to June. Requires a hot dry summer.

(l) **Allium longisepalum** Bertol. see p.147(e).

½ life size Photographed 2 May

⅓ life size Photographed 6 May

Allium karataviense

Allium protensum

Allium akaka

Allium sphaerocephalon

(a) **Allium kharputense** Freyn & Sint. (*Liliaceae*). Native of Turkey and W Iran, growing on stony hillsides from 1500 to 2500m. The obtuse petals and dark ovary are characteristic. Height here 24cm. Source Turkey, Adiyaman, Kahta, towards Nemrut Dağ, Linzee Gordon 5163.

(b) **Allium hirtifolium** Stapf (*Liliaceae*). Native of the Zagros Mts in west and south-west Iran, on rocky hillsides up to 3200m. Flowering stem up to 150cm. Leaves hairy beneath. Very similar to *A. stipitatum* Regel from Afghanistan and Central Asia, but has a smooth not ribbed flower stem, and less tapered petals. Easily grown in a bulb frame or in the open. Both the white and pink forms were collected by Brian Mathew on the Bowles Scholarship Botanical Expedition to Iran in 1963. Source Iran, SW of Arak, BSBE 1840.

(c) **Allium breviscapum** Stapf (*Liliaceae*). Native of Iran, where it is confined to the area of Isfahan. Differs from *A. akaka* in its narrower leaves which are four to six in number and hairy beneath. Easily grown in a bulb frame. Source

Iran, Kuh-i-Alwand, P. Furse 1986.

(d) **Allium ellisii** Hooker (*Liliaceae*). Native of Iran, especially the Elburz mountains. Characterised by its scabrid leaf margin and starry shining flowers like *A. christophii* (p.147), but stems are always much shorter. Cultivation as for (c). Source P. Furse 2571.

(e) **Allium akaka** Gmelin, syn. *A. latifolium* Jaub. & Spach. (*Liliaceae*). Native of E Turkey, Transcaucasia, NW Iran and N Iraq, growing on screes and loose stony slopes in the mountains from 1600 to 3000m, flowering from June to August. Distinguished by its one or two broad glaucous leaves and short stem with a spherical head of pale pink flowers. Cultivation as for (c). Source SE Turkey, Pelli Da., S side of Lake Van, Rix 714. Photographed at 3000m on Artos Dağ, south of Van, in June 1968.

Allium protensum Wendelbo (*Liliaceae*). Native of Central Asia from the Kizil Kum desert to the Pamir-Alai, and northern Afghanistan, from 300 to 3000m, flowering in May and June. This species was for a long time

confused with *A. schubertii* Zucc. from Israel, Syria and Libya, but differs in its shorter stem, and brown rather than purplish flowers. Whereas *A. schubertii* is frost tender, *A. protensum* should be quite hardy provided that it is kept rather dry. Photographed in Tashkent Botanic Garden.

Allium karataviense Regel (*Liliaceae*). Native of Central Asia especially the Alai and western Tien Shan, growing in loose limestone scree, flowering in April and May. Leaves grey-purple. Petals recurved and twisted after flowering. Easily grown in well-drained soil in full sun. See p.152.

Allium sphaerocephalon L. (*Liliaceae*). Native of most of Europe, from England and Belgium to the Caucasus, and N Africa to Israel, growing in dry places and in fields, flowering from June to August. Flowers sometimes replaced by bulbils. Spathe shorter than the pedicels, two-valved; leaves up to 30cm, 1–4mm wide, sheathing the stem. Easily grown in well-drained soil in full sun. Photographed in Greece near Kastoria by Oleg Polunin.

141

⅓ life size Photographed 6 June

(a) Allium neapolitanum Cyr. (*Liliaceae*) (see p.139 (b)). Height here 40cm. Source between Tunis and Tabarka, 50m, Linzee Gordon 465.

(b) Scilla peruviana L. (*Liliaceae*). Native of the western Mediterranean region from Italy and Sicily westwards, growing in damp grassy places, flowering from April to June. Very variable in size and flower colour, from white to dark purple or pale brown in N Africa. The form shown here is probably *S. hughii* Tin. ex Guss. from Isole Egadi. Plant shallow, in a warm sunny place.

(c) Allium regelii Trautr. (*Liliaceae*). Native of Central Asia, especially the Kara Kum desert, Kopet Daǧ and Badgis north of Herat, Afghanistan, especially the Hindu Kush, and NE Iran. It grows on sandy deserts and rocky slopes in the mountains from 800 to 3000m, flowering in May and June. It is unique in its candelabra-like inflorescence, which may have up to six whorls of flowers in a robust specimen. The flowers are either pink, as shown here, or deep purple. Easily grown but probably safer in a bulb frame where it can be kept dry in summer. Source Afghanistan, Hindu Kush, Salang pass, P. Furse 6614.

(d) Allium subhirsutum L. (*Liliaceae*). Native of the Mediterranean region from Spain to Greece, growing on rocky and sandy places, flowering from March to May. Close to *A. trifoliatum* and *A. neapolitanum* (p.139) but *A. subhirsutum* has ciliate leaves and slender not flattened stamen filaments. Easily grown in warm sunny places. Source Greece, Cephalonia.

(e) Allium nigrum Boiss. & Reut. (*Liliaceae*). Native of S Europe eastwards to Iran, growing in fields and among limestone rocks, at 100–2000m, flowering from April to June. With its purple anthers and purplish petals the plant shown here approaches *A. atropurpureum* Wildst. Kit. *A. nigrum* usually has yellowish anthers and white or pink, green-varied petals. Easily grown in a well-drained sunny place. Source W Turkey, between Denizli and Budur, Linzee Gordon 5041.

(f) Allium moly L. (*Liliaceae*). Native of E Spain and SW France where it grows on shady rocks and screes in the mountains, and flowers in May. Cultivation as for (e).

(g) Allium schoenoprasum L. Chives (*Liliaceae*). Native of most of Europe, and usually found in damp meadows in the mountains, forming dense clumps. It is very variable in the wild, and many different forms are grown in gardens for use in cooking and salads. Flowers sometimes white. *A. sibiricum* L., from Kamschatka and Siberia to Japan and across N America, is a more robust tetraploid form.

(h) Allium oreophilum C. A. Meyer, syn. *A. ostrovskianum* Regel (*Liliaceae*). Native of Central Asia, especially the Tien Shan, the Pamir Alai and the Ala Tau, and of eastern Turkey and the Caucasus, growing on stony slopes at 3000–3800m, flowering in July and August. Flowers pinkish, darker in the c.v. 'Zwanenburg' shown here. Easily grown in a sunny place.

(i) Nothoscordum inodorum (Aiton) Nicholson, syn. *Allium fragrans* Vent. (*Liliaceae*). Native of South America, but widely naturalised in Europe and California. *Nothoscordum* differs from *Allium* in its lack of the onion-like smell, and in the petals which are united at the base. Cf. p.145 (i).

½ life size Photographed 29 May

143

⅓ life size Photographed 16 July

(a) **Allium tuberosum** Rottler ex Sprengel, syn. *A. odorum* L. pro parte (*Liliaceae*). Chinese Chives. Widely cultivated in E Asia. Flowers open, starry, capsule obovate, emarginate. Flowers July to October in S England. Grows well in tropical or temperate climates, and appears hardy.

(b) **Ornithogalum narbonense** L. (*Liliaceae*). Native of S Europe, growing in grassy places and waste ground, flowering from May to July. Easily grown and will survive in grass.

(c) **Allium christophii** Trautv., syn. *A. albopilosum* Wright (*Liliaceae*). Native in northern Iran in the central Elburz and N Khorassan, and in the Kopet Daǧ in Soviet Central Asia, growing on rocky slopes from 900 to 2250m. Leaves silky hairy when young, withered by flowering time. Height here 56cm. Easy to grow in hot sunny places.

(d) **Allium ramosum** L., syn. *A. odorum* L. pro parte (*Liliaceae*). Native of Siberia, growing in meadows and on grassy slopes. Flowers not opening flat; petals with a reddish line outside. Ovary ovate, emarginate. Flowers in S England during June and July. Cultivation as (a).

(e) **Allium scorodoprasum** L. subsp. **jajlae** (Vved.) Stearn, syn. *A. jajlae* Vved. Native of the Crimea and the Caucasus, growing on mountain slopes, flowering in June and July.

(f) **Allium cernuum** (*Liliaceae*). Native of North America from New York State to British Columbia southwards to Georgia and Arizona, growing in gravelly and rocky places in the mountains, flowering in July and August. Flowers may be white, pink or purple. Cultivation as (e). Source Columbia River Gorge, Wyoming.

(g) **Allium obliquum** L. (*Liliaceae*). Native of Romania to Siberia and north-western China, growing in meadows, scrub and cliffs, flowering from April to July. Filaments subulate. Cultivation as (e).

(h) **Allium nutans** L. (*Liliaceae*). Native of Siberia and Central Asia, growing in steppes, meadows and stony slopes, flowering in June and July. Inner petals longer than outer. Cultivation as (e).

(i) **Caloscordum neriniflorum** Herbert, syn. *Allium neriniflorum* (Herbert) Baker (*Liliaceae*). Native of E Siberia, Mongolia and China, growing on dry slopes, flowering in July and August. Close to *Allium*, but the stamen filaments are fused to the petals.

(j) **Brodiaea stellaris** Wats. (*Liliaceae*). Native of northern California, from Humboldt to Sonomona counties, on rocky slopes below 1000m, flowering from May to July. Grow in a bulb frame or a warm place outside.

(k) **Triteleia hyacinthina** (Lindl.) Greene (see p.137).

(l) **Triteleia laxa** Benth., syn. *Brodiaea laxa* (Benth.) Wats. Native of western California and S Oregon, growing in heavy soils up to 1200m, flowering from April to June. Flowers deep blue to white. Cultivation as for (j).

(m) **Dichelostemma pulchella** (Salisb.) Heller, syn. *Brodiaea pulchella* Greene (*Liliaceae*). Native of western California and S Oregon, commoner in the west, growing on plains and hillsides, up to c.1800m, flowering from March to May. Cultivation as for (j).

½ life size Photographed 4 August

½ life size Photographed 16 July

(a) Allium paniculatum L. subsp. **paniculatum** (*Liliaceae*). Native of southern Europe northwards to central France, on dry grassy slopes at up to 1000m. Flowering in late summer. Very variable in flower colour. Easily grown in dry sunny places.

(b) Allium cyathophorum var. **farreri** (Stearn) Stearn (*Liliaceae*). Native of north-western China, especially Kansu, where it grows on grassy slopes between 3000 and 3300m. The stamens are fused into a tube at their base. Easily grown in well-drained peaty soil in full sun, kept moist throughout the summer, flowering in late summer.

(c) Allium flavum L. (*Liliaceae*). Native of southern Europe from France to Greece, growing on dry hills and flowering in July. Many dwarf mountain forms have been named, e.g. *A. flavum* var. *minus* Boiss. Easy to grow in sunny places.

(d) Allium stamineum Boiss. (*Liliaceae*). Native of Greece, Turkey and the S Caucasus to Iraq, Arabia and Jordan, growing in steppe, scrub and desert from 100 to 2000m, flowering from May to September. Height up to 30cm. Stamens and style exserted. Easily grown in a bulb frame or pot in the alpine house.

(e) Allium longisepalum Bertol., syn. *A. eriophyllum* Boiss. (*Liliaceae*). Native of E Turkey, N Syria, Iraq, S and W Iran, growing in stony fields and hillsides from 150 to 1000m, flowering in May and June (see also p.139). Very variable. Cultivation as for (l). Source Iran, coll. Ann Ala.

(f) Allium amabile Stapf (*Liliaceae*). Native of SW China, growing in stony alpine meadows at up to 4200m, flowering from July to September. Flowers pink to magenta. Cultivation as for (b).

(g) Allium glumaceum Boiss. & Hausskn. (*Liliaceae*). Native of central Turkey, growing on rocky hillsides at c.2000m. Cultivation as for (a).

(h) Allium cyaneum Regel (*Liliaceae*). Native of NW China from Kansu to Szechuan, growing in open grassland from 2400 to 2700m, flowering from August to October. Suitable for a ledge on the rock garden. Cultivation as for (b).

(i) Allium algirdense Blakelock (*Liliaceae*). Native of high mountains in N Iraq and SE Turkey, where it grows on open stony slopes between 2500 and 3800m, flowering in August and September. The leaves are tubular, up to 10cm long and withered by flowering time. Cultivation as for (d). Source Hakkari, Sat Da., 3000m, Rix 161A.

(j) Allium narcissiflorum Vill., syn. *A. pedemontanum* Willd. (*Liliaceae*). Native of the SW Alps in France and Italy, growing on limestone screes, flowering in June and July. The closely related *A. insubricum* Boiss. & Reut. is found on limestone between Lake Como and Lake Garda. Cultivation as for (b).

(k) Allium callidyctyon C. A. Meyer (*Liliaceae*). Native of central Turkey, Caucasia, Iraq and Iran, growing in dense tufts in rocks and in fields, from 500 to 800m, flowering in August. The leaves which are withered by flowering time appear in autumn and are narrowly tubular, covered with short dense white hairs. The bulbs have a fine woven tunic. Has grown easily in a bulb frame, but is likely to be susceptible to winter damp if planted outside. Source Turkey, Kayseri, south of Pinarbaşi, Rix 1398.

⅓ life size Photographed 6 June

(l) Allium crispum Greene (*Liliaceae*). Native of central California in the inner coast ranges, Santa Barbara and the Sierra Nevada foothills, growing in heavy soil on rolling hills below 800m, flowering from March to May. Height here 20cm, but may be up to 30cm. Grows in good soil in a sunny position, and probably better if protected in summer from too much wet, and in winter from hard frost.

(m) Ornithogalum montanum Cyr. (*Liliaceae*). Native of SE Europe, from Italy to Greece, and Turkey, growing on rocky and grassy slopes, flowering in April and May. Very variable. Leaves glabrous, 8–20mm wide. *O. narbonense* L. is similar, but has a more elongated inflorescence. Easily cultivated in a sunny position or in thin grass. Source W Turkey, Eğredir to Beyşehir, Linzee Gordon 5066.

(n) Ornithogalum sphaerocarpum A. Kerner (*Liliaceae*). Native of south and eastern Europe from France to Czechoslovakia southwards, growing in meadows and scrub, flowering in May and June. Close to *O. pyrenaicum* L., but flowers greenish white not yellowish, and ovary subglobose. Cultivation as (b).

(o) Allium unifolium Kellogg (*Liliaceae*). Native of N California and S Oregon in the coast ranges, growing in moist soils in pine or mixed evergreen forest below 1200m, flowering from May till July. The bulb is very unusual, reforming each year on a short stalk at the side of last year's bulb which has shrunk to almost nothing by flowering time. Grows in good well-drained soil in a sunny position.

(p) Scilla litardieri Breitstr. syn. *S. amethystina* Vis., *S. pratensis* Waldst. & Kit. (*Liliaceae*). Native of W Yugoslavia, growing in meadows and among limestone rocks. The rather similar *S. hyacinthoides* L. has eight to twelve leaves, a taller stem with a laxer 40–150 flowered inflorescence of purplish flowers. Cultivation as for (o).

Eremurus regelii

Eremurus lactiflorus in the Chimgan valley

Eremurus M. Bieb. (*Liliaceae*). The genus is found from Turkey (two spp.) eastwards to the Himalayas, with one species in China and the main concentration (forty-one spp.) in Central Asia. They usually grow on dry, stony, heavily grazed hillsides. The leaves. which are linear and triangular in section, appear in spring; they are not grazed, and so the plants often occur in huge numbers. The roots are long, thick and fleshy, spreading out from a central stock. In cultivation in northern Europe the plants should be grown in sandy soil and protected against late frosts and slugs. A pile of sharp sand or ash over the crowns will help them to survive the wet of winter. In summer after flowering they should be kept as dry as possible. Full sun is important while the leaves are green.

Eremurus cristatus Vved. Native of the western and central Tien Shan, flowering in May. One of the shortest species, about 60cm high in good conditions. Photographed in Tashkent Botanic Garden in April 1979.

Eremurus olgae Regel. Native of N Iran, N Afghanistan and Central Asia especially Tadjikistan, growing on stony hills at 1200–2500m, flowering from May to August. Height 70–100cm. Hybrids with other species are common in the wild, and the 'Shelford hybrids' often cultivated, were derived from *E. olgae × stenophyllus*. Photographed in Afghanistan by C. Grey-Wilson, G.-W. & Hewer 1251.

Eremurus stenophyllus (Boiss. & Buhse) Baker, syn. *E. bungei* Baker. Native of Central Asia, especially the Kopet Dağ, Iran (subsp. *stenophyllus*), Afghanistan, W Pakistan and the Pamir Alai (subsp. *aurantiacus* (Baker) Wendelbo), growing on stony slopes at c.2500m, flowering in June and July. Stem up to 150cm. Photographed in N Afghanistan, Hindu Kush, north of Kenjan, by C. Grey-Wilson.

Eremurus regelii Vved. Native of Central Asia, especially the western Tien Shan, and the western Pamir Alai, growing on earthy hillsides and rocky places at c.1000m, flowering in April and May. Height up to 180cm. Photographed NE of Tashkent, near Aktaş, in May 1980.

Eremurus lactiflorus O. Fedtsch. Native of the western Tien Shan, growing on screes and steep slopes at 1000–2000m, flowering in April and May. Stem 50–100cm. Capsules strongly inflated, c.3.5cm in diameter. Photographed in the Chimgan valley NE of Tashkent, in May 1980.

Eremurus lactiflorus

Eremurus olgae

Eremurus cristatus

Eremurus olgae in the Elburz Mts above Qazvin

Eremurus stenophyllus in the Hindu Kush

149

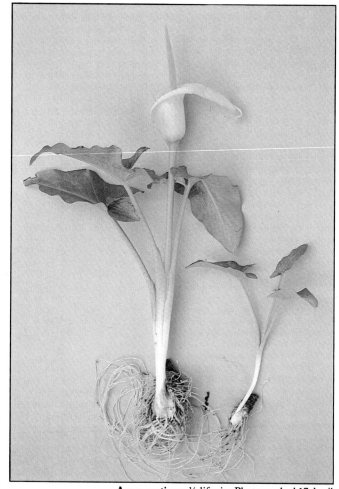

⅓ life size Photographed 28 April

Arum creticum ⅓ life size Photographed 17 April

Gladiolus italicus

Gladiolus atroviolaceus Boiss.

(a) Triteleia ixioides (Ait. fil.) Greene (see p.137). Pedicel length can vary from 1.5 to 7cm.

(b), (c) Zigadenus fremontii, Torr. (*Liliaceae*). Native of California and S Oregon, growing on dry grassy slopes or in scrub, below 1000m, flowering March to May. Very variable. Inflorescence racemose to paniculate, petals 10–12mm long, stamens 5–7mm.

Rhodohypoxis baurii Nel. (*Hypoxidaceae*). Native of southern Africa in Natal and Lesotho, in the Drakensberg mountains growing in grassy peaty soil often on seeping rocks at 1500–3000m, flowering from October to December. Varying in colour from white to deep red and in selected cultivated forms flowers may be 3cm in

diameter. Best grown in pots, kept rather dry in winter and protected from hard frost, and watered well in spring until after flowering. Otherwise can be planted out into a sink each spring and brought in in winter, or left out and given some protection from excess damp and frost.

Gladiolus imbricatus L. (*Iridaceae*). Native of central and eastern Europe from Germany to Greece and the Caucasus, and of Turkey, growing in wet meadows and marshes, flowering from May to July. Distinguished by its dense four to twelve-flowered spike, and obtuse lowest leaf. Flowers sometimes deep purple (cf. *G. atroviolaceus*). Photographed in the N Caucasus, 2000m, June 1980.

Gladiolus atroviolaceus Boiss. (*Iridaceae*). Native of E Turkey, Iraq, Iran and Soviet Armenia, growing in cornfields on dry hillsides, flowering from May to July. The dark flowered species growing in wet meadows, usually at high altitudes, has been distinguished as *G. kotschyanus* Boiss, or as a variety of *G. imbricatus*. Grows happily in a bulb frame, kept dry in summer. Photographed near Erevan, on dry hills, in May 1978.

Gladiolus illyricus Koch (*Iridaceae*). Native of south and west Europe from England southwards, and of the Mediterranean region, growing on heaths, in scrub and open woods, flowering from April to August. Very close to *G. communis*, but usually shorter, up to 50cm,

Gladiolus imbricatus L.　　　　　Gladiolus communis L.　　　　　Gladiolus illyricus Koch.

Rhodohypoxis baurii ½ life size Photographed 6 June

Gladiolus × colvillei

with three to ten flowers on a rarely branched spike. Will naturalise itself in grass in southern England. Photographed by Oleg Polunin.

Gladiolus communis L. (*Iridaceae*). Native of southern Europe from Spain and France to Greece, Turkey and Iran (?), growing in fields and scrub, flowering from April to August. Flowers not all facing one way, not crowded, usually with ten to twenty flowers on the often branched spike. Photographed in the Peloponnese by Roger Phillips.

Arum creticum Boiss. & Held (*Araceae*). Native of the islands of Crete, Samos, Rhodes and Karpathos, where it grows on stony hillsides. The leaves appear in autumn and the flowering stem which may be up to 40cm high appears in spring. Not likely to be confused with any other *Arum* because of its very loosely folded often recurved spathe. The spadix may be yellow (as illustrated) or dark purple, and the spathe white,

yellow or green. Sweetly scented unlike other species. Easily cultivated, but probably better in a pot, protected from severe frost in winter and kept rather dry in summer.

Gladiolus italicus Miller, syn. *G. segetum* Ker-Gawler (*Iridaceae*). A weed of cultivated land from France southwards to N Africa, and eastwards to Romania, Central Asia and Iran, flowering from March to July. Distinguished from other species by having anthers longer than the filaments. Photographed in Turkey near Ankara in May 1972.

Gladiolus × colvillei Sweet (*G. tristis* × *cardinalis*), syn. *G. nanus* hort. (*Iridaceae*). Various coloured hybrids have been derived from these two South African species, in shades of white, pink, crimson and mauve. They are only hardy in the mildest gardens in southern and western Britain. Photographed at Knightshayes, Devonshire.

Eminium intortum

Eminium intortum (Banks & Sol.) O. Kuntze (*Araceae*). Native of southern Turkey and Syria, growing in dry fields and stony places, flowering from March to May. Tuber almost spherical, with a white waxy powder. Has survived, but not grown well in a bulb frame. Photographed in Turkey, near Gaziantep, in May 1970.

151

⅓ life size Photographed 29 May

(a) Gladiolus communis L. subsp. **byzantinus** (Miller) A. P. Hamilton (*Iridaceae*). Native of S Spain, Sicily and N Africa. A form of it with magenta-crimson flowers is commonly cultivated. It requires a very warm sunny position. Subsp. communis see p.151.

(b) Moraea spathacea Ker-Gawler (*Iridaceae*). Native of South Africa, especially the eastern Cape, growing in moist grassy places. Other closely related and very similar species grow in the Drakensberg mountains in bogs. This species seems to be hardy and grows well in deep peaty soil in full sun, and does not require very wet conditions in Europe.

(c) Iris 'Wedgwood'. This is the commonest of the 'Dutch' Irises, and much used for forcing. Derived from crosses between *I. xiphium* L. and *I. tingitana* Boiss. & Reut. Colour ranges from purple and blue to white, yellow, bronze and apricot. Best lifted and dried after flowering, before replanting in early autumn.

(d), (e) Nectaroscordum siculum (Ucria) Lindley (*Liliaceae*). Native of southern Europe from France eastwards to Bulgaria and the Crimea and Turkey, growing in damp shady woods, flowering in May. The plants from Italy westwards have dull greenish-red flowers (subsp. *siculum*) (e), those in Turkey, Bulgaria eastwards (subsp. *bulgaricum* (Janka) Stearn) have whitish flowers shaded with green and pink (d). Both are easily grown in light soil in sun or half-shade.

(f) Allium karataviense Regel (see p.141).

(g) Allium giganteum Regel (*Liliaceae*). Native of Iran, Afghanistan, and Central Asia in Turkomania and the Pamir Alai, growing on gentle slopes at low altitudes, up to 1200m, flowering in April and May. The leaves are glaucous, 5–10cm wide, and the obtuse petals are 5–6mm long. The very similar *A. macleanii* Baker (= *A. elatum* Regel) differs in its shining green leaves, rather shorter ridged stalk, small umbel and longer (6–7mm), subacute tepals. Easily grown in well-drained soil in full sun, and useful for the herbaceous border.

(h) Iris 'Professor Blaauw'. One of the darkest flowered of the 'Dutch' Irises, this variety was raised from *Iris tingitana* Boiss. & Reut. var. *fontanesii* (Gordon) Maire, collected in Morocco.

(i) Arum italicum Miller (*Araceae*). Found throughout south and west Europe and N Africa in hedges and rocky places, often among old walls. The leaves appear in autumn, the flowers in spring. Very variable and may be divided into four subspecies. Subsp. *italicum* shown here has beautifully white-veined leaves which make it a good garden plant; individuals can be found with even more marbling than shown here. This subspecies is often called 'Pictum' or *marmoratum*. The other subspecies do not have marbled leaves. Subsp. *neglectum*, native to southern England, at the foot of the chalk downs, and W Europe, has a flowering stem shorter than the leaves and a greenish-yellow spathe. Subsp. *albispathum* from the Crimea and SW Asia has a spathe pure white inside, and subsp. *byzantinum* from Greece, Turkey and Crete has taller flowering stem and a green spathe marked with purple. Easily grown in sun or dry shade.

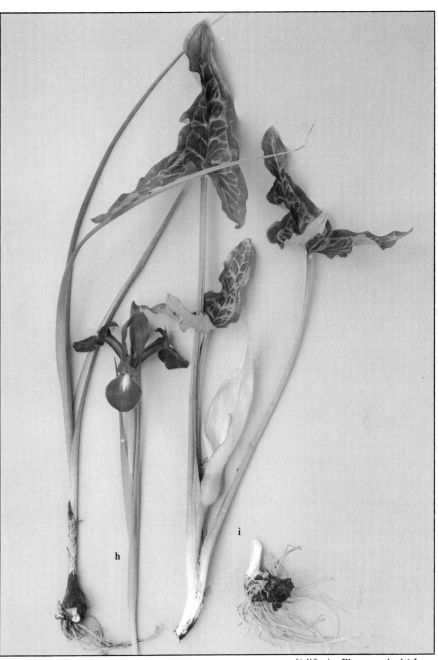

¹⁄₃ life size Photographed 6 June

Iris latifolia, pale form

Iris latifolia

Iris latifolia (Miller) Voss, syn. *I. xiphioides* Ehrh., English Iris (section *xiphion*). Native of the Pyrenees and Cantabrian mountains of northern Spain, growing in damp meadows, flowering in June and July. Flowers larger than the other species of section *xiphion*, with longer falls, 60–75mm. Stem 25–50cm. Flowers in cultivation blue and violet to white. Grows well in any good garden soil. Photographed naturalised in long grass at Great Dixter, Sussex.

½ life size Photographed 29 May

Oxalis depressa

Oxalis laciniata

Roscoea cautleyoides

Roscoea humeana

Roscoea alpina

Oxalis enneaphylla

Roscoea alpina Royle (*Zingiberaceae*). Native of the Himalayas from Kashmir to Sikkim up to 3500m, growing on rocky slopes, flowering in June and July. The flowers open one at a time and the plant is up to 20cm high. Photographed in Garhwal, near Pindari glacier, by Oleg Polunin.

Roscoea humeana Balfour fil. & W. W. Smith (*Zingiberaceae*). Native of China in Szechuan and Yunnan, growing on grassy slopes at up to 3800m, flowering from May to July. Stems up to 60cm. The roots are very fleshy and should be planted at least 15cm deep in well-drained, leafy or peaty soil. Photographed in cultivation by Valerie Finnis.

Roscoea cautleyoides Gagnep. (*Zingiberaceae*). Native of western China, especially the SW Yunnan. The flowers may be yellow or purple. The roots are very fleshy and should be planted about 15cm deep, in well-drained, leafy or peaty soil. Photographed in cultivation by Valerie Finnis.

Oxalis laciniata Cav. (*Oxalidaceae*). Native of Patagonia, growing on grassy screes. The flowers vary in colour from pale blue to deep reddish mauve. Rhizomes fleshy, worm-like. Grows best in light shade in peaty soil. There is an attractive hybrid between this species and *O. enneaphylla*. Photographed in cultivation by Valerie Finnis.

Oxalis enneaphylla Cav. (*Oxalidaceae*). Native of the Falkland Isles and S Chile, growing on heathland and sandy places especially near the sea. Flowers varying from pink to white. The rather similar *Oxalis adenophylla* has less deeply lobed leaflets and often two- or three-flowered stems. Easily grown in a sunny spot in sandy, peaty soil. Photographed by Brinsley Burbidge.

Oxalis depressa Eckl. & Zeyh. syn. *O. inops* Eckl. & Zeyh. (*Oxalidaceae*). Native of S Africa, growing in sandy places near the sea, flowering from February to September. It has a small tuberous rootstock. Easy to grow in a sunny place, and reported to be hardy in southern

England, but can become a weed. Photographed in cultivation by Valerie Finnis.

(a), (c) Arisaema triphyllum (L.) Schott (*Araceae*). Native of most of eastern N America, west to Manitoba, growing in moist woods and bogs, flowering from mid May to early July. The flowers are followed by beautiful shining red berries in a cylindrical cluster. Shown here a small form from New Hampshire. Easily grown in moist leafy soil in shade.

(b) Arisaema ringens (Thunb.) Schott (*Araceae*). Native of China, S Korea and Japan especially the islands of Honshu, Shikoku and Kyushu where it grows in woods near the sea, flowering from March to May. The strange contorted spathe and the tapering tips of the tripartite leaves are characteristic of the species. Forma *praecox* T. Koyama has a plain greenish spathe, and forma *sieboldii* a plain purplish one. Probably one of the hardier species. Grow in leafy soil in shade, kept moist in summer.

155

Arum palaestinum

Arisarum vulgare

¼ life size Photographed 12 July

Dracunculus vulgaris Schott (*Araceae*). Native of the Mediterranean region from Sardinia and Sicily eastwards to S Bulgaria, Greece and S Turkey, growing in scrub and rocky places, flowering in April. Naturalised in S France and Portugal. *Dracunculus muscivorus* (L.fil.) Parl., with a greenish spathe and a spadix covered with hair-like projections, grows in Corsica, Sardinia and the Balearic Islands. Neither are reliably hardy in cold winters, but are easy to grow under a warm wall, and often produce numerous small tubers around the parent. Photographed in Crete by Brinsley Burbidge.

Arisarum vulgare Targ-Tozz. (*Araceae*). Native

of the Mediterranean region and Portugal, flowering from March to May, growing in rocky places. The leaves appear in autumn and are not very hardy, so the plant is better kept in the alpine house or in a warm frame. Photographed by Brinsley Burbidge.

(a) Zantedeschia aethiopica (L.) Sprengel (*Araceae*). Arum Lily. Native of South Africa from the Cape to the Drakensberg mountains, growing in wet marshy places flowering in spring. It varies greatly in its hardiness, but some forms, notably 'Crowborough', seem to be quite hardy in eastern England, especially if planted deep or below water level in which

situation they flower in summer.

(b) Arisaema tortuosum (Wall.) Schott (*Araceae*). Native of the Himalayas from the Punjab to Sikkim, W China and Manipur, growing in forests from 1300 to 2900m, flowering from April to July, sometimes before the beginning of the rains.

Arum conophalloides Kotschy (*Araceae*). Native of Turkey, Syria and Lebanon, growing on rocky slopes at up to 2000m, flowering from April to June. This grew well in cultivation for a few years, but then disappeared. Photographed in Turkey, Van, near Gevaş, in June 1968.

Dracunculus vulgaris

Arum conophalloides

Arum dioscoridis

Eminium albertii

Arum palaestinum Boiss. (*Araceae*). Native of Syria, Lebanon and Israel, growing on shady rocks and walls, flowering in April. Close to *A. diosocidis*, but reputed to be sweet smelling, and spathe always unspotted. Probably requires protection from extremes of cold and wet. Photographed in Lebanon by Oleg Polunin.

Arum dioscoridis Sibth. & Sm. (*Araceae*). Native of southern Turkey, south to Israel, where it grows in hedges and rocky places, flowering in April and May. Leaves emerging in winter from a large rounded tuber. The spathe may vary in colour from almost black as shown here, to yellowish spotted with black at the base. Smells like bad meat. Easy to cultivate under a warm wall or in a bulb frame. Photographed in Lebanon by Oleg Polunin.

Eminium albertii Regel (*Araceae*). Native of Central Asia, especially the Tien Shan and the Pamir Alai, growing on earthy and rocky slopes, flowering from April to June. Will probably grow best in a bulb frame, kept dry in summer. Photographed in Tashkent Botanic Garden in May 1980.

A view of the Himalayas in Sikkim; in the foreground *Rhododendron falconeri*

Lilium polyphyllum

Arisaema concinnum

Arisaema griffithii

Arisaema jacquemontii

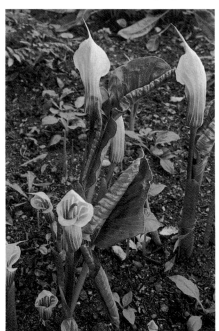

Arisaema speciosum

Arisaema propinquum

Arisaema candidissimum

158

Lilium polyphyllum Royle (*Liliaceae*). Native of the western Himalayas, from Kumaon and Kashmir to Afghanistan, growing on steep grassy slopes and cliffs and forest from 2000 to 4000m, flowering in June and July. Not easy to grow, although quite common in the wild. Photographed in Kashmir near Trunkal by Oleg Polunin.

Arisaema concinnum Schott (*Araceae*). Native of the central and eastern Himalayas from Nepal to Bhutan, growing in clearings in forest from 2400 to 2700m, flowering in April and May. Hardy if well protected by snow or loose leaves. Photographed in Sikkim near Bakhim by Oleg Polunin.

Arisaema speciosum (Wall.) Mart. (*Araceae*) Native of the eastern Himalaya from Nepal to NE India, N Assam and W China, growing in forest at 2300–3500m, flowering from April to June. Photographed in Sikkim near Pemayangtse by Oleg Polunin.

Arisaema jacquemontii Blume (*Araceae*). Native of the Himalayas from Afghanistan to Bhutan, N Assam and SE Tibet, growing on grassy slopes and in open forest from 2700 to 4000m, flowering in June. Probably the hardiest of the Himalayan species. Photographed near Gagaria by Oleg Polunin.

Arisaema griffithii Schott. Native of the eastern Himalayas, growing in forests at around 2500m, flowering in April and May. Photographed in Sikkim by Oleg Polunin.

Arisaema propinquum Schott, (*Araceae*). Native of the Himalayas from Kashmir to Bhutan and S Tibet, growing at 2500–3800m, flowering in May and June. Hardy if well protected by dry leaves in winter. Photograhed in Sikkim by Oleg Polunin.

Arisaema candidissimum W. W. Smith (*Araceae*). Native of western China, especially NW Yunnan and SW Szechuan, growing on steep shady slopes or in open pine forest, flowering in June. The spathe may be pink or white. Although the habitat appears dry, the soil is always wet underneath, and summer drought is probably very harmful to this species. Grows best in leafy soil in shade or half-shade. Photographed in cultivation by Valerie Finnis.

(a) Arisarum proboscoideum (L.) Savi, 'Mouse Plant' (*Araceae*). Native of southern Italy and south-west Spain where it grows in woods and shady places. Forms dense patches of leaves under which the mouse-like inflorescences are hidden. Hardy and easy to grow in shade.

(b) Fritillaria camschatcensis (L.) Ker-Gawler (*Liliaceae*). Native of western N America from Washington northwards to Alaska, along the Kurile Islands and into Kamschatka and northern Japan, growing in moist open woods, in subalpine meadows up to 1800m (in Japan) and grassy places near the sea, flowering in June and July. Very variable in size, and flower colour from purplish to green and black. Grows best in moist peaty soil and a partial shade, never allowed to become dry.

(c) Arisaema sikokianum Fr. & Savi (*Araceae*). Native of Japan, especially the islands of Honshu, Sikoku and Kyushu, growing in woods, flowering in May and June. The very blunt club-shaped spadix and three to five parted leaves are characteristic. Said to be hardy and easily grown, but although introduced in 1938 is very rarely seen in English gardens. A loose leafy soil in shade would be suitable.

½ life size Photographed 14 May

Lilium columbianum

Lilium parvum

Lilium columbianum

Lilium kelloggii

Lilium bolanderi

Lilium washingtonianum

(a), (b) Lilium martagon L. (*Liliaceae*). Native of Europe from France and Portugal eastwards to Turkey, the Caucasus and Siberia, growing in subalpine meadows, woods and scrub, flowering from May to July. The dark wine-red forms (a) have been called *L. cattaniae* (Vis.) Vis. and var. *dalmaticum* Elwes. They come mainly from N Greece, Bulgaria and Yugoslavia, and are stronger growing, earlier flowering and usually have very hairy buds. White forms are frequent in cultivation and particularly beautiful, and other colour forms have been selected. The dull pinkish form shown here (b) is commonest in N Europe. Grows best in good leafy soil in sun or shade, tolerant of lime and probably better in a neutral or alkaline soil.

(c) Lilium pomponium L. Native of S France and NW Italy, growing on steep limestone screes and in scrub, flowering in May. Easily distinguished by its very narrow ciliate leaves and scarlet flowers. Best grown in a warm sunny spot in stony soil, protected from slugs. Source France, near Puget-Theniers, and shot near Vence by Brinsley Burbidge.

Lilium candidum L. Madonna Lily. Native of S Yugoslavia and Greece south to the Lebanon, growing in scrub and on cliffs and rocky slopes at up to 600m, flowering in May. Grows best in a well-drained chalky soil with good fertility, but is rather capricious as to where it will thrive. It often grows very well in cottage gardens, well manured and away from other lilies. The basal leaves usually appear in autumn and remain green through the winter. Photographed at Great Dixter, Sussex.

Lilium columbianum Hanson. Native of western N America from central British Columbia to northern California, in moist soil among rocks, on screes and in scrub and woodland at up to 1600m, flowering in June. Up to 2m high in the wild. Grow in moist well-drained soil, between shrubs. Photographed in California, del Norte Co., in June 1966 by Roger Macfarlane, and (single flower) on Mayne Is., BC, in June 1974 by Brinsley Burbidge.

Lilium kelloggii Purdy. Native of NW California, growing in grassy places, scrub and clearings in redwood forest. Grows in moist well-drained soil between shrubs in half-shade. Photographed in California by Roger Macfarlane.

Lilium parvum Kellogg. Native of California and S Oregon from 1600 to 3000m, growing in wet places and along mountain streams, flowering in June and July. Flowers yellow or orange, to red. Stem up to 2m. Grows best in deep moist sandy soil. Photographed in California by Roger Macfarlane.

Lilium bolanderi S. Watson. Native of the Siskiyou mountains of south Oregon and north California, growing on dry hillsides. Not easy to grow, requiring very well drained, gritty soil, and rather deep planting, about 15cm down. Photographed in California at French Hill in June 1966 by Roger Macfarlane.

Lilium washingtonianum Kellogg, var. **minor**. Native of Oregon and northern California, growing on dry slopes in scrub between 1000 and 2000m flowering in June and July. Flowers white, fading to pinkish-purple in var *purpurascens*. Bulb not creeping. Not easy to grow, requiring very well drained soil in a warm position, with ample moisture before flowering. Photographed in California on Mt Shasta in June 1966 by Roger Macfarlane.

¹/₅ life size Photographed 10 July

Lilium candidum

Lilium pomponium

¼ life size Photographed 12 July

Lilium nepalense

Notholirion macrophyllum

Cardiocrinum giganteum

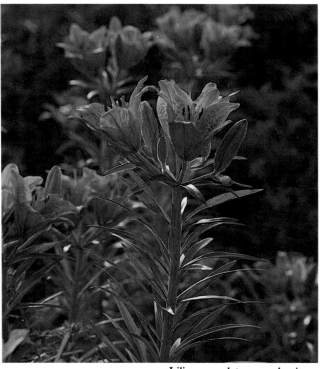

Lilium maculatum var. **dauricum**

(a), (d) **Lilium duchartrei** Franchet (*Liliaceae*). Native of western China from SW Kansu to N Yunnan, growing in moist places, at the edge of forest, in scrub and alpine meadows, flowering in July. The almost umbellate inflorescence is typical. Grow in moist peaty soil among shrubs such as dwarf rhododendrons. The form from Kansu, var. *farreri*, has pure white flowers, and is apparently tolerant of lime. *L. lankongense* Franchet is rather similar, with pink flowers and a stem which creeps underground before emerging with flowers held on horizontal pedicels.

(b) **Lilium tsingtauense** Gilg. Native of Korea and north-eastern China, growing on grassy banks and in open woods. It grows best in a cool peaty soil among dwarf rhododendrons.

(c) **Lilium henrici** Franchet. Native of western China, especially the Yunnan, at 3000–3600m, growing on steep grassy slopes. The flowers are spotted in var. *maculatum* (Evans) Woodcock & Stearn. The plant may have up to nine flowers and be up to 135cm high. This very rare species was derived from seed collected by Forrest's collectors after his death, and has been grown at

Keillour Castle since 1954. It requires a moist well-drained soil and some protection from shrubs.

(e) **Lilium parryi** S. Watson. Native of southern California and Arizona, growing in rich soil by mountain streams at 2000–3000m, flowering in June. Plant in half-shade in very well drained sandy soil with a good quantity of peat or leafmould, in a moist situation. A seedling is shown here. The stem can be up to 2m with over fifteen flowers.

Lilium maculatum Thunb. var. **dauricum**. Native of Japan, mostly around the northern coasts of Honshu, with one locality in the mountains, growing in grassy places and on cliffs. Photographed in Japan, E. Hokkaido, near Shari, c.100m, in July 1978 by Peter Barnes.

Cardiocrinum giganteum (Wallich) Baker, syn. *Lilium giganteum* Wallich (*Liliaceae*). Native of the Himalayas, westwards to Nepal, growing in wet forests and scrub at 1600–3300m, flowering in June and July. Height 2–4m in cultivation. A variety from western China, var. *yunnanense*

Leichtlin, has black slightly shorter stems and bronzy young leaves. Easily grown in rich moist soil with plenty of leafmould. Best in shade. Slugs are very fond of the young leaves, which should also be protected from late frosts. Photographed in Inverewe Gardens, Invernessshire.

Notholirion macrophyllum (D. Don) Boiss. (*Liliaceae*). Native of Nepal, Sikkim, Bhutan and Tibet, growing on grassy slopes at 2700–4400m, flowering in July. Not easy to grow, probably requiring very well drained soil in full light but not hot sun. Photographed in western Nepal by Oleg Polunin.

Lilium nepalense D. Don. Native of Nepal and Kumaon, east to Assam and NE India, growing on steep slopes, often among limestone rocks and bamboos, at 2300–3000m, flowering in June and July. Flower colour varies from all green to about half the flower marked with brown-crimson. The stem often creeps underground before emerging. Keep the bulbs dry in winter, but water well while in growth. Photographed in western Nepal by Oleg Polunin.

Lilium lancifolium Thunb.

Lilium 'Cover Girl'

Lilium 'Black Beauty'

Lilium auratum

Lilium bulbiferum

Lilium mackliniae

Nomocharis aperta

Lilium × testaceum

Lilium lancifolium Thunb., syn. *Lilium tigrinum* Ker-Gawler. This familiar garden lily is sterile triploid, long grown in Japan, and probably originally of hybrid origin, the likely parents being *L. leichtlinii* and *L. maculatum*. It is very tolerant of virus and grows particularly well in northern gardens, in well-drained but rich moist soil, flowering in August and September. It has numerous black stem bulbils. Photographed at Pitmedden, Aberdeenshire.

Lilium 'Cover Girl'. Raised by Oregon Bulb Farms in 1967. A hybrid between *L. speciosum* × *auratum* and *L. auratum* and still one of the finest pink *auratum*-type hybrids. Stems up to 2m, flowers c.25cm in diameter.

Lilium 'Black Beauty'. Raised by L. Woodruff in Oregon in 1957. A hybrid between *L. henryi* and *L. speciosum* which is very vigorous and long lived, with resistance to virus disease inherited from *L. henryi*. Very late flowering, usually August–September in southern England.

Lilium auratum Lindl. Native of Japan, especially Honshu, growing in scrub and grassy places in the mountains. Flowers with broader petals (var. *platyphyllum* Baker) and with red rather than yellow bands (var. *rubrovittatum* Duchartre) occur in the wild, the latter sporadically among the normal form, the former in the south-east of Honshu, growing in volcanic ash. Requires a very well drained acid soil and a warm place in half-shade or among shrubs. Grows better in warmer climates than in England.

Lilium bulbiferum L., syn. *L. croceum* Chaix (*Liliaceae*). Native of central Europe from Spain eastwards to Poland and Yugoslavia, growing in scrub, among bracken and on rocky slopes, flowering in June. Flowers orange to red, with or without bulbils (var. *croceum* (Chaix) Pers.) on the stem. Easily grown in any well-drained soil in sun or half-shade. Tolerant of lime. Photographed in S Switzerland in June 1964.

Lilium mackliniae Sealy. Native of Manipur on Sirhoi peak near Ukrhul, growing on grassy and rocky slopes from 2150 to 2600m, flowering in June. Discovered in 1948 by F. Kingdon Ward, and named after his wife. Plant in leafy well-drained soil in sun or half-shade. Photographed in cultivation by Brian Mathew.

Nomocharis aperta (Franchet) E. H. Wilson (*Liliaceae*). Native of western China, in SW Szechwan and NW Yunnan, and on the Burma–Tibet border, growing in alpine pastures at c.2700m. Flowers usually paler pink than shown here, with scattered spots. Grow in well-drained leaf soil with plenty of moisture at the roots. All *Nomocharis* are alpine plants and grow especially well in E Scotland.

Lilium × testaceum. A hybrid between *L. chalcedonicum* and *L. candidum*, requiring a good well-drained soil in full sun to grow well. It is one of the oldest lily hybrids in cultivation being recorded before 1841. Photographed at Great Dixter, Sussex.

Lilium monadelphum

⅓ life size Photographed 12 July

(a) **Lilium monadelphum** Bieb., syn. *L. szovitsianum* Fisch & Lall. (*Liliaceae*). Native of the Crimea, the northern side of the Caucasus from the Black to the Caspian sea, and the central Caucasus on the south side as far as N Turkey. It grows in woods, scrub and in subalpine meadows, on very steep slopes, at up to 2500m, flowering from June to August. The distinctions between *L. monadelphum* and *L. szovitsianum* do not seem to hold good in the wild. In the large population of several thousand plants shown here, plants were found with spotted and unspotted flowers, yellow or orange pollen, and the depth of the flower colour varied somewhat. No flowers with united filaments were seen. The plant shown in (a) is a fine specimen of the cultivated plant grown as *L. szovitsianum*. Photographed in the northern Caucasus, Dongus Orun, near Mt Elbrus, in June 1980, c.2000m. Grow in good garden soil. Long-lived but not easy to establish.

(b) **Lilium pardalinum** Kellogg (*Liliaceae*). Native of western N America from California to British Columbia, growing in marshes and in scrub in the coast ranges, flowering in June and July. Very variable in the wild, in colour from red to orange and yellow and in the amount of spotting. The bulbs creep horizontally, and can increase and make a dense mass if happy. They grow best in wet soil on a slope or in a well-drained soil in a place with a high water table. Stem up to 2.3m high.

Lilium carniolicum Bernh. ex Koch (*Liliaceae*). Native of the SE Alps in Italy and Austria, southwards to Greece, growing on limestone cliffs, in open pine forest, and in mountain meadows, flowering in May and June. The typical plant has red or orange flowers and leaves pubescent on the veins beneath. It comes from the north part of the species range. The more southerly forms have yellow flowers as shown here, and have been called *L. jankae* A. Kerner. Grows best in a very well drained peaty soil in full sun or half-shade. Photographed in Yugoslavia, Somuborsko Gorge, by Oleg Polunin.

Lilium pyrenaicum L. (*Liliaceae*). Native of the Pyrenees in France and Spain (and naturalised in Scotland), growing in alpine meadows and open woods, flowering in June and July. One of the easiest species to grow in northern England and Scotland, growing well in grass in well-drained peaty soil. There is also a reddish form, var. *rubrum* Stocker. Photographed in Andorra by Brinsley Burbidge.

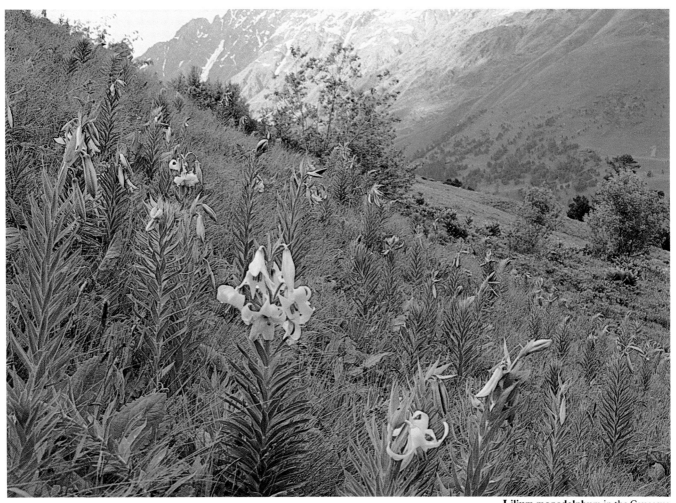

Lilium monadelphum in the Caucasus

Lilium pyrenaicum

Lilium carniolicum

167

¼ life size Photographed 4 August

(a) **Galtonia princeps** Dcne. (*Liliaceae*). Native of eastern S Africa in Natal and Transkei, growing in grassland at up to 1000m, flowering in December. Easy to cultivate, requiring a rich well-drained soil in full sun.

(b) **Tritonia** × **crocosmiflora** (Lemoine) Nicholson, syn. × *Crocosmia crocosmiflora* (Lemoine) N. E. Br. (*Iridaceae*). A hybrid between two species, *T. pottsii* (Baker) Baker from S Africa and *T. aurea* Pappe from central and S Africa. It is now widespread in western Europe in gardens, and naturalised commonly along the Atlantic coast. Other colour forms have been developed in cultivation.

(c) **Crinum** × **powellii** Baker (*Amaryllidaceae*). A garden hybrid between *Crinum moorei* and *C. bulbispermum*, both from South Africa. It is hardy in southern England, growing in any rich moist soil, flowering in July and August. A position in full sun produces more flowers and less of the very lush foliage. Stems up to 1.5m, bulbs up to 20cm in diameter, flask-shaped.

(d) **Habranthus brachyandrus** (Baker) Sealy (*Amaryllidaceae*). Native of S Brazil and Paraguay and NE Argentina, near the Parana river, flowering in January. The long pedicel and large pink flower, purple at the base, are characteristic. Easy to raise from seed, and free flowering in a very warm sunny place. Will survive some frost if kept dry in winter.

(e) **Hippeastrum elwesii** Baker (*Amaryllidaceae*). Native of S Argentina and Chile. This species is almost completely hardy, having survived frost in an alpine house. Easily grown in a pot or a raised bed, best kept dry in winter. The rather similar *H. pratense* has bright red flowers and is hardy in S England. Source Chile, B.C. & W. 4999.

Galtonia candicans Dcne. (*Liliaceae*). Native of southern Africa from Natal and Lesotho to the eastern Cape, growing in moist grassy places up to 2600m, flowering in December. Easy to grow, especially if raised from seed. Hardy in southern England, but very liable to damage from slugs. Plant in full sun.

Tritonia paniculata Klatt, syn. *Cyrtonus paniculatus* (Klatt) N. E. Br. (*Iridaceae*). Native of the Transvaal, Swaziland, Lesotho and Natal, growing in moist grassy places up to c.1800m, flowering in February and March. Height up to 1.5m. Easy in cultivation in moist rich soil; it grows especially well in eastern Scotland, where the photograph shown here was taken.

Galtonia candicans

Tritonia paniculata

169

a b c d e f g

⅓ life size Photographed 24 September

Tropaeolum tuberosum

Tropaeolum speciosum

Tropaeolum azureum

Tropaeolum polyphyllum

Codonoposis convolvulacea

(a), (b), (c) Nerine bowdenii W. Wats. (*Amaryllidaceae*). Native of S Africa, especially the Drakensberg mountains, growing in screes beneath basalt cliffs and on ledges at c.3000m, flowering from March to May. The leaves appear in late winter. The bulbs should be planted on the surface, in a sunny position under a wall. The single flower and seed head (b) are of var. *wellsii* in which the leaves develop with the flowers, also from the Drakensberg. Various cultivars have been named, notably 'Fenwick's var.' with deeper pink flowers; there is also a white form (c).

(d) Nerine crispa hort. (*Amaryllidaceae*). Probably a hybrid of *N. flexuosa* from S Africa. The strap-shaped leaves appear with the very long lasting flowers. Cultivation as for (a).

(e) Amaryllis belladonna L. (*Amaryllidaceae*). Native of South Africa, from Cape Town to Riversdale, growing on rocky hillsides, in scrub and by rivers, flowering from February to April, especially after bush fires. Hardy in southern England, but requires a very warm position to flower well.

(f) Colchicum speciosum 'Album' (*Liliaceae*) (see p.181). Very easy and one of the finest of all autumn-flowering bulbs.

(g) Schizostylis coccinea Backh. & Harv. (*Iridaceae*). Native of southern Africa, especially the Drakensberg mountains, growing on the banks of streams, flowering from January to March. Usually red in the wild, but pink forms are occasionally found. In cultivation it requires a moist soil, growing well with Irises at the edge of water.

Tropaeolum speciosum Poepp. & Endl. Perthweed (*Tropaeolaceae*). Native of southern Chile, and the island of Chiloe, growing in wet forest and scrub, flowering in January and February. The tubers are thin, branched and very brittle. Hardy, and grows better in Scotland or the west of Britain than in SE England, but will grow in a cool shady situation in loose peaty soil. Stems up to 5m. Photographed in Scotland in September 1980.

Tropaeolum polyphyllum Cav. Native of the Andes in Chile, growing in screes. The tubers are elongated; the stems trailing not climbing, up to 40cm long. Hardy in well-drained soil, the tubers planted deeply. Photographed in cultivation by Valerie Finnis.

Tropaeolum tuberosum Ruiz & Pavon. Native of the Andes in Peru and Bolivia, growing on mountain slopes and valleys flowering in

autumn. New tubers are formed annually, at ground level, and if the plant is left outside it should be protected or replanted more deeply. Two forms are cultivated, a short-day plant which begins to flower in October, and day-neutral form which can flower from late June to October (shown here). Height up to 3m. Photographed in cultivation by Valerie Finnis.

Tropaeolum azureum Miers ex Lindl. Native of central Chile, growing in scrub on dry rocky hillsides, flowering in October. The climate here is of Mediterranean type, hot and dry in summer. Tubers spindle-shaped. Tricky in cultivation and hardy only in the warmest gardens. Safer in a pot in the alpine house, kept frost-free. Seeds germinate easily.

Codonopsis convolvulacea Kurz (*Campanulaceae*). Native of Tibet and western China, especially Yunnan and Szechwan, growing in grassland, scrub and bamboo thickets from 1600 to 3500m, flowering in August and September. The climbing stems up to 1.5m long arise from an elongated tuber. Easily grown in sandy peaty soil, kept rather dry in winter, either in a pot or among low shrubs. Var. *forrestii* has larger leaves and a purple ring near the centre of the flower.

(a) **Aconitum volubile** Pallas ex Koelle
(*Ranunculaceae*). Native of E Siberia, Mongolia
and W China, growing in thickets in the
subalpine zone at up to 4000m, flowering from
July to September. Easily grown in sun or shade,
climbing through dwarf shrubs, and simple to
raise from seed.

(b) **Colchicum 'Princess Beatrix'** (? = 'Princess
Astrid'). One of the earliest of the large flowered
hybrids, often flowering in early August. These
hybrids were raised in Holland at the beginning
of the century by crossing *C. speciosum* with
C. bivonae (q.v.v.). All are robust and easily
grown, showing great vigour in good soil. The
leaves are large and resemble *C. speciosum*.
Raised by Zocher & Co., Haarlem, c.1905.

(c) **Eucomis bicolor** Baker (*Liliaceae*). Native of
S Africa, especially the Drakensberg mountains,
growing on moist slopes and grassy places at
c.1800m, flowering from December to March.
Used as a remedy for colic. Easily grown in rich
soil, and one of the hardiest species, requiring
only a slight covering to protect it against very
hard frost.

(d) **Colchicum byzantinum** Ker-Gawler
(*Liliaceae*). An old garden plant of uncertain
origin, possibly a hybrid between *C. autumnale*
and *C. cilicicum*. Very free-flowering and robust,
increasing well. The leaves are large, pleated, up
to 30cm high. The flowers appear in late August.
The long stigmas with bright crimson tips are
characteristic, and distinguish it from large
forms of *C. autumnale* or small forms of
C. cilicicum in which the stigmas are shaded
purplish towards the end. It was named by
Clusius in 1601, who grew corms which had
originally come from Constantinople in 1588.

(e) **Gladiolus papilio.** Hooker fil. (*Iridaceae*).
Native of southern Africa, especially the
Transvaal and Natal, growing in damp grassy
places, at up to 1600m, flowering in February.
Easily grown in good soil in the open and
apparently hardy. In poor soils it will increase
well, but not flower freely. Often damaged by
slugs which eat the young shoots under ground.

Urginea maritima (L.) Baker (*Liliaceae*).
Squill. Native of the Mediterranean region and
Portugal, south to Israel and Jordan, growing on
rocks, dry hills and sandy places, flowering in
August and September. Stem 50–150cm.
Leaves 30–100cm long, up to 10cm wide. Easy
to grow in a warm sunny place, but not
free-flowering in N Europe. Photographed in
Greece, Itea near Delphi, by Oleg Polunin.

Pancratium maritimum L. (*Amaryllidaceae*).
Native of the Mediterranean region, Portugal
and the S Black Sea coast, growing in sand dunes
by the sea, flowering from August to October.
Leaves narrower than *P. illyricum*, up to 50cm
long, evergreen. Easy to grow, but the leaves are
damaged by hard frost, and the English
summers are not usually warm enough to induce
flowering. Photographed by Oleg Polunin.

Cypella herbertii Herbert (*Iridaceae*). Native of
Argentine and Uruguay, growing in damp
grassy places. The hardiest of the species
Cypella, surviving outside in the south of
England if planted in a warm spot, where it
flowers in August. Photographed by Brian
Mathew.

Urginea maritima

Cypella herbertii

Pancratium maritimum

173

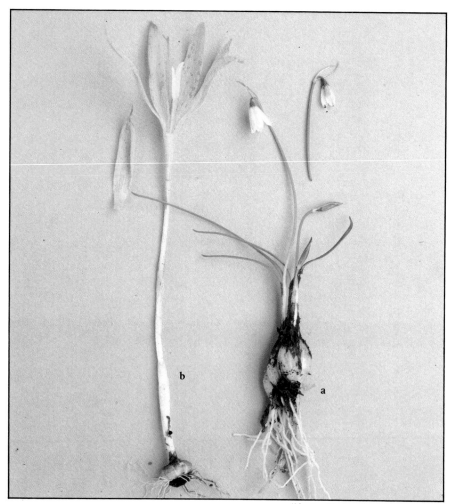

life size Photographed 1 September

½ life size Photographed 19 November

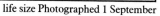

²/₃ life size Photographed 19 November

(a) **Leucojum roseum** F. Martin
(*Amaryllidaceae*). Native of Corsica and
Sardinia, growing in dry grassy and rocky
places, flowering in autumn. Stem up to 12cm;
petals 5–9mm. Grow in a sunny bulb frame or
pot in the alpine house.

(b) **Crocus scharojanii** Ruprecht, syn.
C. lazicus (Boiss. & Bal.), Boiss. (*Iridaceae*).
Native of the Caucasus and NE Turkey,
growing in alpine meadows at up to 3500m,
flowering in August and September. Will grow
well in peaty soil in a bulb frame, but should be
happy in sandy peaty soil outside. Source
SW Caucasus, Klukorsky pass, 1800m, Rix s.n.

(c) **Crocus ochroleucus** Boiss. Native of
S Syria, Lebanon and Israel, growing on rocky
hillsides up to 1000m, flowering in November.
Leaves appearing with the flowers. Cultivation
as (a).

(d) **Narcissus viridiflorus** Schousboe
(*Amaryllidaceae*). Native of SW Spain and
Morocco, on either side of the Straits of
Gibralter, growing in damp fields, flowering in
autumn. Flowers very sweet scented.
Cultivation as (a).

(e) **Crocus melantherus** Boiss. & Orph., syn.
C. crewei Hooker fil. Native of south Greece, the
Cyclades and western Turkey, growing in rocky
places and scrub, flowering from October to
January (see p.21 (a)). Source Peloponnese, SE
of Megalopolis, Rix 2108.

(f) Crocus longiflorus Rafin. Native of
SW Italy, Sicily and Malta, growing in rocky
and grassy places and the edges of woods,
flowering in October and November.
Cultivation as for (a) (see p.179 (p)). Shown
here: a feathered form from Malta.

(g), (h) Crocus laevigatus Bory & Chaub.
Native of S Greece, growing in scrub and on
stony slopes, flowering from October to
January. Corm tunic very hard. Cultivation as
for (a) (see p.179(q)). Shown here are two forms:
(g) from Euboea, near Khalkis, Rix 556, and (h)
a small pale form from Crete.

(i) Crocus nudiflorus Smith. Native of
SW France and Spain, growing in meadows,
flowering in September and October. The bulb
is usually stoloniferous. Leaves three to four,
appearing long after the flowers have faded.
Cultivation as for (b). Will naturalise if happy, in
thin grass.

(j) Crocus speciosus Bieb. Native of the
Crimea, S Caucasus, Turkey and Iran, growing
in woods, scrub, meadows and stony hillsides,
flowering in October and November. Filaments
glabrous. Easily grown in a sunny place or in
thin grass on sandy soil (see p.183). Shown here,
a small form from Crimea.

(k) Crocus serotinus Salisb. subsp. **salzmannii**
(Gay) Mathew, syn. *C. asturicus* Herbert. Native
of west, central and southern Spain, growing on
stony slopes, in scrub and open pine woods,
flowering from September to December.
Cultivation as (b). Source Sierra de
Guadderrama, c.2000m, Rix s.n.

(l) Colchicum corsicum Baker (*Liliaceae*).
Native of Corsica, where it grows in sandy places
in the mountains, flowering in September. The
leaves which appear in winter are three or four in
number, up to 8cm long and 9mm wide, linear
lanceolate. The stigmatic hairs extend a little
down from the tips of the styles. The very
similar *C. alpinum* DC., from the Alps and
mountains of Italy, Corsica, Sardinia and
Sicily, has styles with stigmatic hairs only on
the tip, and usually only two leaves. Cultivation
as for (b).

(m) Habranthus andersonii Herbert
(*Amaryllidaceae*). Native of temperate
S America, probably introduced in Texas.
Flowers may also be pinkish or white with
yellowish apex. Easily grown in a bulb frame,
kept dry in summer, flowering in cultivation
from August to October, and seeding very
freely.

(n) Colchicum boissieri Orph. (*Liliaceae*).
Native of S Greece, especially the Taygetos
mountains in the Peloponnese, where it grows in
scrub and stony hillsides up to 1500m, flowering
from September to December. Usually two
leaves, up to 20cm long and 12cm wide, develop
in winter. Easily distinguished from all other
species except *C. psaridis* Heldr. ex Halacsy by
its strange stoloniferous corm. Cultivation as for
(a). Source Greece, Peloponnese, Brickell 2169.

(o) Colchicum cilicicum Dammer (*Liliaceae*).
Native of southern Turkey in the foothills of the
Tauros mountains at around 1000m, growing
among rocks and on screes in pine woods and
scrub, flowering from October to November.
The leaves are large, up to 30cm high, broadly
lanceolate. Easy to grow in dry sunny places in
well-drained soil.

(p) Colchicum autumnale L. var. 'album (see
p.179 (g)).

½ life size Photographed 17 September

Colchicum pusillum   Crocus karduchorum

(a) **Allium callimischon** Link (*Liliaceae*). Native of Greece (the Peloponnese) and Crete, growing among rocks, flowering September to November. The leaves appear in early autumn; the flower stalk grows in spring, but remains throughout the summer covered in the dead remains of leaves, and the flowers appear from the top of the apparently dead stalk. Subsp. *callimischon* from the Peloponnese has unspotted flowers; subsp. *haemostictum* Stearn illustrated here, from Crete, has spotted petals.

(b) **Umbilicus erectus** DC., syn *Cotyledon lutea* Huds. (*Crassulaceae*). Native of S Italy to NW Africa and E Turkey, growing in rocky places and in woods, at 600–2300m, flowering from June to August. The fleshy kidney-shaped leaves appear in spring from the short tuber. Hardy. Source W Turkey, Izmir, 600m, Rix 1230.

(c) **Crocus kotschyanus** Herbert, subsp. **kotschyanus** (*Iridaceae*). Native of central Turkey, to Lebanon, growing in scrub and rocky places from 500 to 2600m, flowering in September and October. Easily grown in a bulb frame, or sunny place outside.

(d) **Biarum tenuifolium** (L.) Schott (*Araceae*). Native of the Mediterranean region, but absent from France, growing on rocky hillsides at up to 1000m, flowering in late summer or autumn. Here the spathe has been cut open to show the flowers, female below, male above, with sterile filament-like flowers between. Source NW Greece, near Joannina, Rix 1030.

(e) **Sternbergia lutea** (L.) Ker-Gawler (*Amaryllidaceae*). Native of the Mediterranean region, though probably naturalised in France, and west Asia east to Iran and the Pamir Alai, flowering in September and October. The form shown here is unusually tall. Easily grown outside in a sunny spot.

(f) **Merendera pyrenaica** (Pourret) P. Fourn. syn. *M. montana* Lange, *M. bulbocodium* Ramond. (*Liliaceae*). Native of the central Pyrenees, Spain and Portugal, flowering in autumn, on stony hillsides and in dry turf. Easily grown in well-drained soil. Source Sierra de Guadderrama, Rix s.n.

(g) **Sternbergia clusiana** Ker-Gawl ex Spreng. (*Amaryllidaceae*). Native of S Turkey, southwards to Israel and eastwards to Iran, growing on steep rocky slopes and deserts, flowering in October. Leaves about 30cm long, 1cm wide. Cultivation as (h).

Colchicum macrophyllum

Crocus kotschyanus subsp. **cappadocicus**

(h) **Colchicum variegatum** L. (*Liliaceae*). Native of Greece, especially the Aegean islands, Crete, Rhodes and S Turkey, where it grows on rocky hillsides up to 1500m, flowering from September to December. The leaves develop during winter and spring and are three or four in number, spreading, 10–15cm long, 10–20mm wide, with very wavy edges. In nature the flower would have a longer tube than that shown here. *C. agrippinum* hort. ex Baker (see p.181) is probably a hybrid between this and *C. autumnale* L. Easy to grow in dry sunny places in very well drained soil. Source Rhodes, Attaviros, Rix 1262.

(i) **Colchicum parlatoris** Orph. Native of the Peloponnese in southern Greece, growing on rocky hills, flowering from August to November. About four leaves appear in winter or early spring, and are c.1cm wide, and 5–10cm long. This is an unusually broad-leaved form, whereas p.185 (h) is typical. Source S Peloponnese, hills between Neapolis and Monemvasia, Rix 2127.

Crocus karduchorum Kotschy ex Maw (*Iridaceae*). Native of SE Turkey, south of Lake Van, growing on stony slopes in oak scrub c.2000m, flowering in September and October. A beautiful crocus recently rediscovered after

over one hundred years, characterised by its finely divided white stigmata. Photographed near Hizan, by Brian Mathew, BM 9037.

Colchicum macrophyllum B. L. Burtt. Native of Crete, Rhodes and SW Turkey, growing in scrub and on rocky hillsides, flowering from September to November. Leaves three to four, very large, up to 35 × 14cm. Anthers purple, pollen green. Photographed in N Crete near Rethimnon in November 1980 by C. D. Brickell, B. & M. 10,116.

Colchicum pusillum Sieber. Native of Greece and Crete, growing in scrub and on rocky hillsides, flowering in October and November. Leaves three to six, appearing with the flowers, up to 14cm × 2mm. For a bulb frame, or pot in the alpine house. Photographed in NE Crete near Agios Nicolaios by C. D. Brickell in November 1980, B. & M. 10,142.

Crocus kotschyanus Koch, subsp. **cappadocicus** Mathew. Native of central Turkey especially between Kayseri and Malatya, growing on rocky limestone slopes and in alpine turf from 2000 to 2700m, flowering in September. See also p.183 (k). Throat glabrous. Cultivation as for (c). Photographed between Darende and Pinarbaşi by Brian Mathew.

½ life size Photographed 1 September

(a), (b) Cyclamen hederifolium Aiton, syn.
C. neapolitanum Ten. (*Primulaceae*). Native
from S France to Greece and Turkey, growing in
woods and among rocks, flowering in autumn.
The leaves are variously marked and marbled
with silver. Easily grown in sun or shade in stony
leafy soil.

(c) Leucojum autumnale L. (*Amaryllidaceae*).
Native of Spain, Portugal, Sardinia, Sicily and
N Africa, growing in open woods, scrub and
grassy places, flowering from August to
November. Easy in a sunny place outside.

(d) Cyclamen cilicium Boiss. & Held. var.
intaminatum Meikle. Native of south and west
Turkey, growing in pine woods and scrub at
around 1000m. Leaves usually dark green,
unmarked. A flower of var. *cilicium* (p.185), is
shown for comparison.

(e) Cyclamen africanum Boiss. & Reut. Native
of Algeria. Not hardy.

(f) Cyclamen purpurascens Miller, syn.
C. europaeum L., *C. colchicum* Albov,
C. ponticum (Albov) Pobed., *C. fratrense* Halda
& Sojak. Native of France to Yugoslavia
and Poland and in the S Caucasus, growing in
alpine woods on limestone, flowering from June
to October. Tuber rooting all over.
Cultivation as (a).

(g) Colchicum autumnale L. (*Liliaceae*). Native
of most of Europe from southern England and
Portugal to Russia, growing in meadows and
flowering in autumn. Easy to grow in grass.
Source NE Italy, subalpine meadows above
Udine, Rix s.n.

(h) Colchicum kotschyi Boiss. (*Liliaceae*).

(i) Crocus kotschyanus subsp. **hakkariensis**
Mathew (*Iridaceae*). Native of SE Turkey, at
1000–3000m, flowering in September.
Rix 161.

(j) Scilla autumnalis L. (*Liliaceae*). Native of
Europe from England and Hungary
southwards, growing in dry grassy places,
flowering from August to October.

(k) Crocus robertianus C. D. Brickell. Native
of the Pindus mountains of N Greece, growing
in clearings in scrub at c.850m, flowering in
October. Leaves three to four, 4–6mm wide.
Marr 3580.

(l) Crocus tournefortii Gay. Native of most of
the Aegean islands, Crete, Karpathos and
Rhodes, growing in scrub and crevices in rocks,
flowering from September to December.
Cultivation as (i). Source Rhodes, Rix 1251.

(m) Crocus boryi Gay. Native of S and W
Greece to Crete, on stony hillsides in scrub,
flowering in autumn. Cultivation as (i). Source
Peloponnese, near Githion, Rix 512.

(n) Crocus kotschyanus var. **leucopharynx**
B. L. Burtt. Not known in the wild, but
commonly grown. Cultivation as (c).

(o) Crocus caspius Fischer & Meyer. Native of
Iran, on the south coast of the Caspian Sea up to
1300m, in sandy places, meadows and the edges
of forests, flowering in October and November.
Source Iran, Farah Abad, P. Furse 5083.

(p) Crocus longiflorus Rafin (see p.175).

(q) Crocus laevigatus Bory & Chaub. (see p.175
(g)). Source S Peloponnese, Rix 2128.

²⁄₃ life size Photographed 14 October

⅓ life size Photographed 17 September

Crocus vallicola and **Colchicum speciosum** above Trabzon

(a) Colchicum speciosum Steven (*Liliaceae*).
Native of the Caucasus, northern Turkey and
Iran, growing in subalpine meadows and stony
slopes, often in huge numbers, at up to 3000m.
The flowers appear from August to October, the
leaves in spring. They are up to 30cm high,
10cm wide, lanceolate, shining green, four in
number. The petals are untessellated. The form
shown here has been named *C. bornmuelleri*; it
was collected north of Ankara in 1889, and has
been in cultivation ever since. It is larger and has
more white in the throat and green in the tube
than most wild forms, and was the parent of
many of the hybrids. Easily grown in grass or in
normal garden soil, and increases freely when
happy. Photographed in NE Turkey, Zigana
pass, north of Trabzon, by Brian Mathew.

(b) Colchicum agrippinum hort. ex. Baker
(*Liliaceae*). An old garden plant, a hybrid
between *C. variegatum* and another species,
possibly *C. autumnale*. It differs from
C. variegatum in its larger flowers with more
wavy petals, less strongly tessellated, which do
not open as wide; the leaves are narrowly
lanceolate, upright, with only slightly wavy
edges. Easily grown in dry sunny places such as
grassy banks or ledges in the rock garden, and
increases well by proliferation of the corms.

(c) Colchicum lusitanum Brot., syn. *C. tenorii*
hort. (*Liliaceae*). Native of Portugal, Spain and
Italy, growing on dry, stony hillsides, flowering
from September to November. The leaves
which appear in spring are four to five in
number, narrowly linear-lanceolate, up to 35cm
long, 4cm wide, rather smaller than
C. autumnale. The flowers are faintly
tessellated. The plant shown here was grown
under the name *C. tenorii*, but it appears to agree
well with *C. lusitanum*. Easy to grow in sunny
places in good well-drained soil.

(d) Colchicum 'The Giant'. This hybrid is one
of the largest of all Colchicums, raised at the
same time as many of the other hybrids. The tall
white-centred flower is derived from the
speciosum parent, the tessellation and brown
anthers from *bivonae*. The leaves are large,
similar to those of *C. speciosum*. Easy to grow in

Crocus vallicola

any good soil, but flowers better in a warm place
in sun. Raised by Zocker & Co., Haarlem,
c.1905.

(e), (f) Colchicum bivonae Guss., syn.
C. bowlesianum Burtt, *C. visianii* Parl.,
C. latifolium Sibth. & Sm. (*Liliaceae*). Native of
Sardinia, Italy and Yugoslavia to Greece and
NW Turkey, growing in pine woods, and in
scrub at c.500m, flowering from August to
October. The leaves appear in spring, are five to
nine in number spreading and tapering from the
base, up to 25cm long and 4cm wide. A variable
species; the two forms shown here differ in the
number and shape of the flowers and size of the
leaves. Easy to grow in a bulb frame, but less
satisfactory in the open because it is much eaten
by slugs. It requires a very sunny spot and
well-drained soil. Source (e) Greece, foothills of
Mt Olympus, Rix 631 (*C. bowlesianum*): this
form increases very slowly; (f) NW Turkey, S of
Çanakkale, Rix 1217: this form increases
quickly.

(g) Colchicum laetum Steven (*Liliaceae*).
Originally described from S Russia; a species
under this name is grown in gardens, but the
country of origin of the cultivated plants is not
known. The characteristics of the garden plant
shown here are the large bulb and the many
narrow-petalled flowers. The leaves, which

Crocus kotschyanus subsp. **suwarowianus**

emerge in spring, are large, up to 40cm high and
10cm wide, similar to *C. autumnale*. Easily
grown in sunny places in good well-drained soil.

(h) Colchicum 'Conquest' (*Liliaceae*). This is
one of the richest-coloured of all the
large-flowered hybrids, derived from
C. speciosum and *C. bivonae*. It is not as large as
the other hybrids, but equally easy to grow in
any sunny place in good soil. Raised by Zocher
& Co., Haarlem, c.1905.

Crocus vallicola Herbert (*Iridaceae*). Native of
the Caucasus and NE Turkey, growing in
mountain meadows at 1000–3000m, flowering in
August and September. Shoot arising straight
from the centre of the corm (see p.182). Easily
grown outside in sandy peaty soil, but probably
has to be increased by seed. Photographed in NE
Turkey, Zigana pass, above Trabzon, by Brian
Mathew.

Crocus kotschyanus subsp. **suwarowianus**
(C. Koch) Mathew (*Iridaceae*). Native of
western Transcaucasus and NE Turkey, growing
in grassy and earthy places at 2000–3000m,
flowering in September and October. Shoot
arising obliquely from the corm. Petals
purple-veined inside. Easy to grow in a bulb
frame. Photographed in NE Turkey, Ikizdere to
Ispir, 2600m, by Brian Mathew, 9022.

½ life size Photographed 14 October

(a) **Crocus pulchellus** Herbert (*Iridaceae*). Native of the southern Balkans and W Turkey, growing in open woods or meadows, flowering in September and October. Will grow outside, but happier in a bulb frame.

(b)-(e) **Crocus speciosus** Bieb (see p.175). Source (b) wild form, MPR/79/27; (c) 'Oxonian'; (d) commercial form; (e) white form.

(f) **Crocus pallasii** Goldb. Native of E Europe from Crimea, and Romania to Turkey and Syria, growing on stony hillsides, flowering from October to December. Stigma usually red; leaves nine to fourteen, very narrow, greyish. Grow as (a). Source S Turkey, near Malatya, 2000m, Rix 1623.

(g) **Crocus vallicola** Herbert (see p.181).

(h) **Crocus goulimyi** Turrill. Native of the southern Peloponnese growing in rocky places and olive groves, flowering in October and November. Grow as (a).

(i) **Crocus hadriaticus** Herbert. Native of southern Greece, growing on open hillsides and scrub, flowering from October to December. Grow as (a). Source near Sparta, Brickell s.n.

(j) **Crocus cancellatus** Herbert. Native of Greece and Turkey, growing on stony hillsides and in scrub up to 1800m, flowering in October and November. Shown here are var. *cilicicus* (Maw) Maw, from south-east Turkey (mauve), and var. *mazziaricus* (Herbert) Maw from Greece (white). Cultivation as for (a). Source Turkey, Maraş, Berit Dağ, Rix 700, and Greece, SE Peloponnese, Rix 2128.

(k) **Crocus kotschyanus** Koch subsp. **cappadocicus** Mathew (see p.177). Source Kayseri, Binboğa Da., on limestone, Rix 676.

(l) **Crocus banaticus** Gay. Native of Romania, Yugoslavia and western Russia, growing in meadows, woods and scrub, flowering in September and October. Leaves flat, up to 7mm wide. Grows well outside in leafy soil. Source W Romania, c.500m, Marr 3630.

(m) **Crocus niveus** Bowles. Native of the southern Peloponnese, growing among limestone rock and in olive groves, sometimes in great quantity. Flowers white to pale mauve. Grow as (a). Source S Greece, Rix 2135.

(n) **Crocus sativus** L. Saffron. Native range not known. The cultivated Saffron is a sterile triploid, increased vegetatively. Easily grown, but not free-flowering in northern Europe.

(o) **Galanthus nivalis** subsp. **reginae-olgae** (Orph.) Gottl.-Tann., syn. *G. corcyrensis* (G. Beck) F. C. Stern (*Amaryllidaceae*). Native of Sicily and Greece, growing among rocks and in oak scrub, flowering from October to December. Source Greece: shorter plant, Corfu, Rix 464; taller, near Igoumenitsa, Rix 2100.

(p) **Oxalis lobata** Sims (*Oxalidaceae*). Native of Chile, at up to 2000m. Has proved hardy for many years growing in a bulb frame at Wisley.

(q) **Argyropsis candida** (Lindl.) Roem., syn. *Zephyranthes candida* (Lindl.) Herbert (*Amaryllidaceae*). Native of Argentina, growing especially in marshy places along the Rio de la Plata. Hardy and grows best in rich moist soil.

(r) **Crocus medius** Balbis. Native of SE France and NW Italy, growing in grassy places and woods, flowering September to November.

½ life size Photographed 19 November

½ life size Photographed 14 October

(a) **Cyclamen graecum** Link, syn *C. maritimum* Hildebr., *C. pseudomaritimum* Hildebr. *C. pseudograecum* Hildebr. (*Primulaceae*). Native of Greece, Turkey and Cyprus, growing in rocky woods, scrub and clefts in rocks from sea level to c.500m, flowering from September to November. The leaves generally have fine fleshy teeth on the edge; the tuber is very rough with about six fleshy roots emerging from the base. *C. pseudograecum* was described from Crete, *C. maritimum* from wave-splashed limestone rocks in southern Turkey: they are merely minor variants. Easy to grow in a pot or bulb frame, but sometimes shy flowering. Should be very dry and baked in summer and kept rather dry in winter.

(b) **Cyclamen cyprium** Schott & Kotschy. Native of Cyprus, where it grows in woods and rocky places, especially in the Kyrenia range at from 300 to 1200m, flowering in autumn. Reputed to be tender, it is safer grown in a pot and protected from hard frost, but would probably survive in a bulb frame.

(c) **Cyclamen rohlfsianum** Aschers. Native of Libya from Benghazi to Derna, growing on limestone rocks at low altitudes. Not hardy and should be grown in a pot, kept dry in summer and not watered till growth begins. Detailed instructions for the management of this beautiful and rare species are given in the Alpine Garden Society guide, *Cyclamen*.

(d) **Cyclamen cilicium** Boiss. & Held. Native of southern Turkey from Antalya to Adana, growing in pine woods in pockets in limestone rocks at between 700 and 2000m, flowering from September to November. See also var. *intaminatum* Meikle (p.152). Hardy and easy to grow in rather dry places in sun or half-shade in stony soil. Source S Turkey near Akseki, Rix 1325.

(e) **Cyclamen mirabile** Hildebr. Native of SW Turkey around Muğla and Isparta, in pine forest and scrub at between 500 and 1000m, flowering from September to November. Very similar to *C. cilicium*, but the leaves are often clearly toothed and the upper edges of the petals are finely toothed. Grows in the same conditions as suit *C. cilicium* but possibly slightly less hardy.

(f) **Colchicum hierosolymitanum** Feinbrun (*Liliaceae*). Native of southern Turkey, Syria, Lebanon and Israel, growing on stony hillsides and among oak scrub, flowering from September to November. The leaves may be up to twenty in number, and are narrow and linear, about 15cm long, 1cm wide. The flowers appear in succession. The closely related *C. decaisnei* Boiss. and *C. haussknechtii* Boiss. have up to eight broader lanceolate leaves. Has survived and flowered well for ten years in a bulb frame, but not increased, and is always on the point of being killed by botrytis which affects the dead flowers in winter. Source S Turkey, Adana to Gaziantep, Rix 1558.

(g) **Colchicum cupanii** Guss. Native of southern France to Crete, Tunisia and Algeria, growing on rocky hillsides, flowering from September to December. The usually two narrow leaves begin to emerge at the same time as the flowers, and are finally c.15cm long and c.1.5cm wide. Easy to grow in a bulb frame and increases well; not tried outdoors. Source S Italy, Matera to Taranto, Rix 454, and photographed in Crete near Agios Nicolaios by C. D. Brickell in November 1980, B. & M. 10149.

(h) **Colchicum parlatoris** Orph. Native of the Peloponnese in southern Greece, growing on

Sternbergia lutea subsp. **sicula**

Colchicum cupanii

Biarum davisii

rocky slopes flowering from August to November. Usually six to eight leaves appear in autumn after the flowers, and are very narrow (c.3mm wide) and glabrous. Easy to grow, but the dead flowers are susceptible to botrytis. Source S Peloponnese near Neapolis, Rix 2140a.

(i) **Sternbergia colchiciflora** Waldst. & Kit. (*Amaryllidaceae*) (see p.29 (e)). Source N Greece near Joannina, C. D. Brickell 2188.

(j) **Sternbergia lutea** (L.) Ker-Gawler (see p.177). Shown here a narrow-leaved form of subsp. *lutea*. Subspecies *sicula* (Tineo ex Guss.)

D. A. Webb from S Italy, Sicily and Greece has even narrower leaves, 3–5mm wide. Source Greece, Peloponnese, Brickell and Mathew 8140, and subsp. *sicula* photographed in E Crete, Sitia province, in November 1980 by C. D. Brickell.

Biarum davisii Turrill (*Araceae*). Native of Crete, growing in rocky places, flowering in November. The leaves are up to 4cm with a very short stalk and an ovate-oblong blade. Cultivation as for (b). Photographed in Sitia province in 1980 by C. D. Brickell, B. & M. 10,088.

½ life size Photographed 12 January

Hyacinths are hardy and will grow successfully outside, but they are good for forcing indoors to flower from Christmas onwards. They are usually planted in 'bulb fibre', which consists of coarse peat, with shell and charcoal added to keep it 'sweet', in bowls without drainage holes. It is very important that the fibre be well moistened before the bulbs are planted, and that it should not be allowed to dry out; nor should it be sodden, but just moist enough for a drop or two to exude from it if it is squeezed. The bulbs should be planted with their tops on the surface, and when watered the shoot should never be wetted, or the buds will rot.

After planting the bulbs should be put in a dark, cool place (about 10°C) for at least two months while the roots develop. If they are expected to be in flower by Christmas, specially prepared bulbs must be bought, and they should be planted in early September, anyway before the 21st. If planted later the flower stem does not elongate properly as in (**d**) here, and the same happens if the bulbs are brought into heat too soon, or if they are allowed to become dry at any stage of growth. The bowls should be brought into a warmer temperature in as light a place as possible – but not in full sun – about four weeks before they are due to flower; and then after the shoot begins to elongate and the bud appear, they can be put in a warm room.

Varieties vary greatly in the ease with which they can be forced. Roman hyacinths (**g**) are the easiest, and of the other varieties shown here 'Rosalie' (**a**) was the earliest to flower. It is better to plant all bulbs of one variety in each bowl, since it is difficult to get different colours in flower together.

Narcissus are easier. 'Paper White' and 'Soleil d'Or' can be planted in gravel with water up to the base of the bulb. They grow very quickly and after a week or more in the cool can be brought into the house, where they will flower in about five weeks. As many bulbs as will fit should be crowded in for the best show, and it is especially important to get the largest possible bulbs for a good display of flowers. They are only satisfactory outside in the warmest gardens in England, but excellent in the Mediterranean. Other daffodils, tulips, snowdrops and irises can be brought into flower in February and March if kept cool until late December, and forced according to the growers' instructions. *Iris histrioides* 'Major' and *I. danfordiae* are especially good. If the leaves grow up before the flowers appear, the plants should be moved into a cooler place.

(**a**) **'Rosalie'.** Raised by G. van Waveren-Kruyff 1948.

(**b**) **'L'Innocence'.** Raised by V. van der Vinne 1863.

(**c**) **'Pink Pearl'.** Raised by J. W. A. Lefeber 1922.

(**d**) **'Carnegie'.** Raised by A. Lefeber.

(**e**) **'Bismark'.** Raised by D. J. Ziegler 1875.

(**f**) **'Paper White'**, *Narcissus papyraceus* Ker-Gawler (*Amaryllidaceae*). Native of the Mediterranean region, growing in hills and grassy places, flowering from January to May.

(**g**) **'Roman Hyacinth'** *Hyacinthus orientalis* L. (*Liliaceae*). See p.47 for a wild form. There is also a pink form.

(**h**) **'Soleil d'Or'** *Narcissus tazetta* subsp. *aureus* (Loisl.) Baker (*Amaryllidaceae*). Native of S France, NW Italy and Sardinia; close to *N. tazetta*. Flowering January to March.

½ life size Photographed 12 January

Selected bibliography

General books on bulbs

Dwarf Bulbs, Brian Mathew (Batsford 1973)

The Larger Bulbs, Brian Mathew (Batsford 1978)

Collins Guide to Bulbs, Patrick M. Synge (Collins 1961)

Bulbs for the Gardener in the Southern Hemisphere, Sima Eliovson (Howard Timmins, Cape Town 1967)

The Royal Horticultural Society's Dictionary of Gardening, ed. P. M. Synge (OUP 2nd edn. 1965)

The Well-Tempered Garden, Christopher Lloyd (Collins 1970)

Seven Gardens . . ., E. B. Anderson (Michael Joseph 1973)

Floras

Flora Europaea, ed. T. G. Tutin *et al.* (Cambridge 1964–80)

Flora Iranica, ed. K. H. Rechinger (Graz 1963–)

Flora of Turkey, ed. P. H. Davis (Edinburgh 1965–)

Flora of the USSR, ed. V. L. Komarov *et al.* (Moscow and Leningrad 1933–64) (translated into English by Israeli Program for Scientific Translations)

Additamenta et Corrigenda ad 'Floram URSS' (tomi I–XXX), S. K. Czerepanov (Leningrad 1973)

Conspectus Florae Asiae Mediae (tomi II–V) ed. A. I. Vvedensky (Tashkent 1971–76)

Flora of Japan (in English), J. Ohwi (Washington 1965)

A California Flora, P. A. Munz and D. D. Keck (Berkeley and Los Angeles 1959)

Vascular Plants of the Pacific Northwest, C. L. Hitchcock, A. Cronquist, *et al.* (Seattle 1955–69)

Gray's Manual of Botany, M. L. Fernald (New York 1950)

The Flora of South Africa, R. Marloth (Cape Town 1913–32)

Flowers of the Mediterranean, O. Polunin and A. Huxley (Chatto and Windus 1965)

Flowers of South-west Europe, a Field Guide, Oleg Polunin and B. E. Smithies (OUP 1973)

Flowers of Greece and the Balkans, a Field Guide, Oleg Polunin (OUP 1980)

An Enumeration of the Flowering Plants of Nepal (vol. I) H. Hara, W. T. Stearn and L. J. H. Williams (BM (NH) 1978)

Specialist books

Tulips and Irises of Iran, P. Wendelbo (Tehran 1977)

Lilies, P. M. Synge (Batsford 1980)

The Genus Iris, W. R. Dykes (Cambridge University Press 1913)

A Handbook of Crocus and Colchicum for Gardeners, E. A. Bowles (Bodley Head 2nd edn 1952)

Snowdrops and Snowflakes, F. C. Stern (Royal Horticultural Society 1956)

The Daffodil, M. J. Jefferson-Brown (Faber 1951)

Cyclamen: The Genus in the Wild and in Cultivation, D. E. Saunders, revised and amended by R. D. Meikle and C. Grey-Wilson (Alpine Garden Society 1975)

Classified List and International Register of Tulip Names (Royal General Bulbgrowers' Association, Hillegom 1976)

Classified List and International Register of Daffodil Names (Royal Horticultural Society 1969 and later supplements)

Useful journals

The Botanical Magazine (London 1793–); almost every bulb species worth growing has been illustrated here

Hooker's Icones Plantarum (London 1836–); notably vol. XXXIX, parts I and II on Fritillaria, W. B. Turrill and J. R. Sealy 1980

Journal of the Royal Horticultural Society (London 1879–); since 1975 titled *The Garden*

The Plantsman (London 1979–)

Pacific Horticulture (San Francisco 1940–); formerly *Journal of the California Horticultural Society*

The Lily Yearbook (London 1932–79); good articles on all genera of Liliaceae

The Daffodil and Tulip Yearbook (London 1933–); good articles on *Galanthus* and other Amaryllidaceae

The Iris Yearbook (London 1964–) and notes on Iris and Crocus distributed by the Iris Society Species Group

The Lily Yearbook of the North American Lily Society (New York 1948–); only articles on Lilies

The Bulletin of the Alpine Garden Society (London 1930–); many good articles on collecting

The Iranian Journal of Botany (Tehran 1976–)

Other articles

On the Genus Eremurus (Liliaceae) in South-west Asia, Per Wendelbo (Arb. Univ. Bergen no. 5, 1964)

Crocus tournefortii and its allies, Brian Mathew (Kew Bull. 31(4), 775-784, 1977)

Crocus vallicola and its allies, Brian Mathew, (Notes RBG Edinb. 38(3), 387-398, 1980)

Fritillaria in the Eastern Mediterranean region I-IV, E. M. Rix (Kew Bull. 33(4), 585-600, 1979)

Endangered Monocotyledons in Europe and South-west Asia, H. Synge, in C. D. Brickell, D. F. Cutler & M. Gregory (eds), *Petaloid Monocotyledons* (Academic Press 1980)

Neue Scilla-Arten aus dem östlichen Mittlemeerraum, F. Speta (Naturk. Jahrb. Stadt Linz 22, 65-72, 1976); eleven new species described!

Societies and suppliers

Specialist horticultural societies in Great Britain

Royal Horticultural Society
Vincent Square, London SW1P 2PE

Alpine Garden Society
E. M. Upward, Lye End Link, St John's, Woking, Surrey

Scottish Rock Garden Club
Mrs I. Simpson, 48 St Alban's Road, Edinburgh EH9 2LU

British Gladiolus Society
Mrs M. Rowley, 10 Sandbach Road, Thurlwood, Rode Heath, Stoke-on-Trent ST7 3RN

British Iris Society
Species group, Prof. M. Bowley, Brook Orchard, Graffham, Petworth, Sussex

Daffodil Society
D. H. Pearce, 1 Dorset Cottages, Birch Road, Copford, Colchester, Essex

Lily Group of the RHS
c/o RHS, Vincent Square, London SW1P 2PE

Nerine Society
C. A. Norris, Brookend House, Welland, Worcs

Cyclamen Society
Miss G. Nightingale, Lavender House, 47 Lechmere Avenue, Chigwell, Essex

Bulb suppliers and nurseries in Britain

Avon Bulbs, Bathford, Bath BA1 8ED

Broadleigh Gardens, Barr House, Bishop's Hull, Taunton, Somerset

P. J. Christian, Pentre Cottages, Minera, Wrexham, Clwyd, N. Wales

De Jager, The Nurseries, Marden, Kent

Groom Bros Ltd, Spalding, Lincs

Jacques Amand, Beethoven Street, London W10 3LG

Van Tubergen, Willow Bank Wharf, Ranelagh Gardens, London SW6 3JY

Daffodil specialists

Mrs Abel Smith, Orchard House, Letty Green, Hertford

Carncairn Daffodils Ltd, Carncairn Lodge, Broughshane, Ballymena, Co. Antrim BT43 7HS

John Lee, Durley Hall, Stourport-on-Severn, Worcs

Rathowen Daffodils, Knowehead, Dergmoney, Omagh, Co. Tyrone

Other nurseries

Jack Drake, Inshriach, Aviemore, Inverness-shire (for *Nomocharis*)

E. Parker Jervis, Martens Hall Farm, Longwood, Abingdon, Berks (for *Colchicum*)

Washfield Nurseries, Hawkhurst, Kent (for Fritillaries).

Index

Italic type indicates a synonym
* An asterisk indicates
that the plant is
endangered or very rare
in the wild (see p.7)

192